DAVID
HUME

**Purdue University Series
in the History of Philosophy**

General Editors
Arion Kelkel
Joseph J. Kockelmans
Adriaan Peperzak
Calvin O. Schrag
Thomas Seebohm

DAVID HUME

An Introduction to His Philosophical System

Terence Penelhum

Purdue University Press
West Lafayette, Indiana

Printed in the United States of America

Book and cover design by Anita Noble

Library of Congress Cataloging-in-Publication Data
Penelhum, Terence, 1929–
    David Hume: an introduction to his philosophical system / by Terence Penelhum.
        p.   cm. —(Purdue University series in the history of philosophy)
    Includes selections from Hume's works.
    Includes bibliographical references and index.
    ISBN 1–55753–012–2 (alk. paper) —ISBN 1–55753–013–0 (pbk. : alk. paper)
    1. Hume, David, 1711–1776. I. Hume, David, 1711–1776. Selections. 1991. II. Title. III. Series.
    B1498.P45 1991
    192–dc20   91–9096 CIP

To
Edith

CONTENTS

PREFACE

Hume is generally agreed to be the greatest philosopher to have written in English, and he is read very widely indeed by students of philosophy, often early in their studies. This presents problems for anyone contemplating producing a book about him that is intended for students. The ease and grace of his own prose make it absurd for anyone to try to make his points again for him in a more palatable way, as one might do for Kant or Spinoza, and at present there are already a substantial number of scholarly studies of Hume that deal with his work as a whole or examine particular parts of it in detail. The number of such studies continues to grow, and it is a duty for anyone adding to it to explain the need for his or her contribution. I feel this need particularly acutely, since I have already been guilty of adding to the Hume literature myself.

When I was asked to contribute a Hume volume to this series, the fact that it would otherwise have what Antony Flew has called a Hume-shaped gap in it was not enough justification for me, or anyone else, to agree to do it. I have decided to contribute because of several factors. I am convinced from my own study, and from the scholarship of others, that Hume is a highly systematic philosopher, and concentrating too exclusively on one or another of those strands of thought that he tries to combine greatly hampers our understanding of him. This is prevalent partly because he was given to writing in a piecemeal way, especially after the lack of public response to the *Treatise,* and this makes it tempting to ignore those themes that do not obtrude themselves in the passages one is reading. These facts suggest there is room for a volume that presents extracts from his writings and then comments on them in a way that draws particular attention to the relationships between the material that is included and other parts of his thought, and does this in a manner that, while not concealing the commentator's own views, leaves the reader able to make his or her own judgment on how far Hume is successful in blending the various intellectual concerns that motivate him.

Contemporary Hume scholarship is full of controversies, for the clarity of Hume's style does not prevent serious difficulties in interpreting his system as a whole. For example, there are those who see him as a skeptic, and those who strongly deny that he is one; and there are those who see his moral theory as subjectivist, and those who call him a commonsense moral realist. These are fundamental differences of interpretation that naturally affect how one reads arguments that seem to be very clear when one encounters them. So an attempt to relate extracts to the wider concerns found throughout his system is only worthwhile for the student when it shows why such variations exist among the scholars and at least makes sense of interpretations the commentator does not accept himself.

To do all this, one does need quite substantial extracts to comment upon. There is undoubtedly more of Hume to be found in these pages than was expected by the editors of the series when they first planned it. The fact that Hume writes in English has made this less of a problem than it might otherwise be, since there has been no need for translation. But there is still a lot of Hume himself. I have taken it all from the two *Enquiries,* and primarily from the first. These are the works most easily extracted and were intended by Hume himself to be more accessible presentations of his ideas than the *Treatise* had been. The *Treatise* and the *Dialogues* remain indispensable, however, and the aims of this book make it essential to discuss them and quote from them extensively.

I have added an Appendix in which I try to survey some of the most important books and articles on the major themes in Hume's thought. It does not pretend to completeness, but I hope it will serve as an adequate and reasonably up-to-date guide for further reading.

Chapter Two contains some material from the first five pages of an address entitled "David Hume, 1711–76: A Bicentennial Appreciation," which was published in the *Transactions of the Royal Society of Canada* for 1976. I am pleased to acknowledge the Society's permission to reproduce it.

I would like to pay tribute here to the members of the Hume Society, which has always seemed to me a model of what an ongoing scholarly enterprise should be. I first attended one of its meetings in 1974, and have been as often as I could ever since, since the cooperative and serious way in which its meetings have been conducted is such a welcome change from the vast academic circuses in which so many of us have to participate for reasons that are only partially scholarly. Special thanks should go from all of us to James King and Donald Livingston for starting it all off.

I have many debts of gratitude. David Norton has been kind and encouraging in numerous ways. Mrs. Avril Dyson has not only done all the laborious tasks of manuscript preparation, in difficult and changing circumstances, but in so doing has helped bring the department's last remaining technopeasant into the twentieth century before it is quite over. And my wife's love and support have been altogether indispensable, as always. For this no thanks are enough — especially when the time given up to this book came in what was supposed to be the first clear year of retirement.

The selections in this book from the *Enquiry Concerning Human Understanding* and the *Enquiry Concerning the Principles of Morals* are taken from the 1772 edition. This was the last edition seen right through the press by Hume himself and is the one used as the copy text in the forthcoming Princeton edition of Hume's philosophical, political, and literary works, edited by Tom L. Beauchamp, David Fate Norton, and M. A. Stewart. It does not differ significantly from the edition of 1777, except for the fact that section III of the first *Enquiry* has a quite lengthy discussion of the literary implications of the association of ideas. I have included a portion of that discussion. Otherwise, the selections are complete, except for a few of the longer notes. I have modernized spelling occasionally and have modernized punctuation fairly often, though when in doubt I have left the latter alone. I have not Americanized Hume's spelling, however: this preserves uniformity with the quotations from modern editions of Hume's writings (which include some portions of the two *Enquiries* that are not part of the selections).

There are a large number of quotations from Hume. For these it has been necessary to make use of recent editions that are readily accessible to readers so that my quotations can be set in context. These editions are also necessary for readers to consult passages I have referred to but not quoted. There is no doubt that when the Princeton edition is available, it will become standard, however long other versions continue in use. I have been concerned to do nothing that might hinder the widest possible adoption of the new edition, which is the fruit of the finest scholarly labors and the most modern technology. I have therefore tried to cite passages in ways that make them easy to find without page numbers. This means references by book, part, and section numbers in the *Treatise of Human Nature,* and by section or part number in other works. The resulting references are still sometimes too imprecise for readers to locate passages quickly, however; I have therefore developed a compromise. In each case, the reference by book, part, or section is followed by a bracketed reference to the page number in the most readily accessible edition of the work cited.

For the *Treatise of Human Nature,* I have used two editions for quotation and reference: first, that of the Clarendon Press, Oxford, first published in 1888 and edited by L. A. Selby-Bigge (revisions by P. H. Nidditch 1978); second, the Everyman's Library edition, published in two volumes by Dent, London, in 1911. In the quotations, I have preferred the modernized spelling of the Everyman edition, but the Selby-Bigge is rather more widely used. In notes and references, the letter *T* is followed by three numbers: the first, in upper-case roman, is that of the book; the second, in lower-case roman, is that of the part within the book; the third, in arabic, is that of the section within the part. For example, *T* I iv 6 refers to section 6 of part iv of book I of the *Treatise.* This is always followed by a bracket containing first the page reference in Selby-Bigge, indicated by SB and a number, and next the page reference to the Everyman edition, indicated by EL followed by a roman numeral I, II, or III for the book, and a number for the page in the volume where that book appears. For example, *T* I iii 7 (SB 94/EL I 96) indicates that the passage cited comes from section 7 of part iii of book I of the *Treatise,* and can be found on page 94 in Selby-Bigge and page 96 in the first volume of Everyman.

For the two *Enquiries,* citations are noted by the use of *EU* for the *Enquiry Concerning Human Understanding,* and *EM* for the *Enquiry Concerning the Principles of Morals.* Each is followed by the section number in upper-case roman as used by Hume himself, and then by a bracketed reference to the page number in the edition of Selby-Bigge, also published by the Clarendon Press, Oxford (third edition 1975, with revision by P. H. Nidditch): for example, *EU* VIII (SB 95).

For the *Dialogues Concerning Natural Religion,* I use the abbreviation *DNR,* followed by the number of the part, e.g., part II, and then by a bracketed reference to the page number in the edition of Norman Kemp Smith, published in 1947 by Thomas Nelson, Edinburgh, and reprinted by Bobbs-Merrill, Indianapolis (fourteenth printing 1980). An example: *DNR* part IX (KS 189).

The abbreviation *NHR* stands for the *Natural History of Religion*. Reference here is to the relevant part, and the following bracketed reference is to the edition of H. E. Root, published in 1957 by University Press, Stanford, California.

CHAPTER
O   N   E | **Hume's Life**

David Hume was born on 26 April 1711 in Edinburgh.[1] His father
was Joseph Hume, of Ninewells, near Berwick, and the family were
moderately prosperous Border gentry, quite prominent in local affairs, and strict Presbyterians. Hume's father died when David was
only two, and his mother did not remarry. He was a precocious
reader and was sent, with his elder brother John, to Edinburgh University when he was only twelve years old; a more normal age would
have been fourteen.

He describes his intellectual development in his brief autobiog-
raphy, *My Own Life:*

> I passed through the ordinary course of education with success,
> and was seized very early with a passion for literature, which
> has been the ruling passion of my life, and the great source of
> my enjoyments. My studious disposition, my sobriety, and my
> industry, gave my family a notion that the law was a proper
> profession for me; but I found an insurmountable aversion to
> everything but the pursuits of philosophy and general learn-
> ing; and while they fancied I was poring upon Voet and
> Vinnius, Cicero and Virgil were the authors I was secretly de-
> vouring.[2]

Clearly, Hume preferred a literary career to the standard Scottish
destination of the law, and he had acquired a passion for Cicero and
other classical authors. But it is worth pausing to notice other features of his development that he either does not mention or does not
stress. The first is that Hume never saw himself as a philosopher
exclusively, but as someone with a passion for literature and "general learning." He says near the end of the same document that his
"ruling passion" was "my love of literary fame." For him, philosophy
was only part of the literary life he wished, and we might well expect
that this choice would be reflected in his estimate of philosophy's

importance when discussing its role in human life. His detractors, of whom there will always be many (especially among those who have a more exclusive devotion to philosophy), have been inclined to think that he arranged the contents of his philosophical writings to maximize his chances of literary fame at the expense of their philosophical quality.[3] There is a crumb of truth in this, but no more, as we shall see below.

A second and more important fact to notice is that the study of classical authors came, very early, to be a substitute for the religious devotions that he experienced in his home. It is clear that by the time he left the university, he had abandoned all Christian convictions and had formed the lifelong opinion that religion, especially the popular predestinarian Calvinism dominant in the Scotland of his youth, was an unnatural and malign influence in human life and served only to intensify the fears and anxieties that moral reflection should enable us to overcome. He turned for such moral solace to classical writers, especially to Cicero, whose influence on his philosophical system is very deep.

Hume's intellectual environment at Edinburgh was not exclusively classical, however. While the extent and importance of it are a matter of controversy, he clearly absorbed some of the increasing intellectual influence of Newtonian physics.[4] It is generally supposed that it played an important part in the formation of what he described as "a new scene of thought" that completely ousted the law in the center of his attentions in 1729 and was to lead, in an amazingly few years, to his first and greatest philosophical work — *A Treatise of Human Nature*. In the short run, however, the intense intellectual exertions occasioned by the excitement of his philosophical discoveries led to what we would now call a breakdown. He described his symptoms, and his efforts to deal with them, in a remarkable letter that he addressed to a physician (tentatively identified by Mossner as John Arbuthnot).[5] He experienced a "coldness and desertion of the spirit," "scurvy spots" on the fingers, "wateriness in the mouth," and a sudden ravenous appetite that transformed him from a "tall, lean and rawboned" youth into the fat figure who stares at us from the two famous Allan Ramsay portraits. The letter may well not have been sent, but it is a remarkable piece of clinical self-description and shows that Hume had become very fully acquainted with his own nature. But although he correctly diagnosed himself as suffering from the "disease of the learned," his prescription was less successful: he went to Bristol to enter business with a merchant and put philosophy to one side for a time. A few months of the world of business disillusioned him, and he went to France to continue his study and writing. He strove to do this in a manner that would satisfy his philosophical bent without repeating the deep depression that had so damaged him — an attempt that seems to have been a continuing feature of his scholarly life and is of great importance in understanding his philosophical system.

In France he lived first at Rheims and then at La Flèche, a small country town that contained the Jesuit college that had educated René Descartes. Hume lived here on a small allowance from his family and wrote most of the *Treatise*. The importance of French thought for understanding Hume is now well recognized, although for generations he was pigeonholed in the history books as the mere intellectual successor of Locke and Berkeley in Britain. The writers whose study seems to have had the greatest influence on him at this period were Nicolas Malebranche, the Abbé Dubos, and Pierre Bayle.

Hume returned to London in 1737 to arrange for the publication of the *Treatise*. The first two books appeared in 1739, and book III appeared in 1740. Before its publication, Hume removed some material of an overtly antireligious nature (probably what later became section x, "Of Miracles," in the *Enquiry Concerning Human Understanding*) in order to make the work inoffensive to Joseph Butler, the only theological thinker for whom he ever seems to have had real respect; he hoped that Butler would recommend his book and increase its readership. He attempted to call on Butler, then dean of St. Paul's, but Butler was absent, and there is no record of Butler's having read or recommended the *Treatise,* though he did later speak warmly of Hume's other writings. The reception of the *Treatise,* in fact, was a deep disappointment to Hume, who had expected the literary world to share some of his own excitement in his intellectual revolution. "Never literary attempt was more unfortunate," he says, "than my Treatise of Human Nature. It fell dead-born from the press, without reaching such distinction as even to excite a murmur among the zealots."[6] This is an exaggeration. It was noticed enough to give him a reputation for atheism that was to do him great professional damage, in spite of the excisions he had made for Butler's benefit. But his estimate is accurate to the extent that no one appears to have come close to understanding the nature and implications of his main arguments. There was one philosophically interesting and comprehending notice of it, in which it is much praised; this was an anonymous pamphlet that appeared in 1740, under the title *An Abstract of a Book Lately Published, entitled a Treatise of Human Nature,* and it has been shown to the general satisfaction of scholars to have been written by Hume himself in order to generate public interest.[7] It is of considerable value in showing us what Hume himself thought to be the most important aspects of the argument of the first two books of the *Treatise,* but it does not seem to have gained his argument much further notice or acceptance.

Hume retired to Ninewells after this disappointment and began the attempt to present his ideas in a form less likely to stay unnoticed. The result of this attempt was *Essays Moral and Political,* appearing in two volumes in 1741 and 1742. A third volume came out in 1747. This venture was more successful, and Hume was now committed to making his ideas more palatable to the literary world.

In 1745 Hume was considered, but rejected, for the chair of ethics and pneumatical (mental) philosophy at Edinburgh University. His rejection was based on his reputation for irreligion, which was thought to make him unfit to teach the young — an uncanny echo of the verdict against Socrates. In Hume's case, the reputation for irreligion was certainly deserved, although the selection of a relative nonentity in Hume's place was hardly the greatest moment in the history of the university. During the wrangle that preceded the decision, Hume was once more driven to anonymous publication. He wrote a pamphlet called *A Letter from a Gentleman to his Friend in Edinburgh,* in which a supposed third party in the dispute tried to show that Hume's skeptical principles are not the threat to morals or religion that his opponents claimed.[8] It is harder to be sure in this case how far the views in the document are sincere ones, but if they are, they indicate that Hume believed a practical accommodation between his philosophy and established religion was entirely possible.

Hume needed an income and now took the opportunity provided by an invitation to be tutor to the young (and, as it turned out, deranged) Marquess of Annandale. The year he spent in this post helped his finances but was otherwise distressing because of his pupil's mental state and the dishonesty of his agent. Hume was dismissed in 1746 and returned to London on the very day of the Battle of Culloden, which ended the Jacobite rebellion. Although a Scot, Hume had no sympathy for the revolt. He was then asked to take part in two successive missions headed by a relative, Lieutenant-General St. Clair. The first was supposed to be a military expedition against the French in Canada but was downgraded into an abortive raid on the coast of France; the second was a more respectable mission to Vienna and Turin.

These activities improved Hume's financial position, and he was also beginning to achieve some of the literary reputation that he craved. In 1748 he brought out *Philosophical Essays Concerning the Human Understanding,* later to be called *Enquiry Concerning the Human Understanding.* This work was a smoother rewriting of the first two books of the *Treatise.* Book III was similarly re-presented (in this case, it is generally agreed, with changes as well as omissions) in 1751, under the title *Enquiry Concerning the Principles of Morals.* He said, incomprehensibly, that this work was "incomparably the best" of all his writings, but neither it nor his earlier *Enquiry* were very successful, and his literary standing was more improved by *Three Essays Moral and Political* (1748) and *Political Discourses* (1752). Hume was now a resident of Edinburgh once again, and he became keeper of the Library of the Faculty of Advocates there in 1752 — the same year in which he once again failed to get an academic appointment. This time he was rejected for the chair of logic at Glasgow. His literary reputation was truly established, however, by his *History of England,* which appeared in parts in 1754, 1756, 1759, and 1762. It was widely renowned in Hume's own day and throughout the nineteenth century, although it is quite neglected today. It was, in a sense, written backwards: the Stuart reigns were described in those parts that appeared in 1754 and 1756, the Tudors were the subject in 1759, and the centuries from Julius Caesar to Henry VII were the theme in 1762. Hume saw his work as a historian as that of enabling the reader to understand the political institutions of his own day and the need for their preservation in the face of threats, particularly the threats of "enthusiasm," or what we would now call ideological and religious faction. The *History* is shot through with judgments that reflect Hume's deeply felt secularizing bent.

It was his actual and perceived hostility to religion that always threatened to disturb the tranquility and acclaim that Hume enjoyed during the later years of his life. It affected his publications in two important respects. In 1755 two parts of a projected volume of "Five Dissertations" were suppressed when the publisher was pressured by a vociferous watchdog of orthodoxy, William Warburton.[9] More importantly, Hume decided not to publish his greatest work on the philosophy of religion (indeed the greatest work there is on the philosophy of religion) during his own lifetime. The work in question, the *Dialogues Concerning Natural Religion,* was complete in draft form in 1751 but did not appear until 1779, three years after Hume's death. The final version contained many later alterations, but the fact that it was not put into print earlier is clearly the result of a desire to avoid acrimony. There had been a serious attempt to have Hume formally excommunicated by the General Assembly of the Church of Scotland in 1756, but the Moderate Party within the Church, which included many friends of Hume, managed to defeat it.

In 1763 Hume was invited to be personal assistant to Lord Hertford, the new ambassador to France, and he left Scotland to live in Paris for a time. There he became an intellectual hero and a darling of the *salons,* spending time with the most famous figures of the

French Enlightenment, such as Diderot, D'Alembert, and Baron d'Holbach. He became embassy secretary in 1765 and after Hertford's departure was *chargé d'affaires* for a short time. He returned to England accompanied by Jean-Jacques Rousseau, who was fleeing from persecution in Switzerland. Rousseau later accused Hume and others of trying to ruin his reputation, and Hume felt obliged to defend himself in print against the injustice of this accusation, which had no basis outside Rousseau's paranoid imagination and was quite at odds with Hume's character and principles.

Hume's last years were spent in Edinburgh. By this time, Thomas Reid had developed some serious criticisms of Hume's thought, to which Hume did not formally reply, and Reid's pupil, James Beattie, attacked Hume in his *Essay on the Nature and Immutability of Truth* (1770). This work is merely remembered now as the one in whose German translation Kant saw extensive quotations from Hume, which awakened him, as he said, from his "dogmatic slumbers." But in Hume's own day, Beattie's work met with considerable success, and Hume was driven to the unfortunate expedient of disowning the *Treatise,* the target of Beattie's arguments, and insisting that only the *Enquiries* should be taken as representing his mature opinions. Fortunately later philosophers have not followed his advice on the matter. The *Treatise* is established as the greatest philosophical classic in English, although the *Enquiries,* especially the first, are smoother and more elegant performances, frequently anthologized in parts.

Hume contracted bowel cancer in 1775, and although he followed his friends' advice and traveled as far as Bath in search of a cure, he calmly awaited death with no expectation of any life beyond it. His words in *My Own Life* are these:

> I now reckon upon a speedy dissolution. I have suffered very little pain from my disorder; and what is more strange, have, notwithstanding the great decline of my person, never suffered a moment's abatement of my spirits; insomuch, that were I to name the period of my life, which I should most choose to pass over again, I might be tempted to point to this later period. I possess the same ardour as ever in study, and the same gaiety in company. I consider, besides, that a man of sixty-five, by dying, cuts off only a few years of infirmities; and though I see many symptoms of my literary reputation's breaking out at last with additional lustre, I know that I could have but few years to enjoy it. It is difficult to be more detached from life than I am at present.

Hume's quiet was disturbed by a visit from Boswell, who was curious about how someone of Hume's irreligiousness would face death. The interview left Boswell more "disturbed" than Hume was, since

Hume had responded to the intrusion with good humor and even a little teasing and assured him that he had no fear of ceasing to be. Boswell duly reported on all this to Dr. Johnson, who would have none of it. "He lied," said Johnson. "He had a vanity in being thought easy. It is more probable that he lied than that so very improbable a thing should be as a man not afraid of death; of going into an unknown state and not being uneasy at leaving all that he knew. And you are to consider that on his own principle of annihilation, he had no motive not to lie."[10] Though the intensity of Johnson's fears and piety made him especially ferocious in his hostility to Hume, the anecdote demonstrates that Hume's frequent indirectness and irony when writing about religion were not the result of imaginary social risks, but real ones. These same risks were undoubtedly the reason why his close friend, Adam Smith, who was later to write in glowing terms about Hume's personal qualities, nevertheless declined to undertake the publication of the *Dialogues* after Hume's death. It did not see print until his nephew arranged for its publication in 1779.

▮ NOTES

1. My source throughout this chapter is Mossner 1954.

2. *My Own Life* is reproduced in many places, including Mossner 1954, Appendix A.

3. See the conclusion of A. E. Taylor 1927.

4. See Jones 1982 and Noxon 1973.

5. See Hume 1938.

6. *My Own Life.*

7. Hume 1938.

8. Hume 1967.

9. See Mossner 1954, chap. 24.

10. Boswell, *Letters,* vol. 1, 164, quoted in Mossner 1954.

| **Hume and His
Philosophical System**

Hume's philosophy is at present the subject of very wide scholarly interest, and his reputation is higher than it has ever been.
In spite of this, there is a lingering reluctance among philosophers, including many who admit major debts to him, to class
him among the greatest thinkers of the world. I think he does belong among them, but there is no doubt that a judgment like this
still needs to be argued.

As our short biography has indicated, his own contemporaries
could not really take the measure of him: although he was famous
and was lionized and vilified by turns, this was often because his
readers were drawn to those aspects of his work that he made easily
palatable or consciously shocking. By now it is commonplace for philosophers to say that he is the greatest of us ever to have written in
English. But this is an evasive compliment, since English speakers
have always felt that really profound philosophy must be written in
Greek or German! And although twentieth-century admirers of
Hume say warm things about him, they usually do so on the basis of
a very narrow selection of his achievements — confined usually to
his epistemology. Although they owe him so much of their own doctrines and methods, they attend only to those aspects of his work
that can be stated in twentieth-century idiom. Even now, Hume is
rarely appreciated as a *systematic* thinker.

No philosopher can avoid having his successors pick and
choose among his doctrines. This is the price to be paid for being
read by later generations. But in Hume's case, there are special reasons for the uncertainty of his reputation, reasons that have led his
warmest admirers to feel reservations about him. They cannot quite
bring themselves to talk of him in the same breath as Plato or
Aristotle or Aquinas or Spinoza or Kant. Let us see why this is and

why it is mistaken. In doing this we may find clues to the special nature of his system.

One reason why philosophers have never taken Hume altogether seriously is that he does not seem to take *himself* altogether seriously. This is very dangerous for a philosopher: we expect *great* thinkers to manifest the accepted symptoms of profundity — to be solemn and prolix and decently obscure. But Hume's sentences can be understood at the first reading; he apportions the length of his discussions to the importance of his topics; and, most disconcerting of all, he has a sense of humor. He banters and teases, and in style and manner he is the most obviously ironic thinker since Socrates.[1] (There are other parallels: both were accused of impiety, and both were judged unfit to teach the young.) But it is not just that he is engaging and humorous and self-deprecating in the way he writes. What he says is disconcerting. Sometimes he just gives up on a problem and says it is too difficult for him.[2] At other times he will happily admit that an argument is unanswerable but remain quite unaffected by it.[3] And whatever are we to make of a supposedly great thinker who concludes thirty pages of intense argument by saying, "Carelessness and inattention alone can afford us any remedy. For this reason I rely entirely upon them"?[4] Such a person may be greatly gifted. But surely he is frivolous?

What this perception of Hume misses, pardonably enough, is that when he seems to make light of things that others treat with solemnity, this is not the manifestation of temperamental frivolity, but something quite opposite. It is the deliberate application of a doctrine. The doctrine is that of the impotence of philosophical reasoning. One of Hume's central philosophical messages is that we should not take philosophy itself too seriously. This message comes to us from someone who is deeply prone to do this. It is easy to imagine, when we look at the Allan Ramsay portraits of Hume, and when we think of the charming and irreverent and clubbable personality of his later years, that Hume's lightness and irony come from temperamental immunity to philosophical anxieties. But the evidence is otherwise. We have already noticed the revealing letter to Arbuthnot in which Hume wrote of the breakdown occasioned by his absorption in philosophical study in his youth, and his determination to counteract this by a period of activity in business. The same pattern of anxiety and attempted release finds expression in a famous passage at the conclusion of the first book of the *Treatise*. In the fourth part of this book, he has explored, with typical clarity and fearlessness, the consequences of a whole battery of skeptical arguments in the theory of knowledge; he then tells us, in prose in which

I find no trace of irony, that his philosophical perplexities have led him into such melancholy and isolation that he fancies himself "some strange uncouth monster" and is "in the most deplorable condition imaginable." He continues:

> Most fortunately it happens, that since reason is incapable of dispelling these clouds, nature herself suffices to that purpose, and cures me of this philosophical melancholy and delirium, either by relaxing this bent of mind, or by some avocation, and lively impression of my senses, which obliterate all these chimeras. I dine, I play a game of back-gammon, I converse, and am merry with my friends; and when after three or four hours' amusement, I would return to these speculations, they appear so cold, and strained, and ridiculous, that I cannot find it in my heart to enter into them any farther.[5]

At the personal level, then, Hume sees himself as someone with a predilection for philosophical thought. But, unlike others who are so inclined, he does not find that philosophy provides the spiritual anchor and inner peace traditionally claimed for it. On the contrary, since it cannot answer the questions it drives us to ask, it can leave us in bewilderment and despair. It may make us think, as Socrates said, that the unexamined life is not worth living, but it can also make the overexamined life unlivable. The only cure for this despair and stress is a recognition of philosophy's limits and a willingness to be absorbed by common affairs and human society. Fortunately this release is available, for even the philosopher shares a common human nature with the rest of mankind, and a proper apportionment of his time can ensure that the resources of this common nature will overcome the distempers that philosophy can so readily generate.

So the cheery Hume of tradition is real enough, but he is a self-conscious persona. He is the deliberate achievement of a man who knows better, not less well, than his opponents what a hard taskmaster philosophy can be. Such a persona has to be deliberately sustained. Hume sustained it by his social proclivities, by extensive achievements in areas outside philosophy itself, such as economics and history, and by a refusal to engage in controversy with those who assaulted him in print. Above all, he sustained it by systematic theory. It would have been paradoxical if the theory by which Hume kept philosophy in its place were itself wholly philosophical theory. To a considerable extent this is not so. Here we can see a major difference between Hume's negative view of philosophy and that of Wittgenstein in our century. Both men have the same deflationary objective of offering us release from the never-ending uncertainties of philosophical reflection. Both insist that the theories philosophers construct can offer no resting place. But Wittgenstein's remedies are themselves philosophical explorations in a new vein.[6] Hume's are only partially philosophical and largely depend on his understanding of human nature, on what we would now call psychology. It is not that Hume does not take philosophy seriously because he is temperamentally flippant. Rather, he holds as a point of doctrine that it *ought* not to be taken too seriously because it is a potential source of temperamental disorder.

I suggest, then, that we must view Hume's mature personality and his philosophy as of a piece. But this is as much a matter of seeing the personality as a reflection of the doctrines as it is the other way around. It is tempting for those who have a loftier and more positive estimate of philosophy's place in life to choose to dismiss the philosophy as the mere professional reflection of a talented but shallow personality; and equally tempting for those who enjoy doing philosophy but are *untroubled* by its questions to judge him a mere precursor of themselves. Both these temptations lead to deeply mistaken estimates of what he is about, even though the latter might be seen as a result of Hume's own success. Hume does not treat serious problems lightheartedly; he pursues lightheartedness seriously. It is now time to look at the salient features of the theories that determine the strategy of his pursuit.

| The Science of Human Nature

Hume's fundamental theoretical step is to view philosophical reasoning, and indeed reasoning in general, in the wider context of the science of human nature. For he believes that mistaken overestimates of the powers and proper functions of philosophy are themselves symptoms of a failure to recognize the limits of reason in our makeup as human beings. He sees himself as correcting errors on both matters that are as old as philosophical thought itself and were particularly prominent among his own intellectual contemporaries — of whom, nevertheless, some had come to see part of the real truth.

Although he wishes to deflate the claims of reason, and in turn those of philosophy, he does this by making claims of a grandiose, indeed extreme, sort for the science of human nature that is to set things to rights. In the introduction to the *Treatise* (which was subtitled "An Attempt to introduce the experimental Method of Reasoning into Moral Subjects") he says the following:

> Here then is the only expedient, from which we can hope for success in our philosophical researches, to leave the tedious lingering method which we have hitherto followed, and instead of taking now and then a castle or a village on the frontier, to march up directly to the capital or center of these sciences, to

> human nature itself. . . . There is no question of importance
> whose decision is not comprised in the science of man; and
> there is none which can be decided with any certainty before
> we become acquainted with that science. In pretending there-
> fore to explain the principles of human nature, we in effect pro-
> pose a complete system of the sciences, built on a foundation
> almost entirely new, and the only one on which they can stand
> with any security.

The language could hardly be more ambitious, especially for one seeking to set *limits* to the intellectual activity he inherits from his predecessors. How, then, is the ambition he expresses here to be understood?

Using the clues we have so far elicited from his biography, we can say that he considers himself to live at a time in human intellectual history when the study of human nature can become properly scientific; when, as he puts it in the *Treatise* subtitle, it can use the "experimental method." This indicates that in some way or other he will seek to show that the self-understanding hitherto lacking in philosophy can come from the application to our own natures of the method Isaac Newton used with overwhelming success to understand the physical universe. But we must notice that Hume says much more. He says that when we acquire this understanding, it will yield an "entirely new" foundation for the solution of all other questions on which we have to reach decisions — including, by implication, the very study of the physical world that Newton has pursued so successfully. Here Hume echoes a famous name of antiquity: Protagoras, to whom we owe the dictum, "Man is the measure of all things, of things that are that they are, and of things that are not that they are not."[7] This dictum, whatever its detailed interpretation, is the classic expression of the view that one's beliefs are the product of one's nature as a human being and a member of society, and that none of us is able to stand apart from his or her nature as so constituted. What we believe to be true and what we judge to be good are determined by the sort of beings we are. We are, indeed, in part rational beings. Neither Hume nor Protagoras denies this. But our intellectual powers do not enable us to function in independence of the setting of our intellect in our total organic makeup or of the setting each of us has in the society of our place and time. Hume thinks he now has available a way of determining what our nature is and of stating with scientific accuracy what it allows our reason to do and what it prevents our reason from doing. So the science of human nature will reveal the powers and limits of all natural science; and it will do this by showing how far our beliefs are determined by the nature of the mind that knows the world, as well as by the nature of the world it knows. So Hume, although he seems to be full of hubris as he spells out his intellectual purposes, is in fact seeking to set limits to our intellectual endeavors by reminding us that we are not pure intellects but beings whose intellects are circumscribed by other elements in our natures, natures that can be studied with accuracy for the first time.

Hume is not the first to make grandiose claims about putting the whole of human knowledge on a new footing. Descartes had done the same in the preceding century. To understand Hume it is valuable to compare their claims and their programs. Both think that science can tell us only about the principles that govern natural events and can tell us nothing about any ultimate purposes they fulfill; but Descartes sees this as a way of preserving religious orthodoxy from conflict with science (and of protecting science from ecclesiastical interference), whereas Hume sees it as a reason for doubting whether any knowledge of ultimate purposes is possible at all. Both believe there is a sharp distinction to be drawn between the world of public physical events and the world of private mental events; Hume, indeed, seems simply to inherit this from Descartes.[8] But its implications are quite differently understood in each case.

Descartes tries to build a guarantee of the certainty of scientific principles by arguing from our knowledge of our own ideas to our possession of the idea of God, the reality of the deity corresponding to that idea, and the assurance that he would not deceive us if we reason with suitable conscientiousness. This metaphysical route is quite alien to Hume. For although Descartes claims we have certain knowledge of the nature of our own mental contents, the science he uses this knowledge to guarantee is not a science *of the mind;* on the contrary, his distinction between mind and body is so conceived that it implies science is confined in its scope to the material world, and the mind or soul is defined in terms of self-consciousness, simplicity, and freedom, all of which are alien to the matter studied by the physicist. Hume views the simplicity and freedom that Descartes ascribes to the mind as myths, and sees little more in the self-consciousness Descartes ascribes to the mind than our familiar ability to observe and report on our own mental processes. Hence for him there is no reason to suppose there cannot be a science of mind. There can. For Hume such a science will be a Newtonian discipline: it will be observational in character; it will deal with the ultimate corpuscular units that we find when we peer into the world of mental phenomena; and it will locate a principle that accounts for the constant changes that occur in the mental realm, as Newton's principle of gravitation accounts for those in the physical realm.

Hume calls the units of mental life *perceptions,* and he distinguishes among them between *impressions* and *ideas.* The principle governing their change, the mental analogue of gravitation, is *association.* The details of this theory will concern us at a later stage. For the moment, we can note simply that Hume ascribes the greatest importance to the doctrine of association, saying of it, "Here is a kind of *attraction,* which in the mental world will be found to have as extraordinary effects as in the natural, and to show itself in as many and as various forms."[9] He was very vain of this principle, saying of it in his anonymous *Abstract* in 1740, "If anything can entitle the author to so glorious a name as that of an 'inventor,' it is the use he makes of the principle of the association of ideas, which enters into most of his philosophy."[10]

Hume's enthusiasm for a Newtonian mental science seems to have waned between the writing of the *Treatise* and the writing of the first *Enquiry,* even though it is still formally present in the latter. But the implications of Hume's method remain, and are, revolutionary. What follows from the acceptance that there is a science of the mental is that what we think, what we feel, and what we will, can all be explained as the effects of causes and as instances of natural law. So the mind of man is a part of nature, not a stranger in it, as it is, at least by implication, in the system of Descartes. This, in its turn, opens a possibility that enables Hume to view the human intellect in a new way. For if the human mind, with its beliefs and commitments, is a part of nature, then it might be that nature determines it to believe things that are (in our post-Darwinian language) biologically adaptive, even if there is no way our intellect, left to itself, could arrive at them or justify them. Beliefs, emotions, choices — all the stock-in-trade of philosophers, may be natural products that we are (again in our language) biologically programmed to produce in a manner that circumvents the perennial philosophical demand for proofs and survives the skeptical criticisms that all attempted proofs (Descartes' included) perennially fail to meet. This suggestion is the essence of Hume's epistemology.

It has, clearly, a positive and a negative side to it. Its negative side preoccupied Hume's own contemporaries and determined the estimate of his thought that dominated philosophy, even in the English-speaking world, in the less critical and more inflationary climate of the nineteenth century.[11] It found an answering echo in the early and middle years of this century, when the more deflationary forms of analytical philosophy made highly selective uses of his epistemology,[12] although even in this era, those who most closely followed the later Wittgenstein saw Hume as a paradigm of the sort of skepticism Wittgenstein is held to have refuted. The place of skepticism in Hume's thought will concern us shortly. The positive features of his philosophy of human nature were ignored for so long that when Norman Kemp Smith drew scholarly attention to them,[13] serious students of Hume tended to stress them in an equally unbalanced way.[14]

Kemp Smith called Hume's philosophical position *naturalism,* and the title has stuck. It is a good enough one, since Hume insists that our nature is part of Nature, and the intellectual powers of which we are so vain and which we tend to overvalue because we think they separate us from the rest of Nature have to be seen as themselves part of it and as the proper subject matter of a science of man. This naturalism is something that he claims to find, to a degree, in some of his own contemporaries, but the fullest form of it is something he regards as his own discovery. In his letter to Arbuthnot, he says that his studies of the ancient moralists (he lists Cicero, Seneca, and Plutarch) convinced him that moral reflection should not be based only upon "invention," but needed a foundation in knowledge of the actual realities of human nature. His own study of that nature was to convince him that most philosophers needed to abandon what we may, following Nicholas Capaldi, identify as the rationalist view of it.[15]

❙ The Primacy of the Passions

The rationalist view of human nature derives historically from Socrates and Plato. It was Socrates who said that the unexamined life was not worth living and that the key to goodness and happiness was the understanding of oneself. It is important to bear in mind that Hume stands squarely in the Socratic tradition in this. Where he differs from the mainstream of that tradition, as it has come down from Plato, is in his view of what such an understanding of oneself reveals, and how it is to be achieved. (Here he can be compared to Freud, who is also a Socratic figure, but one with his own views about the outcome of the quest for self-knowledge.) In the *Phaedo,* Plato has Socrates deny emphatically that there can be any true knowledge of the world of the human soul that is not teleological in its form or that confines itself to consideration of causal sequences.[16] The setting for this denial is a dialogue that seeks to prove the human soul is alien to the natural order and does not belong within it; and that the philosopher, who understands his own nature, will face death unperturbedly because he sees it as a release from that order. During this life, the philosopher will wean the soul from its affinities to the body, whose desires and passions are hindrances that blind it to those objects whose reality it knew before it was imprisoned within it. This view, shorn of the doctrine of pre-existence, and more or less Christianized in its theology, has been prodigiously influential in Western culture. In Hume's day, it was most obviously represented in Descartes and in such writers as the Cambridge Platonists.[17] In its early modern form, it laid stress upon the intrinsic opposition between reason and the passions; the importance of acquiring knowledge through a priori intellectual activity rather than through empirical observation; and upon the separateness, self-consciousness, and freedom of the inner self.

Hume rejects this understanding of humanity at almost every point. While he is sufficiently Cartesian to assume the reality of the inner mental life, his system is one that denies the very possibility, not merely the desirability, of reason emancipating us from our emotions and desires. One of his most famous dicta is that "[r]eason is, and ought only to be the slave of the passions, and can never pretend to any other office than to serve and obey them."[18] Nothing could be more self-consciously opposed to the picture we inherit from Plato of an autonomous rational soul able to say yes or no, and being best off saying no, to its feelings. Hume believes that it is always passion, and never reason, that provides the moving power for human action. This does not mean that reason has no role in conduct and choice, but that its role is (as he says) a *subordinate* one. When this is recognized, the puritan repression with which the rationalist view of our nature is so often associated can be seen for what it is: a source of stress, melancholy, and antisocial distempers — most particularly if it is allied with a life-denying religious tradition, which Hume thought Christianity to be. The way to discern the natural roles and the relationship of reason and the passions is to observe our actual psychological workings. Such a study will show us that reason's natural role is to assist in the expression and satisfaction of our emotional nature and to facilitate the workings of those social conventions that ensure such expression is of common benefit; not to erect artificial barriers to this expression by developing metaphysical schemes that encourage antisocial practices like the cultivation of the "monkish virtues" of solitude and mortification. Left to itself in a culture permeated by religion, reason will do just this: the slave will get above himself.

Hume is telling us, as Wittgenstein was later to do, to *look and see* what goes on and not be blinded by traditional philosophical preconceptions about what must be there. It is his resolution in doing this, in epistemology and in ethics and in religion, that has made him such a disconcerting thinker to his readers. Unlike Wittgenstein, who is equally profound about epistemology but has much less to say about ethics and religion, Hume saw his way of making us look and see as a scientific one. In spite of his self-estimate as an innovator, he was consciously adapting the theories

of others, in particular, those of Francis Hutcheson, his elder contemporary.[19] Hutcheson had argued for the key role of the emotions
(or sentiments) in morality, and Hume enthusiastically follows him
in this. But, as Kemp Smith again has made clear, he does not confine this to the analysis of morals but sees its implications as being
equally deep in the theory of knowledge.

This was largely overlooked by generations of readers, in part
because of the order in which the *Treatise* presents its arguments.
Book I deals with the theory of knowledge, book II with the theory of
the passions, and book III with the nature of morals and human society. While there is not too much excuse for ignoring the import of
the theory of the emotions for the analysis of morals, it is more excusable for a reader not to see, in spite of plenteous hints, that the
associationist doctrines that are developed in their most uniformly
positive form in book II are essential also in book I, which has, therefore, a positive side as well as a negative one. Hence, for the most
part, the image of Hume as the heedless destroyer, casting down the
idol of reason without erecting anything in its stead. The key to the
Humean philosophy is the belief that the scientific study of man will
show that we are creatures of passion, in whom the role of reason,
though essential, corrective, and indeed positive, is far more limited
than tradition and vanity combine to make us think, and that this
will be clear to us if we apply to the study of how we acquire our beliefs about the world the same principles that explain the generation
and interplay of the passions within us. Though he might not have
been pleased to know it, Hume's views are a deep anticipation of the
Romantic movement, though he develops them before the peak of
the Age of Reason. His belief in the science of man is not merely held
alongside his belief in the primacy of the passions but in his view
proves the truth of that belief.

| Hume and Skepticism

We have so far seen Hume as someone with a positive program of
human science that places us firmly within the natural order, by
revealing the primacy of the passions and the subordinate status of
reason. I have also said that Hume stands in the Socratic tradition
of self-examination but not in the rationalist version of that tradition bequeathed to us by Plato. This will enable us to take the measure of the skeptical side of David Hume. For he was judged to be a
skeptic in his own day and has been assumed to be one, with or without examination, by students of philosophy ever since. The positive
side of his teachings, which we have noted first, has convinced some
contemporary scholars that in spite of this standard reading of him,

he is not a skeptic at all. This is a fundamental issue of interpretation that cannot be dealt with fully here, but some attempt to assess it must be made.[20]

There is no doubt, in my view, that Hume is a skeptic of some sort, and that his skepticism is what makes him the disturbing and exciting thinker that he is. He calls himself a skeptic in the first *Enquiry;* and in that work he offers a consecutive argument that is divided into several sections, one of which is headed "Sceptical Doubts concerning the Operation of the Understanding," and the next is headed "Sceptical Solution of these Doubts." The sections that precede these contain a simplified version of the relevant parts of the science of man as this was earlier expounded in the first book of the *Treatise.* This somewhat puzzling combination suggests a point of fundamental importance: that Hume sees his science of man as something that is fully compatible with his skepticism, and that the skepticism is the source of doubts that can be *solved* without the skepticism being itself *refuted.* So the scientific naturalism (emphasized by Kemp Smith) and the skepticism about the powers of reason (emphasized in Hume's own time by Thomas Reid in particular, and since by almost everyone else) are not, in Hume's eyes, at odds with one another. It is not as strange as it looks to suggest this if one is not previously committed to some understanding of what skepticism is that rules out such a combination. For if skepticism is thought of, initially, as a philosophical theory that the powers of human reason are more limited than we usually think, this is something that can be *part* of a deflationary science of man and need not undermine it.

What, then, *is* skepticism, and what version of it does Hume espouse? In our own day, skepticism is often personified by philosophers in a mythical personage called The Skeptic, who tends to reject, or at least doubt, some fundamental belief of common sense that philosophers consider it their duty to justify (or, if they follow G. E. Moore or the Wittgenstein of *On Certainty,* to insist is indubitable). Such a position is recognized by all parties to the subsequent arguments as one that is held by no one actually existing. But Skepticism was not always like this. There was, in the first place, a lengthy and flourishing tradition of Skeptic thought in the ancient world, and its practitioners are readily identified, if not very much read. The school is traced by tradition to Pyrrho of Elis (c. 365–270 B.C.), whose views are known only by anecdote, and it received its fullest documentary expression in the writings of Sextus Empiricus, about 200 A.D. Augustine (in *Contra Academicos*) thought it important to try to refute Skeptic arguments almost two hundred years after this. One of the most important students of Skeptic thought was Cicero, whom we have already seen as one of Hume's major influences.[21]

Classical Skepticism was not the merely theoretical exercise that The Skeptic in modern times represents. Skeptics saw themselves as followers of Socrates, and those studied by Cicero were members of the Academy, the school founded by Plato himself. Skepticism was, in fact, one of the schools of thought competing for allegiance in Hellenistic times, when philosophy was primarily characterized by moral rather than theoretical or metaphysical concerns. Its main competitors for the allegiance of the intelligentsia were Epicureanism and Stoicism. Each sought to show the wise man the way to achieve inner peace (called by the Skeptics *ataraxia,* or unperturbedness); this was thought by all to be the ideal to be pursued in a large cosmopolitan society where the intimate connection between the individual happiness of the citizen and the politics of the small city-state could no longer be taken for granted as it had been by Plato and Aristotle. The way to this inner peace was envisaged quite differently by the three schools. To the Epicurean, it could be found by so controlling one's circumstances that one was able to pursue simple pleasures and avoid activities that aimed at unattainable or oversophisticated satisfactions. The Stoic saw inner calm as coming from an understanding of one's place in the cosmos, the adjustment of one's will to the destiny that the cosmic reason laid down, and the elimination of the competing demands of emotion and desire. The Skeptic saw peace as the consequence of the suspension of judgment (*epoché*). To the Skeptic, stress and anxiety were the result of commitment: in particular, commitment to dogmas or theoretical claims about reality that are supposed to ground the pursuit of those objectives that men claim to be good. Faction and conflict come from competing claims to have attained truth: from competing forms of what he called Dogmatism. The way to avoid such stress is to understand that human reason cannot attain to the knowledge of reality that Dogmatists insist they have: the Skeptic declines to dogmatize.

Skepticism, then, emerged in history as a philosophical movement with a practical objective that saw philosophy itself as a source of anxiety when incorrectly practiced. Skeptics in this tradition saw themselves as living according to nature. Unlike the Stoic, who saw human nature exemplified in the wise man who is wholly rational and free of passion, the Skeptic saw the life of the undogmatic man as characterized by "moderate affection": immoderate affections arise through dogma (we might now say ideology). This is something that the plain man is prone to embrace without reflection and which the philosophical mind can readily worsen; but the proper use of reasoning can free us from it — if, that is, we use reason to undermine its own pretensions as we find them expressed in the dogmatic systems.

I believe this to represent Hume's own philosophical position very closely, as well as being close to the way he represents the position of the Skeptic in his essay of that name.[22] But simple identification is too easy.

I have described skepticism in a way that is, on the surface, paradoxical in well-known ways. Its essence seems to be the cultivation of a theory to the effect that theories about reality are beyond us and should be avoided, and the pursuit of a moral objective that can only be reached by deciding that we cannot know what is good to pursue. Is the Skeptic not just like the Cretan who tells us all Cretans are liars? Much of Skeptic argument is designed to reveal the fallacies in other philosophical positions without falling into self-contradiction in this obvious way. The clearest example of the way in which this was attempted is to be found in the *Outlines of Pyrrhonism* of Sextus Empiricus.[23] Sextus presents Pyrrhonism not as a philosophical theory (which would be self-refuting) but as a *stance*. The Skeptic (the word originally meant not a doubter but an enquirer) is someone who, after satiation with philosophical argument, has found himself free of perturbation. He has, over and over, examined the arguments of the schools for and against various understandings of reality and has come to find himself equally drawn both ways. As a result, he has suspended judgment, and *ataraxia* has supervened upon this. He now has returned to the conventional attitudes that he exemplifies as a denizen of his time and place, but no longer sees them as having any more cosmic backing than those of others. He assents to what his fellows assent to, but in an undogmatic or beliefless way. He lives by nature, yielding to appearances (*phainomena*) but claiming no access to realities behind them.

> Adhering, then, to appearances, we live in accordance with the normal rules of life, undogmatically, seeing that we cannot remain wholly inactive. And it would seem that this regulation of life is fourfold, and that one part of it lies in the guidance of Nature, another in the constraint of the passions, another in the tradition of laws and customs, another in the instruction of the arts. Nature's guidance is that by which we are naturally capable of sensation and thought; constraint of the passions is that whereby hunger drives us to food and thirst to drink; traditions of customs and laws, that whereby we regard piety in the conduct of life as good, but impiety as an evil; instruction of the arts, that whereby we are not inactive in such arts as we adopt. But we make all these statements undogmatically.[24]

This mode of life minimizes stress, though it does not eliminate it:

> We do not suppose, however, that the Skeptic is wholly untroubled; but we say that he is troubled by things unavoidable; for we grant that he is cold at times and thirsty, and suffers various affections of that kind. But even in these cases, where ordinary people are afflicted by two circumstances — namely by the affections themselves and, in no less a degree, by the belief that these conditions are evil by nature — the Skeptic, by his rejection of the added belief in the natural badness of all these conditions, escapes here too with less discomfort. Hence we say that, while in regard to matters of opinion the Skeptic's End is quietude, in regard to things unavoidable it is "moderate affection."[25]

These quotations make it clear that the Skeptic sees himself as having benefited from his lengthy exposure to philosophy and that his final stance is not a mere return to some prephilosophical innocence. He has now seen that the search for a cosmic support for his opinions (or for alternatives to them) is fruitless, and the equipoise that has brought him to suspense and quietude has reconciled him to living with his former opinions without such justification. But that has (or so he thinks) freed him from belief; and in this freedom he is both more fortunate than his fellow philosophers, the Dogmatists, and more fortunate than his unphilosophical fellow citizens. His assent is mere cultural acquiescence, not conviction. This assent has relativistic implications and is in practice culturally conservative.

The quotations also make clear that the notion of "appearances" will include, but not *only* include, sense-appearances. It will include the way things look, and the way they sound; but it will also include what seems good or evil or useful. The Skeptic will yield to appearances in this sense (which includes conventional opinions) while having no view about how things are. (This, importantly, will include acquiescence in the state religion, in which he will participate in the same beliefless manner.) An essential part of this stance is that it does not deny — indeed raises no question about — the existence of ultimate truth, nor does it involve a formal denial of the possibility of our learning it; it merely involves refraining from claiming to *have learned* it. Classical Skepticism takes for granted that there *is* a reality that seems to be thus-and-so to us, and that it appears to people in various ways; many of its anti-Dogmatic arguments hinge on emphasizing the multitude of such seemings, thus assuming a multiplicity of persons and societies who experience them. So Sextus and the Pyrrhonists he represents are not phenomenalists in the modern sense: that is, they are not thinkers who identify appearances with realities (as Berkeley did) or who claim that statements about realities are reducible in meaning to statements about appearances (as some twentieth-century positivists have claimed). For to the Pyrrhonists a claim to truth is a claim that some preferred appearance corresponds to the way reality is, and they have abandoned all such claims.

This Skeptic tradition is easy to misunderstand today, since the commonest reading of skepticism is one that makes the skeptic doubtful about the very existence of an external world beyond his own perceptions and about the existence of other minds beside his own. This reading of Skepticism is due to Descartes.[27] Descartes was anxious to establish the certainty of the mathematical sciences and their right to claim truth about physical realities. He faced a philosophical community in which Pyrrhonism had been revived because of a great interest in the recently discovered writings of Sextus. He undertook to refute Pyrrhonism and tried to do so in the *Meditations* by raising neo-Pyrrhonian doubts about the senses, and then about the reason. He raised these doubts explicitly as purely theoretical exercises that no one in his right mind can take seriously in practice. Descartes' refutation of Pyrrhonism depends on assuming, for the purposes of argument, that every proposition that can be questioned is false, and then seeing that there are two truths that cannot be doubted and therefore must be judged as established, even by a resolute doubter: these are his own existence as a thinking being, and the fact that although his thoughts and perceptions may correspond to nothing without, he cannot be in error about what his mental contents (or ideas) are. So the Cartesian skeptic turns into someone who cannot deny that he knows his own existence and knows his own ideas; he has the problem of discovering whether any of the ideas he has correspond to realities in a world outside his mind. The Cartesian skeptic faces what has often been called the egocentric predicament: how does he even know there is an external world and that there are other minds in it like his own? Descartes' escape route is through the doctrine of clear and distinct ideas whose veracity is guaranteed by a proof of God's existence. This proof itself, notoriously, depends on the claim that the idea of God is (uniquely) one that could not be in the mind if there were no perfect Being without to correspond to it. The problem of epistemology for Descartes' successors was that of finding an alternative escape route from the egocentric predicament. No one, Hume included, wholly avoided thinking of the refutation of Skepticism in the terms that Descartes set.

There is no doubt that these terms transformed the reading of what Skepticism is. The Pyrrhonian Skeptic did not query the existence of an outer reality or that of a community of perceivers; what he suspended judgment on was whether he, or other members of that community, perceived it as it is. Judgments were about that reality, not about the way it seemed. The Cartesian skeptic, who adopts his skepticism as a temporary theoretical expedient, sees a way to claim knowledge of reality by insisting first that his very doubts entail real knowledge of himself and his mental states. In post-Cartesian epistemology, Descartes has increasingly defined the interpretation of what skepticism is and of what could constitute an answer to it; but it is a gross error not to recognize that in the seventeenth and eighteenth centuries, philosophy was not thought to have begun with Descartes, and his understanding of what it entailed was only partially victorious.

We can now return to Hume. I think Antony Flew is right to insist that Hume is, in certain respects, a Cartesian. The form which his science of human nature takes is largely determined by the Cartesian assumption that "mind is more certainly known than body";[27] that is, that it is the outer world, not the inner world, that is problematic. When he writes about the identity of persons in the sixth section of part iv of book I of the *Treatise,* he goes further in Descartes' direction of separating the mental and the physical, saying that persons are "nothing but a bundle or collection of different perceptions." And in section xii of the first *Enquiry* he says that the "slightest philosophy" shows us that "[n]othing can ever be present to the mind but an image or perception." This, too, could only be asserted with such an air of obviousness to fellow philosophers by a post-Cartesian epistemologist. But it is a deep mistake to suppose that Hume saw his task as refuting skepticism, as Descartes conceived it, by another argument.

Hume was clearly aware of the Pyrrhonist tradition, and many of his arguments against the powers of reason and the reliability of the senses are Pyrrhonian in origin. But there is no clear evidence that he did much reading in Sextus himself.[28] We do know that he read extensively in Pierre Bayle and, of course, Cicero. A lack of direct study of Sextus is the likeliest reason for his appearing to misinterpret what Pyrrhonism was. He does not show any clear awareness that the Skeptic as Sextus presents him takes a stand that incorporates accommodations to the demands of practice and a kind of acceptance of appearances. As a consequence of this, he says that Pyrrhonism is unlivable and treats it, after the manner of Descartes, as a theoretical exercise that cannot be regarded as practically serious. The most extreme statement of this view of it is to be found in the *Letter from a Gentleman:*

> First, as to the Scepticism with which the author is charged, I
> must observe that the doctrine of the Pyrrhonians or Sceptics
> have been regarded in all ages as principles of mere curiosity,
> or a kind of jeu d'esprit, without any influence on a man's

steady principles or conduct of life. In reality, a philosopher who affects to doubt of the maxims of common reason, or even of his senses, declares sufficiently that he is not in earnest, and that he intends not to advance an opinion which he would recommend as standards of judgement and action.[29]

This document, however, is one we should regard with suspicion as a statement of Hume's real views, since its purpose is to downplay the seriousness of those features of the *Treatise* that made the Edinburgh electors suspicious of him. To do this he has to assume the attitude he elsewhere expresses in his famous remark in the conclusion of part iv of book I of the *Treatise* that "the errors in religion are dangerous; those in philosophy only ridiculous." A serious reading of this whole section, however, readily shows that the bravado of this remark does not reveal the whole of Hume's state of mind. Part iv is full of skeptical argument, and it is after exploring its implications in great detail that we find the following passage:

> The intense view of these manifold contradictions and imperfections in human reason has so wrought upon me, and heated my brain, that I am ready to reject all belief and reasoning, and can look upon no opinion even as more probable or likely than another. Where am I, or what? From what causes do I derive my existence, and to what condition shall I return? Whose favour shall I court, and whose anger must I dread? What beings surround me? and on whom have I any influence, or who have any influence on me? I am confounded with all these questions, and begin to fancy myself in the most deplorable condition imaginable, environed with the deepest darkness, and utterly deprived of the use of every member and faculty.[30]

It is at this point that he tells us how nature dispels these clouds of melancholy and despair by absorbing him in social life. (See above, page 10.) This is not the writing of someone for whom Skepticism is a mere *jeu d'esprit,* but one for whom it is a source of real disturbance. And the disturbance is that of a mind bewildered and disoriented by intellectual uncertainties, not liberated by them. It is a mind quite opposite in its character from that presented to us by Sextus, which was one restored to a natural quietude and moderation by suspense of judgment. To Hume, finding no opinion more probable than another does not lead to quietude; it is, on the contrary, an unnatural state. It is not natural for us to live belieflessly; it is natural to *believe.*

This does not mean that we *cannot* be held in suspense by argument, or the problem would not arise. It means that we find it intolerable (or Hume does) when we are. And it also means, as Descartes had said long since, that the skeptic's unnatural doubts can only be sustained in the study and will melt away in the contexts of common life. So we find the Hume of the *Treatise* dealing with its stresses by recommending that if, like him, we have a predilection for philosophy, we indulge it only moderately and alternate it with other pursuits and recreations. The stressfulness of the state of doubt, and the relief obtainable outside the study, are not just brute facts about us, however. There is some explanation of them in the fact that we are, fortunately, programmed to believe. It is this that makes skepticism unnatural and saves us from its dangers. Part iv of book I of the *Treatise* contains accounts of how our fundamental belief in distinct and independent physical objects arises and how we come to take for granted that our minds persist through time. Part iii had already contained a detailed account of the genesis of our belief in the reign of causal necessity in the world, an account presented again in the first *Enquiry*. Hume's science of human nature shows how nature's program of belief formation works itself out.

The account, especially to a rationalist eye, is very unflattering. It makes heavy use of the role of habit, laziness, and confusion. The key beliefs of common life are not due to reason; that is to say, the skeptics are right in showing us that there are no good reasons for them, and even if philosophers had done better in their attempts to provide good reasons when trying to answer the skeptics, the reasons they have offered are quite unknown to anyone else and were not themselves the causes of those philosophers' original convictions. We do not hold these beliefs *for reasons,* but *from causes,* and these causes so entrench the beliefs that skeptical criticisms cannot dislodge them for more than short periods in the study. These causes operate through the mechanism of the association of ideas, which is the key to all our mental operations and is to be seen at work most clearly in the genesis of the passions, as he describes this in book II of the *Treatise*. But in drawing on this mechanism to explain how our fundamental beliefs arise, Hume shows, as he puts it, that "belief is more properly an act of the sensitive, than of the cognitive part of our natures.[31]

It is here, alone, that we can find an answer to the skeptic; and it is an answer, but not a refutation. To many philosophers only a refutation will do; but Hume does not think there is one to be had; and for this reason, the title of skeptic is not one he himself rejects. This leaves many questions. The two most obvious are these: To what beliefs, exactly, does nature commit us? (What is it that we cannot *not* believe?) And does this mean that we can offer *no good reasons* for preferring some beliefs about our world to others?

On the first of these questions, it is tempting to write as though Hume thinks our natural beliefs are very *general* ones: the belief that there is (some sort of) external world, the belief that the self (somehow understood) does persist, identical, through time, and that the world around us, and we ourselves as members of it, in some way form a causal system. This is not mistaken, in that Hume does think these beliefs are to be attributed to everyone. But it is erroneous if it is taken to suggest that each of us explicitly holds such philosophical generalities. What each of us does, rather, is to believe without question that this or that set of perceptions represents a real external object, that it is a set of perceptions that is had by the same person (myself) that saw that object yesterday, and that it is caused to be that way because of events in the object and its environment that have brought it about in a necessary manner. The general beliefs manifest themselves in particular beliefs. But these beliefs, Hume thinks, are in many respects in need of correction; and we correct them, and systematize them when corrected, in science. Philosophical reflection plays its part in this. For example, in his tortuous discussion of perception in the second section of part iv of book I of the *Treatise* (a minefield for interpreters), he makes it clear that the nonphilosopher's assumption that our perceptions, and the objects they represent, are identical is readily shown to be *false* by the old skeptical device of pressing one's eyeballs and noting that there are then two images; philosophers then develop the theory that there exist both continuing objects and fleeting perceptions, and that these have some features in common but not all. This scheme cannot be shown to be true without assuming the reality of external objects without demonstration; but the experiment shows that the initial form of that belief in the plain person's mind requires correction. So the cavils of the skeptic can lead to an improvement in the reliability of our beliefs. But they cannot dislodge (even though they can show to be groundless) the basic belief in the reality of the external object. We can, as he puts it, ask, "what causes induce us to believe in the existence of body? but it is vain to ask whether there be body or not? That is a point which we must take for granted in all our reasonings."[32]

This leads Hume, in the closing section XII of the first *Enquiry,* to describe his own position as *mitigated skepticism.* He contrasts it with Pyrrhonian skepticism, offering as examples of Pyrrhonian arguments those he has himself used earlier in the work to show that our belief in causal necessity is not rationally grounded. He insists that such arguments can only engender a "momentary amazement and confusion," that re-entry into common life quickly dissipates. He then tells us that the experience of skeptical doubt can have healthy results if it generates a sense of the weakness of reason and a willingness to see both sides of a question — roughly, a wise reluctance to be dogmatic. It may also lead us to confine our intellectual attentions to topics where we have some hope of success. We should avoid "all distant and high enquiries" and confine ourselves to "common life, and to such subjects as fall under daily practice and experience." By learning from the fact that Pyrrhonian doubts are unanswerable, but that "instinct," and it alone, can rescue us from the despair they lead to, we can recognize that "philosophical decisions are nothing but the reflections of common life, methodized and corrected."

This rather pedestrian picture of what philosophers should be about is the picture offered us in our own century by positivist thinkers, and it is what Hume says we should learn from the experience of following him through all the ramifications of those parts of his own writings that are so exciting to read! It is a change from the Hume of the closing pages of book I of the *Treatise,* who copes with his anxieties by being Pyrrhonian and dogmatic by turns, and alternating his activities.[33] Mitigated skepticism involves trying to contain philosophy by confining its subject matter. It turns out that the appropriate subject matter is "abstract reasoning concerning quantity or number" (that is, pure mathematics) or "experimental reasoning concerning matter of fact and existence" (that is, observational science). He ends the *Enquiry* by telling us that when we encounter any volume "of divinity or school metaphysics, for instance," and find its author does not confine himself to these, we have only one course. "Commit it then to the flames: for it can contain nothing but sophistry and illusion."

The rhetoric here shows us one way in which Hume is always happy and consistent in his skepticism. He rejects, and gives reason for rejecting, "divinity and school metaphysics": speculative activities where reason goes far beyond its powers, and no amount of methodizing or correcting will put things right. Hume's ambivalence about skepticism comes when its criticisms seem to undermine the methodizable commitments of common life — where, according to his final determination of what true philosophy is, it serves our instincts and does not try to flout them. He has another name for this mitigated skepticism: "academical" skepticism.

We do know that Hume read Cicero avidly. It is most likely that it is Skepticism as Cicero describes it and supports it, in the *Academics* and the dialogue *On the Nature of the Gods* (which served as a model for Hume's own *Dialogues*), that Hume thought he had found the form of Skepticism that both articulated and contained skeptical doubts. Cicero is a sympathetic reporter of the Skepticism that was dominant, for a period, in the history of the Academy, the ancient university founded by Plato. The most famous figure of this phase of Skepticism was Carneades (c. 219–129 B.C.). Sextus, writing three centuries later, accuses the Academic Skeptics of compromising the purity of Pyrrhonism. According to Sextus' account, although the Academics, in opposition to the Stoics, did say that there is no way human reason can apprehend the reality behind appearances, they said *this* dogmatically in the way a true Pyrrhonian would not; and, more importantly, they said that the phenomena of sense-perception, though unsure guides to reality, can be divided into the more and the less probable.[34] The most probable are those that are initially persuasive, are tested (as we might say, confirmed by ancillary observations), and are not reversible (or disconfirmed by contrary observations); this, as Sextus reports it, represents a practical concession to Dogmatism, and an inconsistent one. Whether Sextus' partisan reportage is accurate, and whether, if he is reported accurately, Carneades was inconsistently dogmatic, it is true that Cicero's account of his views seems more or less to coincide with the account of Sextus; and Cicero is clearly defending Carneades against the charge that his views are unlivable in practice. He says:

> His [i.e., Carneades'] view is that there is no presentation of such a sort as to result in perception, but many that result in a judgment of probability. For it is contrary to nature for nothing to be probable, and entails that entire subversion of life of which you, Lucullus, were speaking; accordingly, even many sense-percepts must be deemed probable, if only it be held in mind that no sense-presentation has such a character as a false presentation could not also have. . . . Thus the wise man will make use of whatever apparently probable presentation he encounters, if nothing presents itself that is contrary to that probability.[35]

The conditions for a judgment of probability would seem to correspond to those methodizations and corrections that Hume thinks reason can properly add to the assent our instincts prompt up to make to our perceptions. Hume agrees with both Pyrrhonians and Academics that reason is unable to generate any assurance that perceptions correspond to realities; he says, in opposition to both, that our instinctive natures force us to assent in spite of this; and he follows the apparent Academic compromise of maintaining that reason is able to modify the form of this assent by refining it in the light of the regularities we encounter in daily experience, much as the Academic seemed to modify the practical effects of suspense of judgment.

This neo-Academic position on skepticism is the one Hume offers us at the close of the first *Enquiry,* and he no doubt thinks he has exemplified it in the earlier parts of that work, which we shall be examining in detail. It is a complex position, and may well be an inconsistent one. At the very least, it expresses a philosophical mind quite overtly torn between competing influences and seeking a practical as well as a theoretical resolution of them. For that reason, it has to be understood as the major modern example of a philosophy developed, in the Hellenistic tradition, as a saving way of life. The essence of that way of life is the insistence that we have no rational choice but the acceptance of our nature the way it is, with all its limitations.

We have had to spend more time on Hume's attitude to skepticism than on other features of his system because of the complexity and ambivalence of his responses to it. Two other themes are of almost equal importance but can be treated more briefly here because the problems of interpretation are less severe. These are Hume's views on values and ethics, and his multifaceted critique of religion.

| Reason, Passion, and Value

I have so far presented Hume as a thinker who places the concerns of epistemology and metaphysics within the context of a science of human nature because he thinks that such a science shows us to be creatures who are *of* the world, as well as *in* it, and who lay up anxieties for ourselves if we insist, in the footsteps of Plato, that we are essentially intellectual beings in an alien world of feeling and instinct. His skepticism has to be seen as a part of this overall scheme of thought, its main function being to show us the severe limitations of reason, which, properly understood and used, is the handmaiden, or slave, not of theology but of passion. This scheme also determines his theory of value.

His opinions on this matter manifest the positive features of his science of human nature more than the skeptical strains in his thought. The classical skeptics included judgments of good and evil, along with other judgments, as attempts to characterize reality when all we have access to are appearances; and they stressed, as Protagoras had stressed, that the appearances of good and evil vary radically from one society to another, recommending the thinker to yield to the conventions of his own community without commitment on their ultimate truth. Some of this tradition is reflected in Hume; but the central and best-known feature of his value theory is one that contrasts judgments of value with judgments of fact and does not assimilate them.

The classical Skeptic position is one that implies at least the possibility that there are ultimate moral truths, while saying they are presently beyond us and we have to manage without them. While Hume accepts such an implication with regard to truths about the material world, he sees himself as demystifying values by firmly locating them within human nature itself. In this sense, at least, David Norton is right in maintaining that Hume is a commonsense moralist rather than a moral skeptic.[36] He seeks to show that the moral attitudes of the polite society of his own day are best understood, and best sustained, by a recognition that they are founded in our nature as his science interprets it, and not by the more fashionable resort to rationalism. In arguing for this in the *Treatise,* he engages in some attention-getting rhetoric that has led more to notoriety than to understanding. The famous statement that reason is the slave of the passions is a part of this. So also is the remark that "[i]t is not contrary to reason to prefer the destruction of the whole world to the scratching of my finger."[37] By the time dicta like these are explained, their shock value vanishes; but since Hume was not above using shock value to get attention, he has not served himself well.

His general position is, in rough outline, as follows. There is a sharp and crucial difference between what we say when we talk about matters of fact, such as "the being of a God" or "human affairs," and what we say when we say what is good or bad or right or wrong;[38] this difference is marked, says Hume, by the transition from the words "is" and "is not" to the words "ought" and "ought not." This transition needs to be noted and justified by philosophers. Rationalists seek to justify it by holding that there is a separate realm of moral truths, to which reason has access, and of which it expresses its knowledge in moral utterances. Hume believes that such a supposed realm of values is mythical, and that even if it were not, the rationalist account would still leave unexplained the essential connection of value judgments with our choices and actions. He claims that his own study of human nature can explain that connection and can reveal a completely different source for our evaluations. The reason of man, he claims, can only reveal the relations of our ideas and correct our understanding of matters of fact. Motivation to choice and action is always a matter for the passions — for desire, for love and hate, and pride and shame, and benevolence and malice. It is these that, in simple or complicated ways, lead to our actions, even though our reason can and does do much to generate them, augment them, or lessen them.

No rationalist has ever denied, of course, that much of our behavior is determined by what Hume calls the passions — especially if this concept includes within it (as it does for Hume) our desires or wants. What rationalists maintain is that reason gives us an alternative source of motivation to action in the form of an ability to choose what is good for us (which we call prudent action), even when our desires pull us toward something harmful, and in the even loftier form of an ability to choose what we *ought* to do (which we call moral action or action from conscience or obligation). In these cases reason triumphs over the passions. In these cases we are not acting *in passivity,* as slaves of desire, but in full *autonomy,* to use the phrase favored later by Kant. Hume has to give his own account of these facts, which he does not deny.

His account is one designed to dispense with the rationalist picture of the passions as inner but alien forces that assault the sanctuary of the self unless reason overcomes them. He thinks the mind is merely the theatre where our thoughts and feelings occur, and his moral psychology is one that sees character as a regular preponderance of certain passions over others, whether the character is good or bad. So he construes those occasions when we choose prudently or dutifully as occasions where the passions that rule us are those conducive to our long-term good, or those that lead to moral approval. The "appetite to good and aversion to evil" is one of our desires, and moral approval and disapproval are emotions directed at the characters of others, and even of ourselves, and are a form of love and hatred.[39]

The details of Hume's account are complex, but their basic thrust is clear: those instances of wise choice that the rationalist commends are just as much examples of passions determining conduct as those the rationalist deplores. If this seems implausible, Hume thinks this is because rationalist prejudice makes us interpret human passions too much in terms of those occasions when strong feeling overcomes the desire for good and leads to inner conflict. An overconcentration on such occasions leads us to confuse the efficacy of a passion with its felt intensity. But intensity, or violence, as Hume calls it, is not the same as strength. In *his* view, a passion is strong when we act from it and weak when we do not. The cases the rationalist points to are cases where the stronger passion, such as the desire for good, wins out over the more violent one, such as the craving for a drug. Hume's theory of the passions, therefore, requires a distinction between violent and *calm* passions; and he believes that rationalists intellectualize calm passions and overestimate the importance of violent ones.[40]

It is here that we find the closest connection between his belief in a science of human nature and his doctrine of the primacy of passion. It is not merely that a dispassionate investigation of our nature shows us that the rationalist has failed to observe it correctly. If the rationalist were right, there could be no science of human nature at all; for the paradigm of fully human conduct would be action that involved the victory of *the self* over the passions that sought to master it. So they are viewed as somehow external to it, and it is thought to have the power to assert its freedom and independence from the natural motives within it. (Kant's analysis of moral conduct clearly has this metaphysical implication.[41]) Hume denies we have this freedom with regard to our passions, just as he denies we have the ability to resist our natural instinct to believe.

If it is passion and not reason that generates choice and action, our evaluative, and in particular our moral, utterances will be connected with our actions in the way that they are because they also are manifestations of passion. Since passions are inner states of the self, not outer facts veiled from us by such inner states, the limitations of reason in the moral sphere do not entail any form of skepticism, as they do in the sphere of physical knowledge. Hence Hume does not follow the classical skeptics in holding that in judgments of good and evil and right and wrong we are confined to appearances that may or may not represent outer realities. For in matters of value, the appearances *are* the realities. The rationalist may say that our moral ideas are representations of objective facts or relations, but the science of man, in Hume's view, can tell us what they really are, how they arise, and how they lead to action. What it reveals, once more, is that they are passions, or, in the language of the second *Enquiry*, sentiments. There is a clear sense in which this is not skepticism but a theory that locates the realities of which we speak in a place that is accessible, namely within ourselves. No doubt a rationalist has good enough reason to call the Humean view of values skeptical because it does entail the rejection of moral realities external to the agent and revealed by reason; but in Hume's system, the hidden features of perceived outer objects have no counterparts in the realm of ethics, so skepticism here has no place.

It is also true that in Hume's account of morals the sentiments we express in our moral judgments arise in us on occasions that are determined by our perceptions of the outer world; in particular, our perceptions of human acts and their consequences. These are infected by the same fallibility that attends all human perception in Hume's philosophy; but they are also as probable as other perceptions may be. It is the judgments we make about these nonmoral facts that are properly the subject of moral *argument;* our evaluations themselves, since they are passions, are neither true nor false, reasonable nor unreasonable. Hume's account of morality is the ancestor, then, of twentieth-century ethical emotivism, which has not moved forward so very much from his initial formulations of it: "To have the sense of virtue, is nothing but to feel a satisfaction of a particular kind from the contemplation of a character. The very feeling constitutes our praise or admiration."[42] "The hypothesis which we embrace is plain. It maintains that morality is determined by sentiment. It defines virtue to be whatever mental action or quality gives to a spectator the pleasing sentiment of approbation, and vice the contrary."[43] Hume's emotivism has an important consequence. The peculiarly moral emotion is that of approbation or approval. It arises from "the contemplation of a character." So when we call a character virtuous, we are expressing a feeling that we have when acknowledging a set pattern of choice and behavior. For this to happen, that pattern has to be present and established already. So the virtues (like the vices) pre-exist the moral sentiments, which arise from their recognition. They cannot, then, for the most part, be the *sources* of morally good conduct. Hume, then, can have no sympathy for theories, typically rationalist ones, that trace moral conduct to the sense of rightness or to conscience; for the sentiment that Hume would identify with this is a reactive and not an originating one. We have, for the most part, to look for the sources of virtuous behavior elsewhere, in other sentiments, such as benevolence, and in the imaginative participation in the passions of others that he calls (in the *Treatise*) sympathy. So Hume's ethics is not, for the most part, an ethic of duty, but one that is founded on the recognition of the prevalence of socially beneficial habits and practices.

But although this is true for the most part, it is not true altogether. A simple example will make this clear. Our natural benevolence will often lead us to give to the needy, and this sort of action is the result of what Hume would call a natural virtue — an independently generated habit of benign behavior. But we do not think it appropriate to give our money to the needy when we owe it to our banker, even though our banker is manifestly not needy, and we have no natural inclination to give it to him. The banker still gets our money, and should. (Or so Hume thinks.) Here we do seem motivated by a sense of duty, and by nothing else. This is a fact of social observation, and Hume, in his ethical writings, broadens the concept of the science of man to include social and political behavior. But since the action we do is not natural to us because we have no independent motive for performing it, the source of our motive here is a problem. At least it is a problem for Hume, who differs here quite fundamentally from Joseph Butler, who would have seen such a case as an example of the *natural* superiority of conscience.[44] Hume says the motivation here is acquired socially. The story of how this arises is the story of the origins of *justice,* which occupies most of book III of the *Treatise* and is clearly seen by him as the major intellectual problem of ethics. Justice, unlike benevolence, is an *artificial* virtue, and Hume claims it arises because we all come to accept, through self-interest, the restraints of social life (and in particular those of property) through the recognition of the ill effects of their absence. Justice, ultimately, is something we often value not in itself, but because we *dis*approve of individual and social situations where the rules that embody it are not followed. A much briefer outline of Hume's views on this crucial topic than the one found in the third book of the *Treatise* is embodied in the appendix "Some Farther Considerations with regard to Justice" in the second *Enquiry*, which is included here.

| Hume and Religion

There can be no doubt that Hume is an antireligious thinker and a determined and consistent secularizer. Not only did he abandon his religious loyalties very early; but he also formed, and always retained, the conviction that religion, as he understood it, is an unhealthy and frequently dangerous influence on individual mental health and on social harmony. His secularizing program pervades all his work. As a historian, he viewed the previous two centuries as periods when political stability was constantly under threat from the competing forces of "superstition" (Catholicism) and "enthusiasm" (Protestantism). His science of human nature relies entirely (in his view) on observation, and references to the workings of providence are wholly absent from it, as such references are absent from the workings of Cartesian and Newtonian physical science. He is venomous in his denunciation of the "monkish virtues" of self-denial, solitude, and mortification,[45] which he sees as destructive practices that undermine the social defenses that shield us from anxiety.

He extends his human science to include a pioneering study of the origins and development of religious belief: the *Natural History of Religion*. In that work he argues that religion is due, as our commonsense beliefs are due, to nonrational causes. But the nonrational causes are not found universally because religion is not a universal phenomenon. (The implication of this is that reasoning may dislodge it in a manner impossible for commonsense beliefs.) Its sources are the fears produced by extraordinary and alarming phenomena, such as diseases and earthquakes, that humans cannot control or understand. These phenomena are due to unknown causes that uninformed primitives ascribe to some "invisible intelligent power" like themselves. "Men," says Hume, "are much oftener thrown on their knees by the melancholy than by the agreeable passions."[46] The resulting forms of religion are, predictably, polytheistic, and monotheism is a later development. It comes about through the competitive dominance of the worshippers of one deity over the claims of others. This is not a rational cause either, but once monotheism is established, it enlists the support of reason in a way polytheism does not attempt, and it spawns theological systems that are full of "absurdity and contradiction," and a fount of intolerance, persecution, and hypocrisy. Hume here follows the classical Skeptics in seeing polytheistic religion as a relatively undamaging set of ritualistic accommodations that vary from one community to another and do not much engage the intellectual, and he clearly regards monotheism as a far more dangerous and destructive force.

One of the evil results of monotheism is the way that, in Hume's view, it corrupts philosophical thought. One example is the need, created by the demands of worship (when this includes inner as well as external submission), to pronounce everything commanded by God to be good, even the acts of persecution by which God's superiority is forced upon the unorthodox. "The heart secretly detests such measures of cruel and implacable vengeance; but the judgment dares not but pronounce them perfect and adorable."[47] Given this assessment of the way the pathological forces that generate religion foul the nest of reason, it is impossible to take at face value Hume's statement at the beginning of the *Natural History* that "[t]he whole frame of nature bespeaks an intelligent author; and no rational enquirer can, after serious reflection, suspend his belief a moment with regard to the primary principles of genuine theism and religion. But the other question, concerning the origin of religion in human nature, is exposed to some more difficulty."[48] Hume is ostensibly telling us that even though religion is due to psychological forces that initially make every believer a polytheist, there is a rational argument, based on the observation of nature, that shows monotheism to be true. It seems clear, however, that this assessment contradicts his judgment later in the work that theism generates corrupt and self-deceiving forms of philosophical thought; and most readers would now judge Hume to be patently insincere in this passage. (In general, Hume makes his verbally positive comments on religion, or philosophical apologies for it, in passages such as this, which deal with aspects of religion that are not the center of attention in the work in which they appear.)

In a work like the *Natural History,* whose antireligiousness is very hard to miss, it is a little puzzling that such nominal deference to religious thinking is present at all. The commonest explanation of this is that Hume elects, as Kemp Smith puts it, to follow a "general policy of stating his sceptical positions with the least possible emphasis compatible with definiteness."[49] This in turn is commonly understood as a tactic intended to deflect the attention of his orthodox enemies away from the real intent of his work. Undoubtedly there is some truth in this, but like most interpretations of Hume, it is too simple. Two other factors should be taken into account.

In the first place, although Hume was deeply hostile to the predestinarian Calvinism that permeated the popular Scots culture of his day, he was also aware that the lettered community to which he belonged contained more benign and cultivated influences. The attempt to have him publicly condemned by the Kirk failed. Hume was also keenly aware that some of the political stability that he so greatly valued came from the cementing influence of the established churches in England and Scotland. His social conservatism made him temperamentally unsuited to the abrasive, crusading atheism of the French Enlightenment. Indeed, he never accepted the title of "atheist." There is a famous story that he visited Baron Holbach, the freethinker, in Paris, and remarked while there that he did not think anyone was a real atheist; he was met with the reply that fifteen of them were sitting with him at the table.[50]

Atheists were far too confident about what did not exist for Hume to feel at home with them intellectually, and far too eager to risk conflict by saying so for him to feel at home with them socially. The result of this is a distinction between "true" and "false" religion that he makes much of in the *Dialogues.* Although it is coded language, I think that for Hume, true religion is the secularized, undisturbing religion of polite Christian intellectuals, and false religion is the superstitious or enthusiastic religion of popular pulpits. True religion is not *true,* but it is beneficent enough not to attack.

Secondly, Hume lived in an era in which, to the Scots and English, atheism was largely unthinkable. Although there was a good deal of hostility to revealed religion among intellectuals, this did not take the anticlerical forms it took in Europe and was commonly combined with a belief in God. Many critics of orthodox Christianity were deists, who thought the reality of God could be established by argument, and that biblical revelation was an unnecessary addition to a simple acknowledgment of God and His commands. Some deists maintained a formal connection with the church. There were, therefore, a large number of nominally religious persons whose ethical and social thinking were congenial to Hume. If asked, they would universally agree that the existence of God could be shown by appeal to the so-called argument from design. This argument was based upon the order, beauty, and adaptation we can observe in nature, which (it was claimed) could not be explained without invoking the intelligent creative power of a divine mind. The consensus on this argument was to continue long after Hume demonstrated in the *Dialogues* that it is seriously defective. It is reiterated, for example, by Paley, in his *Natural Theology,* first published in 1802, and a mandatory theological text for many years afterwards. Joseph Butler, one of the few theologians for whom Hume shows respect, argued against the deists' rejection of biblical revelation in his *Analogy of Religion* of 1736; he was able to base many of his most telling retorts to them on the assumption that they took the cogency of the design argument for granted as much as he did. Faced with such a deeply held item of received wisdom, Hume devoted some of his finest and most considered reflection to the examination of the argument and was self-conscious about being in a minority of one in rejecting it. This self-consciousness is undoubtedly one of the sources of the ambiguity of some of the closing passages of the *Dialogues,* and of Hume's diffidence and indirection when writing on religious themes.

The section of the first *Enquiry* entitled "Of a Particular Providence and of a Future State," which is included here, contains a preview of some of the key arguments of the *Dialogues.* In it, Hume maintains that the design argument fails to show that the existence of a creator can be inferred from our world by standards of reasoning like those we use in the sciences. He also maintains that even if it were successful as his contemporaries believed, it would not yield any moral judgments that could not as well be made without it. And just as the *Dialogues* embodies Hume's views but does it indirectly by the use of a dialogue form in which Hume himself does not appear, so section XI of the *Enquiry* softens the blows it delivers by the use of a supposed speech by Epicurus about the implications of a philosophical belief in "Jupiter."

❙ N O T E S

1. This judgment has to be qualified a little when we consider the *Enquiries.* They are written with the limitations, as well as the expectations, of Hume's literary audience in mind. But the irony is still easily detectable.

2. He does this, for example, in the appendix to the *Treatise,* with reference both to the problem of personal identity and that of the nature of belief.

3. He says about Berkeley's arguments that they "admit of no answer and produce no conviction." *EU* XII, footnote (SB 155).

4. *T* I iv 2 (SB 218/EL I 209).

5. *T* I iv 7 (SB 269/EL I 254).

6. For a revealing comparison between the two, see Jones 1982, chap. 5.

7. Burnet 1928, chap. 7.

8. Flew 1986, chaps. 1 and 6.

9. *T* I i 5 (SB 12/EL I 21).

10. *Abstract* 31.

11. See, for example, the editorial introductions to Hume's writings by T. H. Green 1878 and L. A. Selby-Bigge 1888 and 1893.

12. Most famously A. J. Ayer 1936 and 1940.

13. Norman Kemp Smith 1905 and 1941.

14. I think this has been true of the otherwise fine studies of Capaldi 1975, Beauchamp and Rosenberg 1981, and Wilson 1979, 1983, and 1986a.

15. Capaldi 1975, 32–44.

16. Plato, *Phaedo* 95a4–102a9, 1975.

17. Most particularly Ralph Cudworth and Henry More. See Passmore 1967.

18. *T* II iii 3 (SB 415/EL II 127).

19. On this see particularly Norman Kemp Smith 1941 and Norton 1982, chap. 2.

20. Contrast here Capaldi 1975, especially chap. 10, and Stove 1975 and 1976. My own views on this theme are worked out in Penelhum 1979.

21. See Sextus Empiricus 1933, Augustine 1943, and Cicero 1933; for studies of classical skepticism see most particularly Burnyeat 1983, Schofield, Burnyeat, and Barnes 1980, Annas and Barnes 1985, Stough 1969.

22. See "The Sceptic" in Green and Grose 1882, vol. 3, 213–31.

23. Sextus 1933, vol. 1.

24. Sextus 1933, vol. 1, 17.

25. Sextus 1933, vol. 1, 21.

26. Burnyeat 1982; see also Popkin 1979 and 1980b.

27. Flew 1986. See the title of Descartes' *Second Meditation:* many editions.

28. There is a footnote reference to Sextus in *EM* section IV, but the quoted sentence is about the Stoics.

29. *Letter from a Gentleman,* 19.

30. *T* I iv 7 (SB 268–69/EL I 253).

31. *T* I iv 1 (SB 183/EL I 179).

32. *T* I iv 22 (SB 187/EL I 183). This position is repeated in *EU* section XII.

33. Popkin 1951.

34. Sextus 1933, 139–45.

35. Cicero 1933, 595.

36. Norton 1982.

37. *T* II iii 3 (SB 416/EL II 128).

38. *T* III i 1 (SB 469/EL III 177).

39. See *T* II iii 3 (SB 417/EL II 129) and III iii 5 (SB 614/EL III 307); also Chapter Five below.

40. Árdal 1966, chap. 5.

41. Kant 1949 and Paton 1948, chap. 26.

42. *T* III i 2 (SB 471/EL III 179).

43. *EM* appendix I (SB 289).

44. Butler 1900, vol. I, especially sermons 1–4.

45. *EM* IX (SB 270).

46. *NHR* III (Root 31).

47. *NHR* XIII (Root 67).

48. *NHR,* author's introduction (Root 21).

49. *DNR,* 73.

50. *DNR,* 37–38.

CHAPTER
THREE | **The Science of Mind**

Text
Enquiry Concerning
Human Understanding

Section II
Of the Origin of Ideas

Every one will readily allow, that there is a considerable difference between the perceptions of the mind, when a man feels the pain of excessive heat, or the pleasure of moderate warmth, and when he afterwards recalls to his memory this sensation, or anticipates it by his imagination. These faculties may mimic or copy the perceptions of the senses; but they never can entirely reach the force and vivacity of the original sentiment. The utmost we say of them, even when they operate with greatest vigour, is, that they represent their object in so lively a manner, that we could almost say we feel or see it. But, except the mind be disordered by disease or madness, they never can arrive at such a pitch of vivacity, as to render these perceptions altogether undistinguishable. All the colours of poetry, however splendid, can never paint natural objects in such a manner as to make the description be taken for a real landscape. The most lively thought is still inferior to the dullest sensation.

We may observe a like distinction to run through all the other perceptions of the mind. A man in a fit of anger, is actuated in a very different manner from one who only thinks of that emotion. If you tell me, that any person is in love, I easily understand your meaning, and form a just conception of his situation; but never can mistake that conception for the real disorders and agitations of the passion. When we reflect on our past sentiments and affections, our thought is a faithful mirror, and copies its objects truly; but the colours which it employs are faint and dull, in comparison of those in which our original perceptions were clothed. It requires no nice discernment or metaphysical head to mark the distinction between them.

Here therefore we may divide all the perceptions of the mind into two classes or species, which are distinguished by their different degrees of force and vivacity. The less forcible and lively are commonly denominated *thoughts* or *ideas*. The other species want a

| 39

name in our language, and in most others; I suppose, because it was not requisite for any but philosophical purposes, to rank them under a general term or appellation. Let us, therefore, use a little freedom, and call them *impressions;* employing that word in a sense somewhat different from the usual. By the term *impression,* then, I mean all our more lively perceptions, when we hear, or see, or feel, or love, or hate, or desire, or will. And impressions are distinguished from ideas, which are the less lively perceptions, of which we are conscious, when we reflect on any of those sensations or movements above mentioned.

Nothing, at first view, may seem more unbounded than the thought of man, which not only escapes all human power and authority, but is not even restrained within the limits of nature and reality. To form monsters, and join incongruous shapes and appearances, costs the imagination no more trouble than to conceive the most natural and familiar objects. And while the body is confined to one planet, along which it creeps with pain and difficulty, the thought can in an instant transport us into the most distant regions of the universe; or even beyond the universe, into the unbounded chaos, where nature is supposed to lie in total confusion. What never was seen, or heard of, may yet be conceived; nor is any thing beyond the power of thought, except what implies an absolute contradiction.

But though our thought seems to possess this unbounded liberty, we shall find, upon a nearer examination, that it is really confined within very narrow limits, and that all this creative power of the mind amounts to no more than the faculty of compounding, transposing, augmenting, or diminishing the materials afforded us by the senses and experience. When we think of a golden mountain, we only join two consistent ideas, *gold,* and *mountain,* with which we were formerly acquainted. A virtuous horse we can conceive, because, from our own feeling, we can conceive virtue; and this we may unite to the figure and shape of a horse, which is an animal familiar to us. In short, all the materials of thinking are derived either from our outward or inward sentiment. The mixture and composition of these belongs alone to the mind and will. Or, to express myself in philosophical language, all our ideas or more feeble perceptions are copies of our impressions or more lively ones.

To prove this, the two following arguments will, I hope, be sufficient. First, when we analyze our thoughts or ideas, however compounded or sublime, we always find that they resolve themselves into such simple ideas as were copied from a precedent feeling or sentiment. Even those ideas, which, at first view, seem the most wide of this origin, are found, upon a nearer scrutiny, to be derived from it. The idea of God, as meaning an infinitely intelligent, wise, and good Being, arises from reflecting on the operations of our own mind, and augmenting, without limit, those qualities of goodness and wisdom. We may prosecute this enquiry to what length we please; where we shall always find, that every idea which we examine is copied from a similar impression. Those who would assert that this position is not universally true nor without exception, have only one, and that an easy method of refuting it — by producing that idea, which, in their opinion, is not derived from this source. It will then be incumbent on us, if we would maintain our doctrine, to produce the impression, or lively perception, which corresponds to it.

Secondly, if it happen, from a defect of the organ, that a man is not susceptible of any species of sensation, we always find that he is as little susceptible of the correspondent ideas. A blind man can form no notion of colours, a deaf man of sounds. Restore either of them that sense in which he is deficient; by opening this new inlet for his sensations, you also open an inlet for the ideas, and he finds no difficulty in conceiving these objects. The case is the same, if the object, proper for exciting any sensation, has never been applied to the organ. A Laplander or Negro has no notion of the relish of wine. And though there are few or no instances of a like deficiency in the mind, where a person has never felt or is wholly incapable of a sentiment or passion that belongs to his species, yet we find the same observation to take place in a less degree. A man of mild manners can form no idea of inveterate revenge or cruelty, nor can a selfish heart easily conceive the heights of friendship and generosity. It is readily allowed, that other beings may possess many senses of which we can have no conception; because the ideas of them have never been introduced to us in the only manner by which an idea can have access to the mind, to wit, by the actual feeling and sensation.

There is, however, one contradictory phenomenon, which may prove that it is not absolutely impossible for ideas to arise, independent of their correspondent impressions. I believe it will readily be allowed, that the several distinct ideas of colour, which enter by the eye, or those of sound, which are conveyed by the ear, are really different from each other, though, at the same time, resembling. Now if this be true of different colours, it must be no less so of the different shades of the same colour, and each shade produces a distinct idea, independent of the rest. For if this should be denied, it is possible, by the continual graduation of shades, to run a colour insensibly into what is most remote from it; and if you will not allow any of the means to be different, you cannot, without absurdity, deny the extremes to be the same. Suppose, therefore, a person to have enjoyed his sight for thirty years, and to have become perfectly acquainted with colours of all kinds except one particular shade of blue, for instance, which it never has been his fortune to meet with. Let all the different shades of that colour, except that single one, be placed before him, descending gradually from the deepest to the lightest; it is plain that he will perceive a blank, where that shade is wanting, and will be sensible that there is a greater distance in that place between the contiguous colours than in any other. Now I ask, whether it be possible for him, from his own imagination, to supply this deficiency, and raise up to himself the idea of that particular shade, though it had never been conveyed to him by his senses? I believe there are few but will be of opinion that he can, and this may serve as a proof that the simple ideas are not always, in every instance, derived from the correspondent impressions; though this instance is so singular, that it is scarcely worth our observing, and does not merit that for it alone we should alter our general maxim.

Here, therefore, is a proposition, which not only seems, in itself, simple and intelligible, but, if a proper use were made of it, might render every dispute equally intelligible, and banish all that jargon, which has so long taken possession of metaphysical reasonings, and drawn disgrace upon them. All ideas, especially abstract ones, are naturally faint and obscure, the mind has but a slender hold of them, they are apt to be confounded with other resembling ideas; and when we have often employed any term, though without a distinct meaning, we are apt to imagine it has a determinate idea annexed to it. On the contrary, all impressions, that is, all sensations, either outward or inward, are strong and vivid; and limits between them are more exactly determined; nor is it easy to fall into any error or mistake with regard to them. When we entertain, therefore, any suspicion that a philosophical term is employed without any meaning or idea (as is but too frequent), we need but enquire, *from what impression is that supposed idea derived?* And if it be impossible to assign any, this will serve to confirm our suspicion. By bringing ideas into so clear a light we may reasonably hope to remove all dispute, which may arise, concerning their nature and reality.[1]

▌NOTES

1. It is probable that no more was meant by those who denied innate ideas, than that all ideas were copies of our impressions; though it must be confessed, that the terms which they employed were not chosen with such caution, nor so exactly defined, as to prevent all mistakes about their doctrine. For what is meant by *innate?* If innate be equivalent to natural, then all the perceptions and ideas of the mind must be allowed to be innate or natural, in whatever sense we take the later word, whether in opposition to what is uncommon, artificial, or miraculous. If by innate be meant contemporary to our birth, the dispute seems to be frivolous, nor is it worth while to enquire at what time thinking begins, whether before, at, or after our birth. Again, the word *idea,* seems to be commonly taken in a very loose sense, by Locke and others, as standing for any of our perceptions, our sensations and passions, as well as thoughts. Now in this sense, I should desire to know, what can be meant by asserting, that self-love, or resentment of injuries, or the passion between the sexes is not innate?

But admitting these terms, *impressions* and *ideas,* in the sense above explained, and understanding by *innate,* what is original or copied from no precedent perception, then may we assert that all our impressions are innate, and our ideas not innate.

To be ingenuous, I must own it to be my opinion, that Locke was betrayed into this question by the schoolmen, who, making use of undefined terms, draw out their disputes to a tedious length, without ever touching the point in question. A like ambiguity and circumlocution seem to run through that philosopher's reasonings on this as well as most other subjects.

Section III
Of the Association of Ideas

It is evident that there is a principle of connection between the different thoughts or ideas of the mind, and that, in their appearance to the memory or imagination, they introduce each other with a certain degree of method and regularity. In our more serious thinking or discourse this is so observable, that any particular thought, which breaks in upon the regular tract or chain of ideas, is immediately remarked and rejected. And even in our wildest and most wandering reveries, nay in our very dreams, we shall find, if we reflect, that the imagination ran not altogether at adventures, but that there was still a connection upheld among the different ideas, which succeeded each other. Were the loosest and freest conversation to be transcribed, there would immediately be observed something which connected it in all its transitions. Or where this is wanting, the person who broke the thread of discourse might still inform you, that there had secretly revolved in his mind a succession of thought, which had gradually led him from the subject of conversation. Among different languages, even where we cannot suspect the least connection or communication, it is found, that the words, expressive of ideas the most compounded, do yet nearly correspond to each other: a certain proof that the simple ideas, comprehended in the compound ones, were bound together by some universal principle, which had an equal influence on all mankind.

Though it be too obvious to escape observation, that different ideas are connected together, I do not find that any philosopher has attempted to enumerate or class all the principles of association — a subject, however, that seems worthy of curiosity. To me, there appear to be only three principles of connection among ideas, namely, *resemblance, contiguity* in time or place, and *cause* or *effect.*

That these principles serve to connect ideas will not, I believe, be much doubted. A picture naturally leads our thoughts to the original;[1] the mention of one apartment in a building naturally introduces an enquiry or discourse concerning the others;[2] and if we think of a wound, we can scarcely forbear reflecting on the pain which follows it.[3] But that this enumeration is complete, and that there are no other principles of association except these, may be difficult to prove to the satisfaction of the reader, or even to a man's own satisfaction. All we can do, in such cases, is to run over several instances, and examine carefully the principle which binds the different thoughts to each other, never stopping till we render the principle as general as possible.[4] The more instances we examine, and the more care we employ, the more assurance shall we acquire, that the enumeration, which we form from the whole, is complete and entire. Instead of entering into a detail of this kind, which would lead into many useless subtleties, we shall consider some of the effects of this connection upon the passions and imagination, where we may open a field of speculation more entertaining, and perhaps more instructive, than the other.

As a man is a reasonable being, and is continually in pursuit of happiness, which he hopes to obtain by the gratification of some passion or affection, he seldom acts or speaks or thinks without a purpose and intention. He has still some object in view, and however improper the means may sometimes be, which he chooses for the attainment of his end, he never loses view of an end; nor will he so much as throw away his thoughts or reflections, where he hopes not to reap some satisfaction from them.

In all compositions of genius, therefore, it is requisite that the writer have some plan or object; and though he may be hurried from this plan by the vehemence of thought, as in an ode, or drop it carelessly, as in an epistle or essay, there must appear some aim or intention in his first setting out, if not in the composition of the whole work. A production without a design would resemble more the ravings of a madman, than the sober efforts of genius and learning.

As this rule admits of no exception, it follows that, in narrative compositions, the events or actions which the writer relates, must be connected together by some bond or tie. They must be related to each other in the imagination, and form a kind of *unity,* which may bring them under one plan or view, and which may be the object or end of the writer in his first undertaking.

This connecting principle among the several events which form the subject of a poem or history, may be very different according to the different designs of the poet or historian. Ovid has formed his plan upon the connecting principle of resemblance. Every fabulous transformation produced by the miraculous power of the gods falls within the compass of his work. There needs but this one circumstance in any event to bring it under his original plan or intention.

An annalist or historian who should undertake to write the history of Europe during any century, would be influenced by the connection of contiguity in time and place. All events which happen in that portion of space and period of time, are comprehended in his design, though in other respects different and unconnected. They have still a species of unity, amidst all their diversity.

But the most usual species of connection among the different events which enter into any narrative composition, is that of cause and effect; while the historian traces the series of actions according to their natural order, remounts to their secret springs and principles, and delineates their most remote consequences. He chooses for his subject a certain portion of that great chain of events, which compose the history of mankind; each link in this chain he endeavors to touch in his narration; sometimes unavoidable ignorance renders all his attempts fruitless; sometimes he supplies by conjecture what is wanting in knowledge; and always he is sensible that the more unbroken the chain is, which he presents to his reader, the more perfect is his production. He sees that the knowledge of causes is not only the most satisfactory, this relation or connection being the strongest of all others, but also the most instructive, since it is by this knowledge alone we are enabled to control events, and govern futurity.

| NOTES

1. Resemblance.
2. Contiguity.
3. Cause and effect.
4. For instance, contrast or contrariety is also a connection among ideas: but it may, perhaps, be considered as a mixture of *causation* and *resemblance*. Where two objects are contrary, the one destroys the other; that is, the cause of its annihilation, and the idea of the annihilation of an object, implies the idea of its former existence.

| *Commentary*

In sections II and III of the first *Enquiry*, Hume gives us the elements of his mental science. These are the elements from which he constructed the skeptical arguments by which he was best known in his own day and which have been thought to be the core of his philosophy by countless readers since. He does indeed show himself here to be the inheritor of the work of Locke and Berkeley, as Reid and his other critics maintained. In certain key respects, Hume merely takes over the Lockean "way of ideas" and uses it for his own, partially skeptical, purposes, drawing the logical conclusions from it that he has been said to draw by generations of university teachers. This is only one facet of his system, but it is a real and prominent one.

I *Impressions and Ideas*

Section II is a recasting of sections 1–3 of part i of book I of the *Treatise*. Hume introduces here a technical vocabulary that is a refinement on that of John Locke. He says that in doing this he is restoring the common usage of the word "idea," which Locke had stretched too widely. It is best to begin by recounting briefly what Hume inherits from him.

In his *Essay Concerning Human Understanding* (1691) Locke set out to discover the powers and limits of the human intellect.[1] The basic thrust of the *Essay* (if a work as prolix and full of competing concerns can be said to have one) is that the way to see what the mind can do is to see what it *does* do. Locke, like other thinkers of his time, derives from Descartes a fundamental dualism of mind and body and assumes that the knowledge we have is an inner state that properly represents *within* the mind the nature of the world *outside* the mind. What is problematic is how we can come to know the outer world, and how extensive and reliable our knowledge is. What goes on in the mind itself is transparent to us, even though there are some confusions and disagreements that philosophers in particular may have about the details of what passes within. Inevitably, Locke holds that we learn about the outer world by having mental contents within that *represent* it. Not all the contents of the mind do this: when we are in error, or dream, or fantasize, our mental contents, however they get there, do not correctly represent outer reality to us. Locke needs a general term to cover all the contents of the mind and uses the term "idea" for this. An idea is anything in the mind. The vagueness of the term, thus stretched, is something he himself apologizes for: "Before I proceed on to what I have thought on this subject, I must here in the entrance beg pardon of my reader for the frequent use of the word *idea*, which he will find in the following treatise. It being that term which, I think, serves best to stand for whatsoever is the *object* of the understanding when a man thinks, I have used it to express whatever is meant by *phantasm, notion, species, or whatever it is which the mind can be employed*

about in thinking; and I could not avoid frequently using it."[2]
Locke tries to reduce the vagueness by classifying ideas into
groups. He distinguishes between simple and complex ideas, the
latter being in some way composed from the former, and he
distinguishes between ideas of sensation and ideas of reflection. In
the latter division, the former class are those ideas that we have
when our bodies are acted upon by outer objects and we have
visual or auditory or other sensations; and the latter are the ideas
we have when we feel emotions, or are aware of our own mental
processes, or when we remember, dream, or imagine, or use in
some other way ideas that are copies of those we have first had in
sensory experience. One of Hume's motives in his own classification is to provide for greater clarity in the discussion of this latter
class.

Locke holds that our knowledge is limited to those matters of
which we can have ideas and that all our ideas come from *experience.* This claim, which, of course, is the essence of empiricism, is
less clear than it looks; but it cannot mean that all knowledge
comes from sensory experience, given that there are ideas of
mental processes as well as of physical ones. Locke begins the
Essay with an attack on the Cartesian doctrine of *innate* ideas.
Descartes held that the mental contents that generate true knowledge, such as (in his view) the fundamental mathematical concepts
and the idea of God, are innate in the mind. Given the mathematical and theological silence of newborn infants, he has some problem defining this notion, but its main thrust is negative: the truths
of theology and mathematics are not derived from experience, but
are, in philosophical parlance, a priori, even though our facility in
reflecting on them may not show itself until we reach some degree
of maturity. Descartes' position has obvious affinities with the
Platonic doctrine of reminiscence as well as with the Stoic doctrine
of kataleptic phantasms and is an integral part of his answer to
the redefined skepticism of his first Meditation.[3] Locke interprets
the doctrine in largely psychological terms and insists that all the
ideas we have, including mathematical and moral ideas, arise in
the mind through experience, whatever the mind may subsequently do with them.[4] In spite of a patronizing comment on Locke,
Hume is in fundamental agreement with him in these matters,
although his own version of that agreement does not emerge in the
Enquiry until section IV.

The doctrine of ideas, in spite of its obvious attractiveness and
commonsense look, is notoriously skeptical in its results. It is clear
that our knowledge of the outer world comes through the ideas of
sensation we have, which must yield accurate judgments about the

objects in the world that cause them if we are to have knowledge of those objects. How, then, do we know if they do? The theory allows us no access to the outer world except through the ideas in the mind that represent it to us; but how can we ever be in a position to know which of those ideas represent it as it is and which do not? *In the theory,* no comparison between them is possible.

Locke compounds his own difficulty by making an important distinction between primary and secondary qualities. The primary qualities are those qualities allegedly in objects that are, roughly speaking, measurable, such as size, shape, and motion, and the secondary qualities are those that are not quantifiable, such as color and taste. Locke says that the primary qualities are features of our ideas of sensation *and* of the objects that cause them, but that the secondary qualities, though obviously features of our ideas, are not features of the objects, although the objects will have configurations of primary qualities that cause our sensations. Locke is influenced here by developing theories about the corpuscular constitution of physical objects and the physiology of perception: the primary qualities are those qualities that such theories suggest are really *in* things and are measurable by science, and the secondary qualities are those that are merely part of our *experience* of them.[5] Whatever Locke's motives for the distinction, however, the arguments he offers for it are weak ones, and Berkeley, in his *Principles of Human Knowledge* (1710), was able to argue very effectively that our sensory experience of the primary qualities and that of the secondary qualities could not be separated. He went further, of course, holding that the belief in a material world beyond the experiences of minds was baseless, the universe consisting of God, finite minds, and their ideas. Hume accepts the force of Berkeley's arguments but rejects their conclusion. He rightly judges them to be skeptical in their force, even though Berkeley believed that he was refuting skepticism and bolstering theism by using them. Hume's judgment on them was that they "admit of no answer, and produce no conviction."[6]

Hume's vocabulary is intended to provide for greater clarity in describing the workings of our mental life and the relationships between the elements of it. For Locke's "ideas," Hume substitutes the term "perceptions." It is not the happiest of terms for him to have chosen, since it carries a suggestion that can create ambiguity. It implies that the mental items it names have objects; perceptions, in ordinary speech, are *of* something. Hume is frequently forced to remind us that perceptions are self-contained realities on their own account and carry no reference or implication beyond themselves, in his opinion. But the verbal suggestion that there is some other real entity, mental or physical, to which the perception has reference sometimes leads Hume to talk about mental processes in ways that seem plausible only because of it.[7]

More important for our purposes is the distinction Hume makes within perceptions. He divides them into *impressions* and *ideas.* Many of his most important arguments make vital use of this distinction. Its importance is indicated in the very title of the section: what concerns Hume is where our *ideas* originate, and his basic thesis is that they all originate ultimately from impressions because they are all copies of them or are wholly composed of parts that are. This thesis is not different from Locke's claim that all our complex ideas derive from simple ideas of sensation or simple ideas of reflection, and no doubt Hume assumes that his readers will recognize that he is making the same point that Locke was making and follow him subsequently in being more consistent than Locke was in drawing out its implications.

But he has a problem, or appears to have. Locke, however inconsistent he may be in this, presupposes the reality of an external physical world and can therefore expect us to understand what an idea of sensation is without difficulty: it is an idea we have when our senses are affected by outer objects. He can also, in consequence, assume we can understand him when he tells us that our simple ideas of reflection arise when we are aware of our own mental operations or our own emotions — when, that is, new ideas arise within us that are not due directly to the action of outer objects upon us but to our responses to that action and to our subsequent mental activities. But Hume writes after much philosophical discussion of the skeptical results of Locke's teachings. He appears to want to define the difference between impressions and ideas without making the source of impressions the criterion for distinguishing them. He therefore seeks a defining difference that is internal to the impressions and ideas themselves.

If the overall interpretation of Hume outlined earlier is a correct one, there is no real need for this. For Hume holds, in fact, that although Berkeley was right that the reality of the external world cannot be proved, none of us is able to doubt it seriously. "It is in vain to ask, Whether there be body or not? That is a point which we must take for granted in all our reasonings."[8] Since this is his view, there is nothing formally inconsistent in his making use of the fact of external objects in the classification of the contents of the mind.

To some extent, of course, he does. In the *Enquiry,* his first example, that of heat, is ambiguous between a condition of the outer atmosphere and the inner experience of the perceiver; but when he later has cause to emphasize the results of certain kinds of sensory deprivation, he is forced to refer to the fact that outer objects cannot excite the relevant organs in the bodies of the blind and the deaf and to the fact that the "Laplander or Negro" has not tasted wine. It is not at all clear that anything in his system makes it improper for him to do this. But Hume is anxious to show that our nature overcomes the skeptical doubts that, but for our instincts, would interfere with our power to live. And the arguments that show how such doubts arise are (or at least include) the arguments that showed the skeptical implications of Locke's version of the ideal theory. If we look at the discussion of perceptual skepticism in section 2 of part iv of book I of the *Treatise,* we find that both Hume's perceptual skepticism and his account of those forces that enable our instinct to overcome it depend on a set of arguments that occupy the first thirteen paragraphs of the section. These arguments are designed to prove that our belief in the existence of outer objects does not come from the senses and therefore requires special explanation. Outer objects have distinct and continued existence, that is, they do not depend on the perceiver for their existence, and they continue to exist when not perceived. These features, says Hume, cannot be shown us by our senses, which "convey to us nothing but a single perception, and never give us the least intimation of any thing beyond." This is true even in the case of our awareness of our own bodies because "properly speaking, it is not our body we perceive, when we regard our limbs and members, but certain impressions, which enter by the senses; so that the ascribing a real and corporeal existence to these impressions, or to their objects, is an act of the mind . . . difficult to explain."

So Hume's account of how we come to a belief in outer objects is one in which, although we are presented only with perceptions that do not carry marks of coming from an external source, we come to ascribe to some of them an existence that is distinct from their presentation to us.[9] The details of this account, which is not duplicated in the *Enquiry,* need not concern us here. What is of importance is the fact that Hume follows Locke in holding that we are confined to perceptions in our mental life, and if we hold beliefs about a world beyond them, which we do, they have to have been developed by reason or instinct from an initial awareness that is so confined. This is how he conceives his skeptical problems and their possible solutions. He therefore seeks to classify the perceptions themselves in ways that only refer to discernible differences between them, not to their origins.

In addition to this, Hume, like Locke and other post-Cartesians, assumes that in some way our knowledge of our own minds is unproblematic. In the *Treatise* discussion just mentioned, while arguing that the senses cannot be the source of our belief in distinct external things, he says, "Upon this head we may observe, that all sensations are felt by the mind, such as they really are, and that when we doubt whether they present themselves as distinct objects, or as mere impressions, the difficulty is not concerning their nature, but concerning their relations and situation."

The *nature* of our perceptions is not something on which we are subject to the error that can infect our *interpretation* of them.[10] In the seventh section of the *Enquiry,* we have a much blunter statement, that "consciousness never deceives." The context of this is an argument that consciousness would reveal something in our experience to us, if it were really there; so we cannot have *un*conscious perceptions. Here we have a view that is at least the linear descendant of Descartes' assertion that mind is known more certainly than body is.

It is hard to be sure of the exact scope or implication of Hume's claim that consciousness cannot deceive us. While it does seem to mean that we cannot have a perception without being aware of it, and are in some manner the ultimate authority on the characteristics our perceptions have, it is also clear that he does think we can make mistakes about our perceptions when we reflect on them or introspect. We can, for example, believe very firmly that we have an impression of power when we do not (a point made much of in section VII); we can think an idea copies one impression when it copies another; we can readily overlook the separateness of our impressions and thus identify similar but distinct ones. Such errors generate false philosophical theories, but it is a forced reading of Hume's texts to suppose he thinks only philosophers are liable to them. But Hume is not to be expected to yield a systematic theory on these questions, any more than are his predecessors. For the present, it is enough to note that the unique access each person has to his or her perceptions is another reason Hume will have had for thinking that he should, and that he can, classify them without reference beyond them.

I do not think these considerations *compel* Hume to make his distinction between impressions and ideas a purely internal one, but they make it easy enough to see why he does this. The criterion he uses for the distinction is that of relative force, liveliness, or vivacity. Impressions are lively, ideas faint. He makes it clear from the start that impressions comprise the "perceptions of the senses" and the emotions, such as anger; ideas comprise the perceptions of the memory and the imagination. The criterion is not a very happy one, but although Hume recognizes this, he insists that no candid reader can really doubt the truth of what he says. One cannot help being reminded here of Locke's testy response to those who said that his representative theory of perception left him with no criterion for distinguishing real perception from illusions: that everyone knows the difference between being in a fire and merely dreaming that one is in one.[11] Perhaps we do all know the difference between the two kinds of perceptions Hume distinguishes, but such familiarity does nothing to show that it is force and vivacity that enables us to tell them apart. Hume admits himself that in dreams or madness, ideas may approach impression in their vividness, and that sometimes our sensory impressions are faint. We can easily enough think of other near-exceptions: occasions, for example, when a radical change of attitude toward someone causes us to recall vividly something that person said to us on a past occasion, when the remark was only barely noticed at the time.

Hume compounds his own difficulty in his theory of the passions in book II of the *Treatise;* he there says that all passions are impressions, each a distinct and unique one, but in order to make such unemotional conditions as the appetite for the good qualify as passions, he makes the vital distinction between violent and calm ones. Calm passions are passions that occur without being very disturbing or noticeable, even though they are effective in changing our conduct. It is hard not to read "calm" as equivalent to "faint" and "violent" as equivalent to "lively," in which case something like the original distinction between impressions and ideas becomes essential for an internal classification of impressions. And the very same principle is used in his account of sympathy to explain how it is that, in his view, some ideas *turn into* impressions: I may form an idea of another person's emotion, and through recognition of his affinity to myself this idea may become so enlivened that it turns into an experience of the same passion within myself.[12]

Finally, Hume's appeals to the familiarity of the two kinds of perception themselves suggest differing understandings of the classification. In the *Enquiry,* he says that the most vivid poetry can never paint natural objects in a way that makes its description one we can mistake for a real landscape. This equates the difference with that between the experience of the real and the experience of the imaginary, which makes inescapable external reference, and in any case omits those impressions that are passions. In the *Treatise,* he says in his first paragraph that we can all recognize the distinction between feeling and thinking. This does not omit the passions and suggests, as MacNabb says, that Hume is reaching for a distinction between "what we think about, the given, and our thoughts about it, or the symbols by means of which these thoughts are thought."[13] The notion of a given is not itself the easiest to define, but we could reasonably try to do it negatively and suggest that an idea is a perception that in some manner has a reference to a preceding perception, whereas an impression does not. On the face of it, this looks hard to square with calling the passions impressions, since a passion like anger seems to have reference to a prior injury built into it; but Hume denies this, insisting that although a passion may arise as a result of other perceptions that occasion it, it is itself a self-contained state. So MacNabb may be right.[14]

Hume does not spend much time on justifying his distinction, however. He is too eager to put it to use. The use to which he puts it is stated with crispness and elegance in the last paragraph of section II, one of the best-known of his methodological pronouncements.

The repositories, or factories, of ideas are the memory and imagination. The ideas they contain may often seem to be different from all the impressions we have previously had, but in practice we find that even in the most extravagant fancies of imagining or dreaming, or in the loftiest thoughts of theology, the ideas we use are never more than rearrangements of elements that were previously encountered in our impressions, though in different combinations. So if we allow for a difference between simple and complex impressions, and simple and complex ideas, we can say that all our simple ideas are copies of previous impressions; and hence that all our complex ideas are direct copies of previous impressions, or are composed of simpler elements that are.

All ideas, then, are copies of previous impressions. This apparently bland psychological generalization is now used by Hume as a potentially devastating ground for dismissing a large number of philosophical questions and theories. He performs this shift by the simple device of saying, or rather of assuming, that the meaning of a "term" is to be identified with "a determinate idea annexed to it." If we are suspicious, he says, that a philosopher is using a term without clear meaning, "as is but too frequent," we can test this by asking from what impression the idea supposedly annexed to it is derived. This will tell us whether the term is meaningful or not. It will also tell us what its meaning is, though Hume does not say that here: we may find, as he later argues with regard to the idea of necessary connection, that the impression the idea comes from is not always the one we would expect.

Philosophy, Psychology, and Meaning

Since Hume announces the principle that all ideas are copies of impressions to be a critical tool that can make havoc of much metaphysics, it is natural for twentieth-century readers to regard him as engaged on the same enterprise as the logical positivists in the decade before the Second World War. They erected the notorious verification principle as a criterion for distinguishing "factually meaningful" sentences from meaningless or nonsensical ones.[15] The criterion functioned, or was supposed to function, by forcing us to determine whether or not the sentences in question could be verified or falsified by reference to sense experience. Since one important result of its application was thought to be the reduction of philosophical activity to the analysis of commonsense and scientific statements, which looks very close to Hume's program of methodizing and correcting the beliefs of common life, his mitigated skepticism has been equated with positivism in the minds of very many readers, who have lamented that his insights, thus interpreted, are wrapped up in psychological language. He is thus taken to have been confused at critical points between philosophy and psychology.

As a general criticism of Hume this is totally inaccurate, even if, from time to time, he does indeed take a question to belong to psychology when it does not. The psychological thesis that as believing and feeling beings we are determined primarily by instinct and only secondarily by reason is fundamental to his system and would be wildly distorted if translated into the language of linguistic analysis. To argue, as we shall see him doing, that our key beliefs are not due to reason, he does maintain that no good reasons for those beliefs can be found by philosophers; but he then engages in the provision of accounts of how these beliefs are determined by our instincts. Such accounts themselves involve showing how our intellects are from time to time led into confusions and mistakes and ill-grounded inferences. This is certainly a *mixture* of philosophy (as this is likely to be understood now) and psychology; but it is not a program that involves a *confusion* between them.

The primary psychological thrust of Hume's method needs to be recognized before we assess his use of the impressions-ideas principle, especially the major application he makes of it in the central sections of the *Enquiry*. Hume's question, "From what impression is that supposed idea derived?" may get the answer "None," but it may equally well get the answer "Not from an impression of the sort you suppose, but another." In this way he argues that the idea of necessary connection arises from the impression of a mental process (what he calls in the *Treatise* an impression of reflection), not an impression of a sensory character.[16] An argument of this sort uses the impressions-ideas principle not to dismiss a key concept of philosophy and common life as meaningless but to reinterpret its real place in our lives. The purpose and method are irreducibly psychological.

This does not mean that the radical surgery of positivism cannot emerge from Hume's use of this principle on occasion, or that his psychologism never leads him into errors. We just have to be careful in attributing to him theories that have been developed by others whose objectives are different from his. For all his hostility to traditional theism, for example, Hume does not follow the positivist example of dismissing theological propositions as nonsensical. He specifically says, without any obvious irony, that the idea of God is developed from ideas of our own mental operations, which in turn derive from impressions of reflection. He saves his crypto-positivism for strictly philosophical concepts like that of substance[17] and rationalist conceptions of the self.[18] His critiques of representative theories of perception[19] and his attacks on the improper extension of our ideas of causation to the Deity[20] are far subtler than the dismissive condemnation of them that would follow from a simple application of the verification principle. He is very sensitive of our pretensions to know about things that are beyond us; but he does not express this sensitivity by pretending he cannot understand us when we yield to them.

But although Hume is more sparing in the destructive use of his impressions-ideas principle than his recent admirers, the fact that he does use it in this way at all shows that there is a problem about its status. The verification principle was criticized for being arbitrary and self-defeating because declarations of it appear to violate it. If the principle is itself verifiable, then we would have to ensure by examining cases that all meaningful statements satisfied it; but such an investigation could only avoid question begging if we could determine which statements were meaningful without depending on it. Similarly, if Hume says that the idea of substance is empty because no impression of substance can be found, we can ask why the absence of an impression proves this. Merely to assert that it does, without grounds, is arbitrary and dogmatic. But if the principle is supposed to be a generalization based on experience, we should be able to test it by looking for exceptions to it. Then a curiosity like Hume's missing shade of blue becomes important, for it seems to be a clear example of an idea that *does not* come from a previous impression. His candor in introducing it may be charming, but his airy dismissal of it is unfortunate. For why should a metaphysician not say, equally, that *his* idea of substance has a clear content, in spite of not coming from an impression? Do I prove him wrong merely by saying *I* do not understand it?

This leads us into another and more serious problem, of which recent commentators have made a good deal. How do we tell whether someone is using words with understanding? When we are dealing with people who are using words in a way that betrays they do not understand them (even though the rest of us do), or are dealing with people who use words we do not understand (and we suspect that they do not either), there are ways in which we can test these things. These ways are necessarily public, even in cases like the use of color adjectives. We can test a person's understanding of terms by seeing whether he or she can conform to the conventions governing the use of the relevant words in our language or can make clear to us the special conventions attached to those words he or she is using that we do not ourselves yet understand. We have to be sure they and we are familiar with the words' *use.* Such an exercise does not seem to involve reference even to the presence, let alone to the *production,* of any *images* that the speaker has. Meaning is a function of expressions in language; language is unconventional, and conventions require a public world, inhabited by language-users who are part of a rule-governed society whose practices they all share. Hume seems, however, to see the question of whether someone understands terms to be a matter of what images that person has in consciousness. He has, the argument goes, a private-language view of meaning.[21]

Donald Livingston has argued vigorously against this interpretation.[22] He points out that in book III of the *Treatise* Hume emphasizes the conventional status of morals and stresses the conventional character of moral discourse. He also argues that Hume, as a thinker who never himself questions the reality of a world of common objects and personal community, has no need to follow Locke or Descartes in judging what he calls perceptions to be logically private phenomena whose location in a common world is problematic. If that is so, then Hume's insistence on the conventional character of language and his doctrine of impressions and ideas are not inconsistent, but parts of a possible theory of language whose inner connections Hume had not worked out because semantic questions as such held little interest for him. I think

Livingston's arguments are weighty; against them is the fact that in section 2 of part iv of book I of the *Treatise,* Hume assumes the obligation of accounting for our belief in a common world of objects when we begin, he supposes, with impressions that cannot "produce the opinion of a distinct existence." This at least suggests most naturally that he would think any aspects of meaning that depended on convention would follow, and not precede, the emergence of the belief in a common world. Unless such a primitive belief were wholly inarticulate or nonverbal, it would have to begin with ideas that were the basis of some form of verbalizable thinking that was private in its sources, however much it had to be supplemented at a more developed stage of consciousness. Here again we have a situation where the beliefs Hume says we cannot do without intrude themselves into his account of their origins in ways that at least risk inconsistency. Although this is a basic question of interpretation, I leave the matter here, as debate among interpreters is so far inconclusive.

| *Association and the Self*

The description of the association of ideas in the first *Enquiry* is a pared-down version of sections 4 to 7 of part i of book I of the *Treatise.* The 1772 edition contains a quite extended discussion of how the theory of association can illuminate literary devices and traditions; this discussion is partially included in our extract but was eliminated entirely in the 1777 edition. This progressive abridgment of Hume's account is a clear sign that he came to lose interest in the details of his Newtonian psychology, even though he had singled it out for special commendation in the *Abstract.* But we should not overestimate the importance of this change. There is no good reason to think that Hume did not still consider an associationist psychology to be at the heart of his science of human nature and at least to embody an essential confirmation of his opinion that our minds can and must be understood naturalistically, in contrast to rationalist understandings of them. This means, for epistemology, that its application to the genesis of beliefs is still central. In the *Enquiry,* the mechanism is said to explain the origin of our belief in causal necessity in nature, and even though Hume may seem less vain of the theoretical merits of his theory, there is no sign of his having abandoned it, or of the overall Newtonian paradigm it reflects.[23]

But we do have to look at the *Treatise* to understand better how he thought of it. He describes association there as "a kind of attraction, which in the mental world will be found to have as extraordinary effects as in the natural, and to show itself in as many and as various forms." But although the Newtonian analogy is obvious and deliberate, it is never complete. He introduces association as a principle that connects ideas and says it makes the operations of the *imagination* "in some measure uniform." It governs the sequences of our images to a considerable degree, but Hume is clear that imagination can be fanciful and arbitrary, "for nothing is more free than that faculty," as we can see from fables and romances. This seems to mean that the imagination is governed by the principles of association when we are not *imagining:* when, that is, we are not exercising conscious control over it. Occasions when we are not doing so include most exercises of memory and all dreams. The cases that interest him are those of *involuntary* production and succession of images. It is these, for example, that generate our natural beliefs. The analogy with attraction is further weakened, however, when he says that even where association does operate, it is only "a gentle force, which commonly prevails." In practice this seems to mean that Hume is not able to use it to predict how our minds will work but sees it as enabling us to understand how certain mental operations, when recalled in introspection, can be seen to have proceeded.

He says that association operates through three relations: resemblance, contiguity in time or place, and cause and effect. In the *Treatise,* he says these relations exist between "objects," a term much used in the *Enquiry* later, when the principle is applied to our causal beliefs. Because of these qualities, "the mind is conveyed" from one idea to another, or from an impression to an idea, because the idea *to* which it is conveyed is an idea (or is an idea derived from an impression) that resembles (or is of an object that resembles), or has been found contiguous to, or to be the cause or effect of, that impression or idea (or object) *from* which it is conveyed.

The use of this principle in Hume's epistemology is found mainly in three places. The best-known is the account, central to both the *Treatise* and the *Enquiry,* of the genesis of our belief in causal necessity. The relation of cause and effect is one of the three relations that connect ideas in association, yet Hume's account of the origin of our supposed awareness of it seems to reduce it to resemblance, contiguity, and association! But, with this far from minor modification, we can still say that this application is the one where the principle is applied with the least admixture of other principles. In his accounts of our belief in the existence of outer objects and in personal identity, its use is augmented with other hypotheses, such as that of our proneness to prefer smooth to jerky transitions, and sheer intellectual error.[24]

The principle is also employed very ingeniously and in much more detail, in book II of the *Treatise,* in the analyses of the passions. Here it has to be augmented to apply beyond the imagination, as Hume understands that faculty. The passions are impressions, which often arise as a result of the association of ideas, and which also cause one another to arise (as when hatred generates anger, and love leads to benevolence). So Hume claims there is an association of impressions as well as an association of ideas; the two are both at work in the generation of what Hume calls the indirect passions of pride, humility, love, and hatred. When talking of the association of *impressions,* Hume is forced to reduce the number of relevant relations to one, namely resemblance: a passion will call up another that resembles it again; the passage from love to benevolence is a case in point.[25]

The underlying message of these applications is that the associative mechanism is an involuntary one from which we cannot escape, even though we can modify some of its results. Psychologically, he regards it as ultimate and beyond deeper explanation, though he does, in the *Treatise,* indulge in speculation that it may in turn be due to physiological causes in the brain.[26] (To speculate in this way, Hume has to assume that there are bodies, of course. But although the speculation precedes his account of how we come to believe in bodies, it should be emphasized again that there is no circularity in his presupposing something that he consistently maintains is beyond any real doubt for us.) One of the apparent purposes of the discussions of literary forms in the 1772 version of section III of the *Enquiry* is to show how the various classical forms of literary composition derive their effectiveness from the ways they use the different associative relations, thus showing indirectly how basic and pervasive they are.

A careful look at Hume's applications of his doctrine, however, leads into a deep problem in his whole philosophy of mind: that of the nature and status of the mind itself. If we recall the first sentence of section III, it reads: "It is evident that there is a principle of connection between the different thoughts or ideas of the mind, and that, in their appearance to the memory or imagination, they introduce each other with a certain degree of method and regularity." Association, then, appears to be a principle of connection *between ideas* in the mind, which seems here to be merely a sort of place where the succession of ideas plays itself out. This is the picture of our mental life on which Hume wishes to lean to carry out his antirationalist program. According to Hume, the mind itself plays no role in the mental processes that go on in it, especially those that generate belief. Our fundamental epistemic processes are not actions we freely perform but sequences of images that happen in us.

If we look at Hume's actual words, however, we find that although he is fairly consistent in using the language of passivity to speak of these processes, he is far less consistent in speaking of them as processes in which the mind itself has no role. He frequently writes of *the mind being led* from one idea to another rather than of one idea leading to another. In the section before us, he says that when we think of a wound, "we can scarcely forbear reflecting on the pain which follows it" — language suggesting a real self being impelled to pass from the one idea to the other. Another example of this notion is to be found in the midst of Hume's definition of a cause in section VII of the *Enquiry* when he tells us that "[t]he appearance of a cause always conveys the mind, by a customary transition, to the idea of the effect." In these contexts, Hume says, the mind is governed by custom to pass from one idea to another or from an impression to an idea. So even when describing the workings of association itself and depicting the mind as passive, Hume appears to ascribe habits and tendencies to it, not merely to refer to the perceptions it has. His accounts of the formation of our beliefs in the *Treatise* are full of references to the way the mind is prone to confuse one perception with another, to be led by patterns in them to ascribe independence to them, and the like. And in the case of causal beliefs, he tells us that an essential element in our idea of causation comes from the mind's anticipating an effect when a cause occurs, even though the impression of that effect lies in the future.

So Hume frequently ascribes *disposition* and *power* to the mind in the very places where his associationism seems to dispense with the mind's own activities altogether. Because of this, R. P. Wolff has argued that Hume has an unacknowledged theory of mental activity that anticipates much that is later found in Kant.[27] No doubt it could be argued that this is only something that Hume *appears* to have and that when he says things that seem to entail such a theory, he is really making statements in loose and popular language that could be recast in the language of association, impressions, and ideas, thus preserving a Newtonian rather than a Kantian view of the mind.[28] The question can only be answered with assurance if we take into account the import of what Hume says when describing the workings of the passions in book II of the *Treatise* and his account of character and the virtues in book III. Only then could we be sure how far he is, or could be, consistent with the radically Newtonian implications of such comments as the notorious remark he makes in the passage about the "corollaries" of his theory of causation in section 14 of part iii of book I: "The distinction, which we often make, between power and the exercise of it, is without foundation." This seems to deny that powers are real qualities of things or persons.

However this question is to be resolved, it leads in turn to another that has been much more disputed by scholars: the theory of self-identify in Hume's philosophy.

Hume's associationism and his empiricism certainly seem to commit him to the denial of the real existence of a self, mind, or ego, if such terms are taken to denote any sort of entity other than the successive perceptions each of us has. This appears to be at odds with common sense, particularly if we take note of Hume's regular insistence that impressions and ideas are distinct existences, that is, are separate from each other. Hume certainly seems to think that our commonsense belief about ourselves is that each of us retains numerical identity through all the changing perceptions we experience, and that this belief needs special explanation in view of the discontinuities in our mental lives that introspection reveals to us. In *Treatise* I iv 6 he begins a famous discussion of this theme by briskly rejecting the rationalist doctrine of the existence of a simple and identical self that is the owner and observer of all its perceptions. He can find no such entity within; there is no such impression, and therefore no such idea. Each of us, on the contrary, is "nothing but a bundle or collection of different perceptions, which succeed each other with an inconceivable rapidity." The mind, he says, "is a kind of theatre, where several perceptions successively make their appearance, pass, re-pass, glide away and mingle in an infinite variety of postures and situations." But "the comparison of the theatre must not mislead us. They are the successive perceptions only, that constitute the mind."[29]

He then proceeds to offer an explanation of why it is that we form the commonsense belief in "an invariable and uninterrupted existence through the whole course of our lives." What follows is an associationist account of the genesis of this belief that includes key reference to our great "propensity" to mistakes and confusions between continuing unchanging perceptions and successive similar ones, and our invention of notions like the self to conceal it. His account has been criticized on many grounds; since the whole question he is addressing is one of the deepest and most perplexing in philosophy, there is no prospect of a consensus on the strength of his arguments. We must confine ourselves here to the exegetical question of whether or not Hume's own position is internally consistent. On the surface it seems not to be, since Hume at first denies the reality of any self beyond the perceptions one has, but he then proceeds to explain how it is that *we* manage to evolve the firm belief that there is a self. The apparent inconsistency is not present in his accounts of the belief in external objects or causal necessity. In those cases, the problem is one of explaining how *we* come to believe in something that is not presented in *our* impressions. But here the problem is how to describe the origin of a belief in a self-identical mind when there is, it seems, no such mind there to form or have such a belief. Hume seems to have to talk as though what he denies is true in order to show how we can come to believe in it. There is not much doubt that a verbal difficulty exists for Hume here; but in view of the importance he gives to our sense of ourselves when he writes about such emotions as pride and shame and love and hatred,[30] our judgment of the coherence of his whole system hinges to a great extent on how far we think he has the resources to show that the inconsistency is merely a verbal one. The most promising line of defense is that offered by Nelson Pike and others: that there is no formal inconsistency in supposing that a mere series of impressions and ideas might contain within it an idea of the series as a whole and an idea of the unity of that series; since all the mind or self does is *include* perceptions, it might well include these also. The viability of this defense depends in part on the deeper question of whether one can intelligibly talk of perceptions without supposing them to be *someone's* perceptions. Hume certainly holds that one can, but it is by no means obvious that he is correct here.[31]

I *NOTES*

1. See Locke's famous story of the *Essay's* origin in the "Epistle to the Reader" with which it opens. Locke 1959, vol. 1, 32.

2. Locke 1959, vol. 1, 32.

3. See Plato's *Meno,* 1965; also Rist 1969, chap. 8, Stough 1969, chap. 3, Burnyeat 1982, and the essay by Michael Frede in Burnyeat 1983.

4. Mabbott 1973, chap. 9.

5. Mabbott 1973, chap. 2; Bennett 1971, chap. 4.

6. *EU* XII, footnote.

7. For example, his definition of will in *T* III ii 1 (SB 399/EL II 113) makes it unclear whether volition *is* an impression or is a process that gives rise to one.

8. *T* I iv 2, first paragraph.

9. Penelhum 1975a, 62–63.

10. *T* I iv 2 (SB 189/EL I 184). See Bricke 1980, chap. 7.

11. Locke 1959, book 4, chap. 2, paragraph 14 (vol. 2, 185–88).

12. *T* II i 11.

13. MacNabb 1951, 26.

14. See Hume's footnote to *T* I i 1 (SB 2/EL I 12) and his argument against passions being "contrary to reason" in *T* II iii 3 (esp. SB 451/EL II 127).

15. See, for example, Urmson 1966, Ayer 1936.

16. *T* I i 2.

17. *T* I iv 3 ("Of the Ancient Philosophy").

18. *T* I iv 5 ("Of the Immateriality of the Soul") and I iv 6 ("Of Personal Identity").

19. *T* I iv 2 ("Of Skepticism with regard to the senses").

20. *DNR,* passim, also *EU* XI.

21. Ayer 1980, chap. 1; Flew 1961, chap. 2.

22. Livingston 1984, chaps. 3 and 4.

23. Jones 1982, chap. 1.

24. *T* I iv 2 and *T* I iv 6.

25. Capaldi 1975, chap. 6; Penelhum 1975a, chap. 5.

26. *T* I ii 5 (SB 60–61/EL I 65); Bricke 1980, chap. 2.

27. Wolff 1960.

28. This is argued in Wilson 1979. See also Bricke 1980, chap. 3.

29. *T* I iv 6 (SB 253/EL I 249).

30. *T* II ii 2–7.

31. See particularly *T* I ii 6 and *T* I iv 2 (SB 207/EL I 200); also Penelhum 1975a, 62–64. On the whole question of how far Hume can maintain a "Newtonian" view of the self, see Penelhum 1955, 1975b, 1976b, Ashley and Stack 1974, Pike 1967, McIntyre 1979a, Beauchamp 1979, Biro 1979, and McIntyre 1979b.

CHAPTER
F O U R | **Cause and Effect**

Text
Enquiry Concerning
Human Understanding

Section IV
Sceptical Doubts Concerning
the Operations of the Understanding

All the objects of human reason or enquiry may naturally be divided into two kinds, to wit, relations of ideas, and matters of fact. Of the first kind are the sciences of geometry, algebra, and arithmetic, and in short, every affirmation which is either intuitively or demonstratively certain. That the square of the hypotenuse is equal to the square of the two sides, is a proposition which expresses a relation between these figures. That three times five is equal to the half of thirty, expresses a relation between these numbers.

Propositions of this kind are discoverable by the mere operation of thought, without dependence on what is anywhere existent in the universe. Though there never were a circle or triangle in nature, the truths demonstrated by Euclid would for ever retain their certainty and evidence.

Matters of fact, which are the second objects of human reason, are not ascertained in the same manner; nor is our evidence of their truth, however great, of a like nature with the foregoing. The contrary of every matter of fact is still possible, because it can never imply a contradiction, and is conceived by the mind with the same facility and distinctness, as if ever so conformable to reality. That the sun will not rise tomorrow is no less intelligible a proposition, and implies no more contradiction, than the affirmation, that it will rise. We should in vain, therefore, attempt to demonstrate its falsehood. Were it demonstratively false, it would imply a contradiction, and could never be distinctly conceived by the mind.

It may, therefore, be a subject worthy of curiosity, to enquire what is the nature of that evidence which assures us of any real existence and matter of fact, beyond the present testimony of our senses, or the records of our memory. This part of philosophy, it is observable, has been little cultivated, either by the ancients or moderns, and therefore our doubts and errors, in the prosecution of

I 64

so important an enquiry, may be the more excusable, while we march through such difficult paths without any guide or direction. They may even prove useful, by exciting curiosity, and destroying that implicit faith and security, which is the bane of all reasoning and free enquiry. The discovery of defects in the common philosophy, if any such there be, will not, I presume, be a discouragement, but rather an incitement, as is usual, to attempt something more full and satisfactory than has yet been proposed to the public.

All reasonings concerning matter of fact seem to be founded on the relation of cause and effect. By means of that relation alone we can go beyond the evidence of our memory and senses. If you were to ask a man, why he believes any matter of fact, which is absent, (for instance, that his friend is in the country, or in France) he would give you a reason, and this reason would be some other fact, as a letter received from him, or the knowledge of his former resolutions and promises. A man finding a watch or any other machine in a desert island, would conclude that there had once been men on that island. All our reasonings concerning fact are of the same nature. And here it is constantly supposed that there is a connection between the present fact and that which is inferred from it. Were there nothing to bind them together, the inference would be entirely precarious. The hearing of an articulate voice and rational discourse in the dark assures us of the presence of some person. Why? Because these are the effects of the human make and fabric, and closely connected with it. If we anatomize all the other reasonings of this nature, we shall find that they are founded on the relation of cause and effect, and that this relation is either near or remote, direct or collateral. Heat and light are collateral effects of fire, and the one effect may justly be inferred from the other.

If we would satisfy ourselves, therefore, concerning the nature of that evidence, which assures us of matters of fact, we must enquire how we arrive at the knowledge of cause and effect.

I shall venture to affirm, as a general proposition, which admits of no exception, that the knowledge of this relation is not, in any instance, attained by reasonings *a priori,* but arises entirely from experience, when we find that any particular objects are constantly conjoined with each other. Let an object be presented to a man of ever so strong natural reason and abilities; if that object be entirely new to him, he will not be able, by the most accurate examination of its sensible qualities, to discover any of its causes or effects. Adam, though his rational faculties be supposed, at the very first, entirely perfect, could not have inferred from the fluidity and transparency of water that it would suffocate him, or from the light and warmth of fire that it would consume him. No object ever discovers, by the qualities which appear to the senses, either from the causes which produced it, or the effects which will arise from it; nor can our reason, unassisted by experience, ever draw any inference concerning real existence and matter of fact.

This proposition, that causes and effects are discoverable, not by reason but by experience, will readily be admitted with regard to such objects, as we remember to have once been altogether unknown to us, since we must be conscious of the utter inability, which we then lay under, of foretelling what would arise from them. Present two smooth pieces of marble to a man who has no tincture of natural philosophy: he will never discover that they will adhere together in such a manner as to require great force to separate them in a direct line, while they make so small a resistance to a lateral pressure. Such events, as bear little analogy to the common course of nature, are also readily confessed to be known only by experience, nor does any man imagine that the explosion of gunpowder, or the attraction of a lodestone, could ever be discovered by arguments *a priori*. In like manner, when an effect is supposed to depend upon an intricate machinery or secret structure of parts, we make no difficulty in attributing all our knowledge of it to experience. Who will assert that he can give the ultimate reason, why milk or bread is proper nourishment for a man, not for a lion or a tiger?

But the same truth may not appear, at first sight, to have the same evidence with regard to events, which have become familiar to us from our first appearance in the world, which bear a close analogy to the whole course of nature, and which are supposed to depend on the simple qualities of objects, without any secret structure of parts. We are apt to imagine that we could discover these effects by the mere operation of our reason, without experience. We fancy, that were we brought on a sudden into this world, we could at first have inferred that one billiard ball would communicate motion to another upon impulse, and that we needed not to have waited for the event, in order to pronounce with certainty concerning it. Such is the influence of custom, that, where it is strongest, it not only covers our natural ignorance but even conceals itself, and seems not to take place, merely because it is found in the highest degree.

But to convince us that all the laws of nature, and all the operations of bodies without exception, are known only by experience, the following reflections may, perhaps, suffice. Were any object presented to us, and were we required to pronounce concerning the effect, which will result from it, without consulting past observation, after what manner, I beseech you, must the mind proceed in this operation? It must invent or imagine some event, which it ascribes to the object as its effect, and it is plain that this invention must be entirely arbitrary. The mind can never possibly find the effect in the supposed cause, by the most accurate scrutiny and examination. For the effect is totally different from the cause, and consequently can never be discovered in it. Motion in the second billiard ball is a quite distinct event from the motion in the first, nor is there anything in the one to suggest the smallest hint of the other. A stone or piece of metal raised into the air, and left without any support, immediately falls; but to consider the matter *a priori,* is there anything we discover in this situation which can beget the idea of a downward, rather than an upward, or any other motion, in the stone or metal?

And as the first imagination or invention of a particular effect, in all natural operations, is arbitrary, where we consult not experience, so must we also esteem the supposed tie or connection between the cause and effect, which binds them together, and renders it impossible that any other effect could result from the operation of that cause. When I see, for instance, a billiard ball moving in a straight line towards another; even suppose motion in the second ball should by accident be suggested to me, as the result of their contact or impulse, may I not conceive, that a hundred different events might as well follow from the cause? May not both these balls remain at absolute rest? May not the first ball return in a straight line, or leap off from the second in any line or direction? All these suppositions are consistent and conceivable. Why then should we give the preference to one, which is no more consistent or conceivable than the rest? All our reasonings *a priori* will never be able to show us any foundation for this preference.

In a word, then, every effect is a distinct event from its cause. It could not, therefore, be discovered in the cause, and the first invention or conception of it, *a priori,* must be entirely arbitrary. And even after it is suggested, the conjunction of it with the cause must appear equally arbitrary, since there are always many other effects, which, to reason, must seem fully as consistent and natural. In vain, therefore, should we pretend to determine any single event, or infer any cause or effect, without the assistance of observation and experience.

Hence we may discover the reason why no philosopher, who is rational and modest, has ever pretended to assign the ultimate cause of any natural operation, or to show distinctly the action of that power, which produces any single effect in the universe. It is confessed, that the utmost effort of human reason is to reduce the principles, productive of natural phenomena, to a greater simplicity, and to resolve the many particular effects into a few general causes, by means of reasonings from analogy, experience, and observation. But as to the causes of these general causes, we should in vain attempt their discovery, nor shall we ever be able to satisfy ourselves, by any particular explication of them. These ultimate springs and principles are totally shut up from human curiosity and enquiry.

Elasticity, gravity, cohesion of parts, communication of motion by impulse: These are probably the ultimate causes and principles which we shall ever discover in nature, and we may esteem ourselves sufficiently happy, if, by accurate enquiry and reasoning, we can trace up the particular phenomena to, or near to, these general principles. The most perfect philosophy of the natural kind only staves off our ignorance a little longer, as perhaps the most perfect philosophy of the moral or metaphysical kind serves only to discover larger portions of it. Thus the observation of human blindness and weakness is the result of all philosophy, and meets us at every turn, in spite of our endeavours to elude or avoid it.

Nor is geometry, when taken into the assistance of natural philosophy, ever able to remedy this defect, or lead us into the knowledge of ultimate causes, by all that accuracy of reasoning for which it is so justly celebrated. Every part of mixed mathematics proceeds upon the supposition that certain laws are established by nature in her operations, and abstract reasonings are employed, either to assist experience in the discovery of these laws, or to determine their influence in particular instances, where it depends upon any precise degree of distance and quantity. Thus, it is a law of motion, discovered by experience, that the moment of force of any body in motion is in the compound ratio or proportion of its solid contents and its velocity, and consequently, that a small force may remove the greatest obstacle or raise the greatest weight, if, by any contrivance or machinery, we can increase the velocity of that force, so as to make it an overmatch for its antagonist. Geometry assists us in the application of this law, by giving us the just dimensions of all the parts and figures which can enter into any species of machine; but still the discovery of the law itself is owing merely to experience, and all the abstract reasonings in the world could never lead us one step towards the knowledge of it. When we reason *a priori,* and consider merely any object or cause, as it appears to the mind, independent of all observation, it never could suggest to us the notion of any distinct object, such as its effect, much less show us the inseparable and inviolable connection between them. A man must be very sagacious who could discover by reasoning that crystal is the effect of heat, and ice of cold, without being previously acquainted with the operation of these qualities.

| Part II

But we have not yet attained any tolerable satisfaction with regard to the question first proposed. Each solution still gives rise to a new

question as difficult as the foregoing, and leads us on to farther enquiries. When it is asked, What is the nature of all our reasonings
concerning matter of fact? the proper answer seems to be, that they
are founded on the relation of cause and effect. When again it is
asked, What is the foundation of all our reasonings and conclusions
concerning that relation? it may be replied in one word, experience.
But if we still carry on our sifting humor, and ask, What is the foundation of all conclusions from experience? this implies a new question, which may be of more difficult solution and explication.
Philosophers, that give themselves airs of superior wisdom and suf-
ficiency, have a hard task when they encounter persons of inquisitive dispositions, who push them from every corner to which they
retreat, and who are sure at last to bring them to some dangerous
dilemma. The best expedient to prevent this confusion, is to be modest in our pretensions, and even to discover the difficulty ourselves
before it is objected to us. By this means, we may make a kind of
merit of our very ignorance.

I shall content myself, in this section, with an easy task, and
shall pretend only to give a negative answer to the question here
proposed. I say then, that, even after we have experience of the operations of cause and effect, our conclusions from that experience
are not founded on reasoning, or any process of the understanding.
This answer we must endeavour both to explain and to defend.

It must certainly be allowed, that nature has kept us at a great
distance from all her secrets, and has afforded us only the knowledge of a few superficial qualities of objects, while she conceals from
us those powers and principles on which the influence of these objects entirely depends. Our senses inform us of the colour, weight,
and consistence of bread, but neither sense nor reason can ever inform us of those qualities which fit it for the nourishment and support of a human body. Sight or feeling conveys an idea of the actual
motion of bodies, but as to that wonderful force or power, which
would carry on a moving body for ever in a continued change of
place, and which bodies never lose but by communicating it to others
— of this we cannot form the most distant conception. But notwithstanding this ignorance of natural powers[1] and principles, we always presume, when we see like sensible qualities, that they have
like secret powers, and expect that effects, similar to those which we
have experienced, will follow from them. If a body of like colour and
consistence with that bread, which we have formerly eaten, be presented to us, we make no scruple of repeating the experiment, and
foresee, with certainty, like nourishment and support. Now this is a
process of the mind or thought, of which I would willingly know the

foundation. It is allowed on all hands that there is no known connection between the sensible qualities and the secret powers; and consequently, that the mind is not led to form such a conclusion concerning their constant and regular conjunction, by anything which it knows of their nature. As to past experience, it can be allowed to give direct and certain information of those precise objects only, and that precise period of time, which fell under its cognizance; but why this experience should be extended to future times, and to other objects, which for aught we know, may be only in appearance similar — this is the main question on which I would insist. The bread, which I formerly ate, nourished me: that is, a body of such sensible qualities was, at that time, endued with such secret powers; but does it follow, that other bread must also nourish me at another time, and that like sensible qualities must always be attended with like secret powers? The consequence seems nowise necessary. At least, it must be acknowledged that there is here a consequence drawn by the mind, that there is a certain step taken — a process of thought, and an inference, which wants to be explained. These two propositions are far from being the same: I have found that such an object has always been attended with such an effect, and I foresee, that other objects, which are, in appearance, similar, will be attended with similar effects. I shall allow, if you please, that the one proposition may justly be inferred from the other; I know, in fact, that it always is inferred. But if you insist that the inference is made by a chain of reasoning, I desire you to produce that reasoning. The connection between these propositions is not intuitive. There is required a medium, which may enable the mind to draw such an inference, if indeed it be drawn by reasoning and argument. What that medium is, I must confess, passes my comprehension, and it is incumbent on those to produce it, who assert that it really exists, and is the origin of all our conclusions concerning matter of fact.

This negative argument must certainly, in process of time, become altogether convincing, if many penetrating and able philosophers shall turn their enquiries this way and no one be ever able to discover any connecting proposition or intermediate step, which supports the understanding in this conclusion. But as the question is yet new, every reader may not trust so far to his own penetration, as to conclude, because an argument escapes his enquiry, that therefore it does not really exist. For this reason it may be requisite to venture upon a more difficult task, and enumerating all the branches of human knowledge, endeavor to show that none of them can afford such an argument.

All reasonings may be divided into two kinds, namely, demonstrative reasoning, or that concerning relations of ideas, and moral reasoning, or that concerning matter of fact and existence. That there are no demonstrative arguments in the case seems evident; since it implies no contradiction that the course of nature may change, and that an object, seemingly like those which we have experienced, may be attended with different or contrary effects. May I not clearly and distinctly conceive that a body, falling from the clouds, and which, in all other respects, resembles snow, has yet the taste of salt or feeling of fire? Is there any more intelligible proposition than to affirm, that all the trees will flourish in December and January, and decay in May and June? Now whatever is intelligible, and can be distinctly conceived, implies no contradiction, and can never be proved false by any demonstrative argument or abstract reasoning *a priori*.

If we be, therefore, engaged by arguments to put trust in past experience, and make it the standard of our future judgement, these arguments must be probable only, or such as regard matter of fact and real existence, according to the division above mentioned. But that there is no argument of this kind, must appear, if our explication of that species of reasoning be admitted as solid and satisfactory. We have said that all arguments concerning existence are founded on the relation of cause and effect, that our knowledge of that relation is derived entirely from experience, and that all our experimental conclusions proceed upon the supposition that the future will be conformable to the past. To endeavor, therefore, the proof of this last supposition by probable arguments, or arguments regarding existence, must be evidently going in a circle, and taking that for granted, which is the very point in question.

In reality, all arguments from experience are founded on the similarity which we discover among natural objects, and by which we are induced to expect effects similar to those which we have found to follow from such objects. And though none but a fool or madman will ever pretend to dispute the authority of experience, or to reject that great guide of human life, it may surely be allowed a philosopher to have so much curiosity at least as to examine the principle of human nature, which gives this mighty authority to experience, and makes us draw advantage from that similarity which nature has placed among different objects. From causes which appear similar we expect similar effects. This is the sum of all our experimental conclusions. Now it seems evident that, if this conclusion were formed by reason, it would be as perfect at first, and upon one instance, as after ever so long a course of experience. But the case is far otherwise. Nothing so like as eggs; yet no one, on account of this appearing similarity, expects the same taste and relish in all of them. It is only after a long course of uniform experiments in any kind, and we attain a firm reliance and security with regard to a particular event. Now where is that process of reasoning which, from one instance, draws a conclusion so different from that which it infers from a hundred instances that are nowise different from that single one? This question I propose as much for the sake of information, as with an intention of raising difficulties. I cannot find, I cannot imagine any such reasoning. But I keep my mind still open to instruction, if any one will vouchsafe to bestow it on me.

Should it be said that, from a number of uniform experiments, we infer a connection between the sensible qualities and the secret powers: this, I must confess, seems the same difficulty, couched in different terms. The question still recurs, on what process of argument this inference is founded? Where is the medium, the interposing ideas, which join propositions so very wide of each other? It is confessed that the colour, consistence, and other sensible qualities of bread appear not, of themselves, to have any connection with the secret powers of nourishment and support. For otherwise we could infer these secret powers from the first appearance of these sensible qualities, without the aid of experience, contrary to the sentiment of all philosophers, and contrary to plain matter of fact. Here, then, is our natural state of ignorance with regard to the powers and influence of all objects. How is this remedied by experience? It only shows us a number of uniform effects, resulting from certain objects, and teaches us that those particular objects, at that particular time, were endowed with such powers and forces. When a new object, endowed with similar sensible qualities, is produced, we expect similar powers and forces, and look for a like effect. From a body of like colour and consistence with bread we expect like nourishment and support. But this surely is a step or progress of the mind, which wants to be explained. When a man says, "I have found, in all past instances, such sensible qualities conjoined with such secret powers," and when he says, "Similar sensible qualities will always be conjoined with similar secret powers," he is not guilty of a tautology, nor are these propositions in any respect the same. You say that the one proposition is an inference from the other. But you must confess that the inference is not intuitive, neither is it demonstrative. Of what nature is it, then? To say it is experimental, is begging the question. For all inferences from experience suppose, as their foundation, that the future will resemble the past, and that similar powers will be conjoined with similar sensible qualities. If there be any suspicion that the course of nature may change, and that the past may be no rule for the future, all experience becomes useless, and can give rise to no inference or conclusion. It is impossible, therefore, that any arguments from experience can prove this resemblance of the past to the future, since all these arguments are founded on the supposition of that resemblance. Let the course of things be allowed hitherto ever so regular; that alone, without some new argument or inference, proves not that, for the future, it will continue so. In vain do you pretend to have learned the nature of bodies from your past experience. Their secret nature, and consequently all their effects and influence, may change, without any change in their sensible qualities. This happens sometimes, and with regard to some objects; why may it not happen always, and with regard to all objects? What logic, what process of argument secures you against this supposition? My practice, you say, refutes my doubts. But you mistake the purport of my question. As an agent, I am quite satisfied in the point; but as a philosopher, who has some share of curiosity, I will not say scepticism, I want to learn the foundation of this inference. No reading, no enquiry has yet been able to remove my difficulty, or give me satisfaction in a matter of such importance. Can I do better than propose the difficulty to the public, even though, perhaps, I have small hopes of obtaining a solution? We shall at least, by this means, be sensible of our ignorance, if we do not augment our knowledge.

I must confess that a man is guilty of unpardonable arrogance who concludes, because an argument has escaped his own investigation, that therefore it does not really exist. I must also confess that, though all the learned, for several ages, should have employed themselves in fruitless search upon any subject, it may still, perhaps, be rash to conclude positively that the subject must, therefore, pass all human comprehension. Even though we examine all the sources of our knowledge, and conclude them unfit for such a project, there may still remain a suspicion, that the enumeration is not complete, or the examination not accurate. But with regard to the present subject, there are some considerations which seem to remove all this accusation of arrogance or suspicion of mistake.

It is certain that the most ignorant and stupid peasants — nay infants, nay even brute beasts — improve by experience, and learn the qualities of natural objects, by observing the effects which result from them. When a child has felt the sensation of pain from touching the flame of a candle, he will be careful not to put his hand near any candle, but will expect a similar effect from a cause which is similar in its sensible qualities and appearance. If you assert, therefore, that the understanding of the child is led into this conclusion by any process of argument or ratiocination, I may justly require you to produce that argument, nor have you any pretence to refuse so equitable a demand. You cannot say that the argument is abstruse, and may possibly escape your enquiry; since you confess that it is obvious to the capacity of a mere infant. If you hesitate, therefore, a moment, or if, after reflection, you produce any intricate or profound argument, you, in a manner, give up the question, and confess that it is not reasoning which engages us to suppose the past resembling the future, and to expect similar effects from causes which are, to appearance, similar. This is the proposition which I intended to enforce in the present section. If I be right, I pretend not to have made any mighty discovery. And if I be wrong, I must acknowledge myself to be indeed a very backward scholar, since I cannot now discover an argument which, it seems, was perfectly familiar to me long before I was out of my cradle.

▮ NOTES

1. The word, power, is here used in a loose and popular sense. The more accurate explication of it would give additional evidence to this argument. See Section VII.

▮ Section V
Sceptical Solution
of These Doubts
▮ Part I

The passion for philosophy, like that for religion, seems liable to this inconvenience, that, though it aims at the correction of our manners, and extirpation of our vices, it may only serve, by imprudent management, to foster a predominant inclination, and push the mind, with more determined resolution, towards that side which already draws too much, by the bias and propensity of the natural temper. It is certain that, while we aspire to the magnanimous firmness of the philosophic sage, and endeavor to confine our pleasures altogether within our own minds, we may, at last, render our philosophy like that of Epictetus, and other Stoics, only a more refined system of selfishness, and reason ourselves out of all virtue as well as social enjoyment. While we study with attention the vanity of human life, and turn all our thoughts towards the empty and transitory nature of riches and honours, we are, perhaps, all the while flattering our natural indolence, which, hating the bustle of the world, and drudgery of business, seeks a pretence of reason to give itself a full and uncontrolled indulgence. There is, however, one species of philosophy which seems little liable to this inconvenience, and that because it strikes in with no disorderly passion of the human mind, nor can mingle itself with any natural affection or propensity; and that is the

Academic or Sceptical philosophy. The academics always talk of doubt and suspense of judgement, of danger in hasty determinations, of confining to very narrow bounds the enquiries of the understanding, and of renouncing all speculations which lie not within the limits of common life and practice. Nothing, therefore, can be more contrary than such a philosophy to the supine indolence of the mind, its rash arrogance, its lofty pretensions, and its superstitious credulity. Every passion is mortified by it, except the love of truth; and that passion never is, nor can be, carried to too high a degree. It is surprising, therefore, that this philosophy, which, in almost every instance, must be harmless and innocent, should be the subject of so much groundless reproach and obloquy. But, perhaps, the very circumstance which renders it so innocent is what chiefly exposes it to the public hatred and resentment. By flattering no irregular passion, it gains few partisans. By opposing so many vices and follies, it raises to itself abundance of enemies, who stigmatise it as libertine, profane, and irreligious.

Nor need we fear that this philosophy, while it endeavors to limit our enquiries to common life, should ever undermine the reasonings of common life, and carry its doubts so far as to destroy all action, as well as speculation. Nature will always maintain her rights, and prevail in the end over any abstract reasoning whatsoever. Though we should conclude, for instance, as in the foregoing section, that, in all reasonings from experience, there is a step taken by the mind which is not supported by any argument or process of the understanding, there is no danger that these reasonings, on which almost all knowledge depends, will ever be affected by such a discovery. If the mind be not engaged by argument to make this step, it must be induced by some other principle of equal weight and authority, and that principle will preserve its influence as long as human nature remains the same. What that principle is may well be worth the pains of enquiry.

Suppose a person, though endowed with the strongest faculties of reason and reflection, to be brought on a sudden into this world: he would, indeed, immediately observe a continual succession of objects, and one event following another, but he would not be able to discover anything further. He would not, at first, by any reasoning, be able to reach the idea of cause and effect, since the particular powers, by which all natural operations are performed, never appear to the senses; nor is it reasonable to conclude, merely because one event, in one instance, precedes another, that therefore the one is the cause, the other the effect. Their conjunction may be arbitrary and casual. There may be no reason to infer the existence of one from the appearance of the other. And in a word, such a person, without more experience, could never employ his conjecture or reasoning concerning any matter of fact, or be assured of anything beyond what was immediately present to his memory and senses.

Suppose, again, that he has acquired more experience, and has lived so long in the world as to have observed similar objects or events to be constantly conjoined together: what is the consequence of this experience? He immediately infers the existence of one object from the appearance of the other. Yet he has not, by all his experience, acquired any idea or knowledge of the secret power by which the one object produces the other; nor is it by any process of reasoning he is engaged to draw this inference. But still he finds himself determined to draw it, and though he should be convinced that his understanding has no part in the operation, he would nevertheless continue in the same course of thinking. There is some other principle which determines him to form such a conclusion.

This principle is custom or habit. For wherever the repetition of any particular act or operation produces a propensity to renew the same act or operation, without being impelled by any reasoning or process of the understanding, we always say that this propensity is the effect of custom. By employing that word, we pretend not to have given the ultimate reason of such a propensity. We only point out a principle of human nature, which is universally acknowledged, and which is well known by its effects. Perhaps we can push our enquiries no farther, or pretend to give the cause of this cause, but must rest contented with it as the ultimate principle, which we can assign, of all our conclusions from experience. It is sufficient satisfaction, that we can go so far, without repining at the narrowness of our faculties because they will carry us no farther. And it is certain we here advance a very intelligible proposition at least, if not a true one, when we assert that, after the constant conjunction of two objects — heat and flame, for instance, weight and solidity — we are determined by custom alone to expect the one from the appearance of the other. This hypothesis seems even the only one which explains the difficulty, why we draw from a thousand instances, an inference which we are not able to draw from one instance that is in no respect different from them. Reason is incapable of any such variation. The conclusions which it draws from considering one circle are the same which it would form upon surveying all the circles in the universe. But no man, having seen only one body move after being impelled by another, could infer that every other body will move after a like impulse. All inferences from experience, therefore, are effects of custom, not of reasoning.[1]

Custom, then, is the great guide of human life. It is that principle alone which renders our experience useful to us, and makes us expect, for the future, a similar train of events with those which have appeared in the past. Without the influence of custom, we should be entirely ignorant of every matter of fact beyond what is immediately present to the memory and senses. We should never know how to adjust means to ends, or to employ our natural powers in the production of any effect. There would be an end at once of all action, as well as of the chief part of speculation.

But here it may be proper to remark, that though our conclusions from experience carry us beyond our memory and senses, and assure us of matters of fact which happened in the most distant places and most remote ages, yet some fact must always be present to the senses or memory, from which we may first proceed in drawing these conclusions. A man, who should find in a desert country the remains of pompous buildings, would conclude that the country had, in ancient times, been cultivated by civilized inhabitants; but did nothing of this nature occur to him, he could never form such an inference. We learn the events of former ages from history, but then we must peruse the volumes in which this instruction is contained, and thence carry up our inferences from one testimony to another, till we arrive at the eyewitnesses and spectators of these distant events. In a word, if we proceed not upon some fact, present to the memory or senses, our reasonings would be merely hypothetical; and however the particular links might be connected with each other, the whole chain of inferences would have nothing to support it, nor could we ever, by its means, arrive at the knowledge of any real existence. If I ask why you believe any particular matter of fact, which you relate, you must tell me some reason, and this reason will be some other fact, connected with it. But as you cannot proceed after this manner, *in infinitum,* you must at least terminate in some fact, which is present to your memory or senses, or must allow that your belief is entirely without foundation.

What, then, is the conclusion of the whole matter? A simple one — though, it must be confessed, pretty remote from the common theories of philosophy. All belief of matter of fact or real existence is derived merely from some object, present to the memory or senses, and a customary conjunction between that and some other object. Or in other words, having found, in many instances, that any two kinds of objects — flame and heat, snow and cold — have always been conjoined together; if flame or snow be presented anew to the senses, the mind is carried by custom to expect heat or cold, and to believe that such a quality does exist, and will discover itself upon a nearer approach. This belief is the necessary result of placing the mind in such circumstances. It is an operation of the soul, when we are so situated, as unavoidable as to feel the passion of love, when we receive benefits, or hatred, when we meet with injuries. All these operations are a species of natural instincts, which no reasoning or process of the thought and understanding is able either to produce or to prevent.

At this point, it would be very allowable for us to stop our philosophical researches. In most questions we can never make a single step farther, and in all questions we must terminate here at last, after our most restless and curious enquiries. But still our curiosity will be pardonable, perhaps commendable, if it carry us on to still farther researches, and make us examine more accurately the nature of this belief, and of the customary conjunction, whence it is derived. By this means we may meet with some explications and analogies that will give satisfaction, at least to such as love the abstract sciences, and can be entertained with speculations, which, however accurate, may still retain a degree of doubt and uncertainty. As to readers of a different taste, the remaining part of this section is not calculated for them, and the following enquiries may well be understood, though it be neglected.

∎ Part II

Nothing is more free than the imagination of man, and though it cannot exceed that original stock of ideas furnished by the internal and external senses, it has unlimited power of mixing, compounding, separating, and dividing these ideas, in all the varieties of fiction and vision. It can feign a train of events, with all the appearance of reality, ascribe to them a particular time and place, conceive them as existent, and paint them out to itself with every circumstance, that belongs to any historical fact, which it believes with the greatest certainty. Wherein, therefore, consists the difference between such a fiction and belief? It lies not merely in any peculiar idea, which is annexed to such a conception as commands our assent, and which is wanting to every known fiction. For as the mind has authority over all its ideas, it could voluntarily annex this particular idea to any fiction, and consequently be able to believe whatever it pleases, contrary to what we find by daily experience. We can, in our conception, join the head of a man to the body of a horse, but it is not in our power to believe that such an animal has ever really existed.

It follows, therefore, that the difference between fiction and belief lies in some sentiment or feeling, which is annexed to the latter, not to the former, and which depends not on the will, nor can be commanded at pleasure. It must be excited by nature, like all other sentiments; and must arise from the particular situation, in which the mind is placed at any particular juncture. Whenever any object is presented to the memory or senses, it immediately, by the force of custom, carries the imagination to conceive that object, which is usually conjoined to it, and this conception is attended with a feeling or sentiment, different from the loose reveries of the fancy. In this consists the whole nature of belief. For as there is no matter of fact which we believe so firmly that we cannot conceive the contrary, there would be no difference between the conception assented to and that which is rejected, were it not for some sentiment which distinguishes the one from the other. If I see a billiard ball moving towards another, on a smooth table, I can easily conceive it to stop upon contact. This conception implies no contradiction, but still it feels very differently from that conception by which I represent to myself the impulse and the communication of motion from one ball to another.

Were we to attempt a *definition* of this sentiment, we should, perhaps, find it a very difficult, if not an impossible task; in the same manner as if we should endeavor to define the feeling of cold or passion of anger, to a creature who never had any experience of these sentiments. Belief is the true and proper name of this feeling; and no one is ever at a loss to know the meaning of that term, because every man is every moment conscious of the sentiment represented by it. It may not, however, be improper to attempt a *description* of this sentiment, in hopes we may, by that means, arrive at some analogies, which may afford a more perfect explication of it. I say, then, that belief is nothing but a more vivid, lively, forcible, firm, steady conception of an object, than what the imagination alone is ever able to attain. This variety of terms, which may seem so unphilosophical, is intended only to express that act of the mind, which renders realities, or what is taken for such, more present to us than fictions, causes them to weigh more in the thought, and gives them a superior influence on the passions and imagination. Provided we agree about the thing, it is needless to dispute about the terms. The imagination has the command over all its ideas and can join and mix and vary them, in all the ways possible. It may conceive fictitious objects with all the circumstances of place and time. It may set them, in a manner, before our eyes, in their true colours, just as they might have existed. But as it is impossible that this faculty of imagination can ever, of itself, reach belief, it is evident that belief consists not in the peculiar nature or order of ideas, but in the manner of their conception, and in their feeling to the mind. I confess, that it is impossible perfectly to explain this feeling or manner of conception. We may make use of words which express something near it. But its true and proper name, as we observed before, is belief, which is a term that every one sufficiently understands in common life. And in philosophy, we can go no farther than assert, that belief is something felt by the mind, which distinguishes the ideas of the judgement from the fictions of the imagination. It gives them more weight and influence, makes them appear of greater importance, enforces them in the mind, and renders them the governing principle of our actions. I hear at present, for instance, a person's voice, with whom I am acquainted, and the sound comes as from the next room. This impression of my senses immediately conveys my thought to the person, together with all the surrounding objects. I paint them out to myself as existing at present, with the same qualities and relations, of which I formerly knew them possessed. These ideas take faster hold of my mind, than ideas of an enchanted castle. They are very different to the feeling, and have a much greater influence of every kind, either to give pleasure or pain, joy or sorrow.

Let us, then, take in the whole compass of this doctrine, and allow, that the sentiment of belief is nothing but a conception more intense and steady than what attends the mere fictions of the imagination, and that this manner of conception arises from a customary conjunction of the object with something present to the memory or senses. I believe that it will not be difficult, upon these suppositions, to find other operations of the mind analogous to it, and to trace up these phenomena to principles still more general.

We have already observed that nature has established connections among particular ideas, and that no sooner one idea occurs to our thoughts than it introduces its correlative, and carries our attention towards it, by a gentle and insensible movement. These principles of connection or association we have reduced to three, namely, resemblance, contiguity, and causation, which are the only bonds that unite our thoughts together, and beget that regular train of reflection or discourse, which, in a greater or less degree, takes place among all mankind. Now here arises a question, on which the solution of the present difficulty will depend. Does it happen, in all these relations, that, when one of the objects is presented to the senses or memory, the mind is not only carried to the conception of the correlative, but reaches a steadier and stronger conception of it than what otherwise it would have been able to attain? This seems to be the case with that belief which arises from the relation of cause and effect. And if the case be the same with the other relations or principles of association, this may be established as a general law, which takes place in all the operations of the mind.

We may, therefore, observe, as the first experiment to our present purpose, that, upon the appearance of the picture of an absent friend, our idea of him is evidently enlivened by the resemblance, and that every passion, which that idea occasions, whether of joy or sorrow, acquires new force and vigor. In producing this effect, there concur both a relation and a present impression. Where the picture bears him no resemblance, at least was not intended for him, it never so much as conveys our thought to him, and where it is absent, as well as the person, though the mind may pass from the thought of the one to that of the other, it feels its idea to be rather weakened than enlivened by that transition. We take a pleasure in viewing the picture of a friend, when it is set before us, but when it is removed, rather choose to consider him directly than by reflection in an image, which is equally distant and obscure.

The ceremonies of the Roman Catholic religion may be considered as instances of the same nature. The devotees of that superstition usually plead in excuse for the mummeries, with which they are upbraided, that they feel the good effect of those external motions, and postures, and actions, in enlivening their devotion and quickening their fervour, which otherwise would decay, if directed entirely to distant and immaterial objects. We shadow out the objects of our faith, say they, in sensible types and images, and render them more present to us by the immediate presence of these types, than it is possible for us to do merely by an intellectual view and contemplation. Sensible objects have always a greater influence on the fancy than any other, and this influence they readily convey to those ideas to which they are related, and which they resemble. I shall only infer from these practices, and this reasoning that the effect of resemblance in enlivening the ideas is very common; and as in every case a resemblance and a present impression must concur, we are abundantly supplied with experiments to prove the reality of the foregoing principle.

We may add force to these experiments by other of a different kind, in considering the effects of contiguity as well as of resemblance. It is certain that distance diminishes the force of every idea, and that, upon our approach to any object, though it does not discover itself to our senses, it operates upon the mind with an influence, which imitates an immediate impression. The thinking on any object readily transports the mind to what is contiguous, but it is only the actual presence of an object, that transports it with a superior vivacity. When I am a few miles from home, whatever relates to it touches me more nearly than when I am two hundred leagues distant, though even at that distance the reflecting on any thing in the neighborhood of my friends or family naturally produces an idea of them. But as in this latter case, both the objects of the mind are ideas, notwithstanding there is an easy transition between them, that transition alone is not able to give a superior vivacity to any of the ideas, for want of some immediate impression.[2]

No one can doubt but causation has the same influence as the other two relations of resemblance and contiguity. Superstitious people are fond of the relics of saints and holy men, for the same reason, that they seek after types or images, in order to enliven their devotion, and give them a more intimate and strong conception of those exemplary lives, which they desire to imitate. Now it is evident, that one of the best relics which a devotee could procure, would be the handiwork of a saint, and if his clothes and furniture are ever to be considered in this light, it is because they were once at his disposal, and were moved and affected by him — in which respect they are to be considered as imperfect effects, and as connected with him by a shorter chain of consequences than any of those, by which we learn the reality of his existence.

Suppose, that the son of a friend, who had been long dead or absent, were presented to us: it is evident, that this object would instantly revive its correlative idea, and recall to our thoughts all past intimacies and familiarities, in more lively colours than they would otherwise have appeared to us. This is another phenomenon which seems to prove the principle above mentioned.

We may observe, that, in these phenomena, the belief of the correlative object is always presupposed — without which the relation could have no effect. The influence of the picture supposes, that we believe our friend to have once existed. Contiguity to home can never excite our ideas of home, unless we believe that it really exists. Now I assert, that this belief, where it reaches beyond the memory of senses, is of a similar nature, and arises from similar causes, with the transition of thought and vivacity of conception here explained. When I throw a piece of dry wood into a fire, my mind is immediately carried to conceive, that it augments, not extinguishes the flame. This transition of thought from the cause to the effect proceeds not from reason. It derives its origin altogether from custom and experience. And as it first begins from an object, present to the senses, it renders the idea or conception of flame more strong and lively than any loose, floating reverie of the imagination. That idea arises immediately. The thought moves instantly towards it, and conveys to it all that force of conception, which is derived from the impression present to the senses. When a sword is levelled at my breast, does not the idea of wound and pain strike me more strongly, than when a glass of wine is presented to me, even though by accident this idea should occur after the appearance of the latter object? But what is there in this whole matter to cause such a strong conception, except only a present object and a customary transition to the idea of another object, which we have been accustomed to conjoin with the former? This is the whole operation of the mind, in all our conclusions concerning matter of fact and existence, and it is a satisfaction to find some analogies, by which it may be explained. The transition from a present object does in all cases give strength and solidity to the related idea.

Here, then, is a kind of pre-established harmony between the course of nature and the succession of our ideas; and though the powers and forces, by which the former is governed, be wholly unknown to us, yet our thoughts and conceptions have still, we find, gone on in the same train with the other works of nature. Custom is that principle, by which this correspondence has been effected: so necessary to the subsistence of our species, and the regulation of our conduct, in every circumstance and occurrence of human life. Had not the presence of an object instantly excited the idea of those objects, commonly conjoined with it, all our knowledge must have been limited to the narrow sphere of our memory and senses; and we should never have been able to adjust means to ends, or employ our natural powers, either to the producing of good, or avoiding of evil. Those who delight in the discovery and contemplation of final causes, have here ample subject to employ their wonder and admiration.

I shall add, for a further confirmation of the foregoing theory, that, as this operation of the mind, by which we infer like effects from like causes, and vice versa, is so essential to the subsistence of all human creatures, it is not probable, that it could be trusted to the fallacious deductions of our reason, which is slow in its operations, appears not, in any degree, during the first years of infancy, and at best is, in every age and period of human life, extremely liable to error and mistake. It is more conformable to the ordinary wisdom of nature to secure so necessary an act of the mind, by some instinct or mechanical tendency, which may be infallible in its operations, may discover itself at the first appearance of life and thought, and may be independent of all the laboured deductions of the understanding. As nature has taught us the use of our limbs, without giving us the knowledge of the muscles and nerves, by which they are actuated; so has she implanted in us an instinct, which carries forward the thought in a correspondent course to that which she has established among external objects, though we are ignorant of those powers and forces, on which this regular course and succession of objects totally depends.

∎ NOTES

1. Nothing is more usual than for writers, even on moral, political, or physical subjects, to distinguish between reason and experience, and to suppose that these species of argumentation are entirely different from each other. The former are taken from the mere result of our intellectual faculties, which, by considering *a priori* the nature of things, and examining the effects, that must follow from their operation, establish particular principles of science and philosophy. The latter are supposed to be derived entirely from sense and observation, by which we learn what has actually resulted from the operation of particular objects, and are thence able to infer, what will, for the future, result from them. Thus, for instance, the limitations and restraints of civil government, and a legal constitution, may be defended, either from reason, which reflecting on the great frailty and corruption of human nature, teaches, that no man can safely be trusted with unlimited authority, or from experience and history, which inform us of the enormous abuses, that ambition, in every age and country, has been found to make of so imprudent a confidence.

The same distinction between reason and experience is maintained in all our deliberations concerning the conduct of life, while the experienced statesman, general, physician, or merchant is trusted and followed, and the unpractised novice, with whatever natural talents endowed, neglected and despised. Though it be allowed, that reason may form very plausible conjectures with regard to the consequences of such a particular conduct in such particular circumstances, it is still supposed imperfect, without the assistance of experience, which is alone able to give stability and certainty to the maxims derived from study and reflection.

But notwithstanding that this distinction be thus universally received, both in the active and speculative scenes of life, I shall not scruple to pronounce, that it is, at bottom, erroneous, at least superficial.

If we examine those arguments, which, in any of the sciences above mentioned, are supposed to be the mere effects of reasoning and reflection, they will be found to terminate, at last, in some general principle or conclusion, for which we can assign no reason but observation and experience. The only difference between them and those maxims, which are vulgarly esteemed the result of pure experience, is that the former cannot be established without some process of thought, and some reflection on what we have observed, in order to distinguish its circumstances, and trace its consequences, whereas in the latter, the experienced event is exactly and fully similar to that which we infer as the result of any particular situation. The history of a Tiberius or Nero makes us dread a like tyranny, were our monarchs freed from the restraints of laws and senates, but the observation of any fraud or cruelty in private life is sufficient, with the aid of a little thought, to give us the same apprehension; while it serves as an instance of the general corruption of human nature, and shows us the danger which we must incur by reposing an entire confidence in mankind. In both cases, it is experience which is ultimately the foundation of our inference and conclusion.

There is no man so young and unexperienced, as not to have formed, from observation, many general and just maxims concerning human affairs and the conduct of life; but it must be confessed, that, when a man comes to put these in practice, he will be extremely liable to error, till time and farther experience both enlarge these maxims, and teach him their proper use and application. In every situation or incident, there are many particular and seemingly minute circumstances, which the man of greatest talents is, at first, apt to overlook, though on them the justness of his conclusions, and consequently the prudence of his conduct, entirely depend. Not to mention, that, to a young beginner, the general observations and maxims occur not always on the proper occasions, nor can be immediately applied with due calmness and distinction. The truth is, an unexperienced reasoner could be no reasoner at all, were he absolutely unexperienced; and when we assign that character to any one, we mean it only in a comparative sense, and suppose him possessed of experience, in a smaller and more imperfect degree.

2. "Is it natural or is it just an error," he asked, "that we are more moved by seeing those places that are known to have been associated with famous men, than by hearing of their deeds or reading their writings? I am moved in this way myself, now. It comes to my mind that Plato is said to have been the first philosopher to dispute here; and indeed that garden nearby does not merely bring him to memory but seems to make me see him. Here was Speusippus, and Xenocrates, and his pupil Polemo, who sat in that seat over there. Even our own senate-house (I mean the Hostilia, not the new one, which seems smaller to me since it was enlarged) made me think of Scipio, Cato, and Laelius, and above all of my grandfather. Places can remind us of so much; and it is not without reason that the formal training of the memory is based upon them" (Cicero, de Finibus, Book V).

Section VII
Of the Idea of Necessary Connection
Part I

The great advantage of the mathematical sciences above the moral consists in this, that the ideas of the former, being sensible, are always clear and determinate, the smallest distinction between them is immediately perceptible, and the same terms are still expressive of the same ideas, without ambiguity or variation. An oval is never mistaken for a circle, nor a hyperbola for an ellipsis. The isosceles and scalenum are distinguished by boundaries more exact than vice and virtue, right and wrong. If any term be defined in geometry, the mind readily, of itself, substitutes, on all occasions, the definition for the term defined; or even when no definition is employed, the object itself may be presented to the senses, and by that means be steadily and clearly apprehended. But the finer sentiments of the mind, the operations of the understanding, the various agitations of the passions, though really in themselves distinct, easily escape us, when surveyed by reflection; nor is it in our power to recall the original object, as often as we have occasion to contemplate it. Ambiguity, by this means, is gradually introduced into our reasonings, similar objects are readily taken to be the same, and the conclusion becomes at last very wide of the premises.

One may safely, however, affirm, that, if we consider these sciences in a proper light, their advantages and disadvantages nearly compensate each other, and reduce both of them to a state of equality. If the mind, with greater facility, retains the ideas of geometry clear and determinate, it must carry on a much longer and more intricate chain of reasoning, and compare ideas much wider of each other, in order to reach the abstruser truths of that science. And if moral ideas are apt, without extreme care, to fall into obscurity and confusion, the inferences are always much shorter in these disquisitions, and the intermediate steps, which lead to the conclusion, much fewer than in the sciences which treat of quantity and number. In reality, there is scarcely a proposition in Euclid so simple, as not to consist of more parts, than are to be found in any moral reasoning which runs not into chimera and conceit. Where we trace the principles of the human mind through a few steps, we may be very well satisfied with our progress; considering how soon nature throws a bar to all our enquiries concerning causes, and reduces us to an acknowledgment of our ignorance. The chief obstacle, therefore, to our improvement in the moral or metaphysical sciences is the obscurity of the ideas, and ambiguity of the terms. The principal difficulty in the mathematics is the length of inferences and compass of thought, requisite to the forming of any conclusion. And, perhaps, our progress in natural philosophy is chiefly retarded by the want of proper experiments and phenomena, which are often discovered by chance, and cannot always be found, when requisite, even by the most diligent and prudent enquiry. As moral philosophy seems hitherto to have received less improvement than either geometry or physics, we may conclude, that, if there be any difference in this respect among these sciences, the difficulties, which obstruct the progress of the former, require superior care and capacity to be surmounted.

There are no ideas, which occur in metaphysics, more obscure and uncertain, than those of power, force, energy or necessary connection, of which it is every moment necessary for us to treat in all our disquisitions. We shall, therefore, endeavour, in this section, to fix, if possible, the precise meaning of these terms, and thereby remove some part of that obscurity, which is so much complained of in this species of philosophy.

It seems a proposition which will not admit of much dispute, that all our ideas are nothing but copies of our impressions, or, in other words, that it is impossible for us to think of anything, which we have not antecedently felt, either by our external or internal senses. I have endeavoured[1] to explain and prove this proposition, and have expressed my hopes, that, by a proper application of it, men may reach a greater clearness and precision in philosophical reasonings, than what they have hitherto been able to attain. Complex ideas may, perhaps, be well known by definition, which is nothing but an enumeration of those parts or simple ideas, that compose them. But when we have pushed up definitions to the most simple ideas, and find still some ambiguity and obscurity, what resource are we then possessed of? By what invention can we throw light upon these ideas, and render them altogether precise and determinate to our intellectual view? Produce the impressions or original sentiments, from which the ideas are copied. These impressions are all strong and sensible. They admit not of ambiguity. They are not only placed in a full light themselves, but may throw light on their correspondent ideas, which lie in obscurity. And by this means, we may, perhaps, attain a new microscope or species of optics, by which, in the moral sciences, the most minute, and most simple ideas may be so enlarged as to fall readily under our apprehension, and be equally known with the grossest and most sensible ideas, that can be the object of our enquiry.

To be fully acquainted, therefore, with the idea of power or necessary connection, let us examine its impression; and in order to find the impression with greater certainty, let us search for it in all the sources, from which it may possibly be derived.

When we look about us towards external objects, and consider the operation of causes, we are never able, in a single instance, to discover any power or necessary connection — any quality, which binds the effect to the cause, and renders the one an infallible consequence of the other. We only find, that the one does actually, in fact, follow the other. The impulse of one billiard ball is attended with motion in the second. This is the whole that appears to the outward senses. The mind feels no sentiment or inward impression from this succession of objects. Consequently, there is not in any single, particular instance of cause and effect, any thing which can suggest the idea of power or necessary connection.

From the first appearance of an object, we never can conjecture what effect will result from it. But were the power or energy of any cause discoverable by the mind, we could foresee the effect, even without experience, and might, at first, pronounce with certainty concerning it, by the mere dint of thought and reasoning.

In reality, there is no part of matter, that does ever, by its sensible qualities, discover any power or energy, or give us ground to imagine, that it could produce any thing, or be followed by any other object, which we could denominate its effect. Solidity, extension, motion: these qualities are all complete in themselves, and never point out any other event which may result from them. The scenes of the universe are continually shifting, and one object follows another in an uninterrupted succession; but the power or force, which actuates the whole machine, is entirely concealed from us, and never discovers itself in any of the sensible qualities of body. We know, that, in fact, heat is a constant attendant of flame; but what is the connection between them, we have no room so much as to conjecture or imagine. It is impossible, therefore, that the idea of power can be derived from the contemplation of bodies, in single instances of their operation; because no bodies ever discover any power, which can be the original of this idea.[2]

Since, therefore, external objects as they appear to the senses, give us no idea of power or necessary connection, by their operation in particular instances, let us see, whether this idea be derived from reflection on the operations of our own minds, and be copied from any internal impression. It may be said, that we are every moment conscious of internal power, while we feel, that, by the simple command of our will, we can move the organs of our body, or direct the faculties of our mind. An act of volition produces motion in our limbs, or raises a new idea in our imagination. This influence of the will we know by consciousness. Hence we acquire the idea of power or energy, and are certain, that we ourselves and all other intelligent beings are possessed of power. This idea, then, is an idea of reflection, since it arises from reflecting on the operations of our own mind, and on the command which is exercised by will, both over the organs of the body and faculties of the soul.

We shall proceed to examine this pretension; and first with regard to the influence of volition over the organs of the body. This influence, we may observe, is a fact, which, like all other natural events, can be known only by experience, and can never be foreseen from any apparent energy or power in the cause, which connects it with the effect, and renders the one an infallible consequence of the other. The motion of our body follows upon the command of our will. Of this we are every moment conscious. But the means by which this is effected, the energy by which the will performs so extraordinary an operation, of this we are so far from being immediately conscious, that it must for ever escape our most diligent enquiry.

For first, is there any principle in all nature more mysterious than the union of soul with body, by which a supposed spiritual substance acquires such an influence over a material one, that the most refined thought is able to actuate the grossest matter? Were we empowered, by a secret wish, to remove mountains, or control the planets in their orbit, this extensive authority would not be more extraordinary, nor more beyond our comprehension. But if by consciousness we perceived any power or energy in the will, we must know this power; we must know its connection with the effect; we must know the secret union of soul and body, and the nature of both these substances, by which the one is able to operate, in so many instances, upon the other.

Secondly, we are not able to move all the organs of the body with a like authority, though we cannot assign any reason besides experience, for so remarkable a difference between one and the other. Why has the will an influence over the tongue and fingers, not over the heart or liver? This question would never embarrass us, were we conscious of a power in the former case, not in the latter. We should then perceive, independent of experience, why the authority of will over the organs of the body is circumscribed within such particular limits. Being in that case fully acquainted with the power or force, by which it operates, we should also know why its influence reaches precisely to such boundaries, and no further.

A man, suddenly struck with a palsy in the leg or arm, or who had newly lost those members, frequently endeavours, at first, to move them, and employ them in their usual offices. Here he is as much conscious of power to command such limbs, as a man in perfect health is conscious of power to actuate any member which remains in its natural state and condition. But consciousness never deceives. Consequently, neither in the one case nor in the other, are we ever conscious of any power. We learn the influence of our will from experience alone. And experience only teaches us, how one event constantly follows another; without instructing us in the secret connection, which binds them together, and renders them inseparable.

Thirdly, we learn from anatomy, that the immediate object of power in voluntary motion, is not the member itself which is moved, but certain muscles, and nerves, and animal spirits, and, perhaps, something still more minute and more unknown, through which the motion is successively propagated, ere it reach the member itself whose motion is the immediate object of volition. Can there be a more certain proof, that the power, by which this whole operation is performed, so far from being directly and fully known by an inward sentiment or consciousness, is, to the last degree, mysterious and unintelligible? Here the mind wills a certain event. Immediately another event, unknown to ourselves, and totally different from the one intended, is produced. This event produces another, equally unknown. Till at last, through a long succession, the desired event is produced. But if the original power were felt, it must be known. Were it known, its effect must also be known, since all power is relative to its effect. And *vice versa,* if the effect be not known, the power cannot be known nor felt. How indeed can we be conscious of a power to move our limbs, when we have no such power, but only that to move certain animal spirits, which, though they produce at last the motion of our limbs, yet operate in such a manner as is wholly beyond our comprehension?

We may, therefore, conclude from the whole, I hope, without any temerity, though with assurance; that our idea of power is not copied from any sentiment or consciousness of power within ourselves, when we give rise to animal motion, or apply our limbs to their proper use and office. That their motion follows the command of the will is a matter of common experience, like other natural events, but the power or energy by which this is effected, like that in other natural events, is unknown and inconceivable.[3]

Shall we then assert, that we are conscious of a power or energy in our own minds, when, by an act or command of our will, we raise up a new idea, fix the mind to the contemplation of it, turn it on all sides, and at last dismiss it for some other idea, when we think that we have surveyed it with sufficient accuracy? I believe the same arguments will prove, that even this command of the will gives us no real idea of force or energy.

First, it must be allowed, that, when we know a power, we know that very circumstance in the cause, by which it is enabled to produce the effect, for these are supposed to be synonymous. We must, therefore, know both the cause and effect, and the relation between them. But do we pretend to be acquainted with the nature of the human soul and the nature of an idea, or the aptitude of the one to produce the other? This is a real creation, a production of something out of nothing, which implies a power so great, that it may seem, at first sight, beyond the reach of any being less than infinite. At least it must be owned, that such a power is not felt, nor known, nor even conceivable by the mind. We only feel the event, namely, the existence of an idea, consequent to a command of the will, but the manner, in which this operation is performed, the power by which it is produced, is entirely beyond our comprehension.

Secondly, the command of the mind over itself is limited, as well as its command over the body, and these limits are not known by reason, or any acquaintance with the nature of cause and effect, but only by experience and observation, as in all other natural events and in the operation of external objects. Our authority over our sentiments and passions is much weaker than that over our ideas, and even the latter authority is circumscribed within very narrow boundaries. Will any one pretend to assign the ultimate reason of these boundaries, or show why the power is deficient in one case, not in another?

Thirdly, this self-command is very different at different times. A man in health possesses more of it than one languishing with sickness. We are more master of our thoughts in the morning than in the evening, fasting, than after a full meal. Can we give any reason for these variations, except experience? Where then is the power, of which we pretend to be conscious? Is there not here, either in a spiritual or material substance, or both, some secret mechanism or structure of parts, upon which the effect depends, and which, being entirely unknown to us, renders the power or energy of the will equally unknown and incomprehensible?

Volition is surely an act of the mind, with which we are sufficiently acquainted. Reflect upon it. Consider it on all sides. Do you find anything in it like this creative power, by which it raises from nothing a new idea, and with a kind of *fiat*, imitates the omnipotence of its Maker, if I may be allowed so to speak, who called forth into existence all the various scenes of nature? So far from being conscious of this energy in the will, it requires as certain experience as that of which we are possessed, to convince us that such extraordinary effects do ever result from a simple act of volition.

The generality of mankind never find any difficulty in accounting for the more common and familiar operations of nature — such as the descent of heavy bodies, the growth of plants, the generation of animals, or the nourishment of bodies by food, but suppose that, in all these cases, they perceive the very force or energy of the cause, by which it is connected with its effect, and is for ever infallible in its operation. They acquire, by long habit, such a turn of mind, that, upon the appearance of the cause, they immediately expect with assurance its usual attendant, and hardly conceive it possible that any other event could result from it. It is only on the discovery of extraordinary phenomena, such as earthquakes, pestilence, and prodigies of any kind, that they find themselves at a loss to assign a proper cause, and to explain the manner in which the effect is produced by it. It is usual for men, in such difficulties, to have recourse to some invisible intelligent principle[4] as the immediate cause of that event which surprises them, and which, they think, cannot be accounted for from the common powers of nature. But philosophers, who carry the scrutiny a little farther immediately perceive that, even in the most familiar events, the energy of the cause is as unintelligible as in the most unusual, and that we only learn by experience the frequent conjunction of objects, without being ever able to comprehend anything like connection between them. Here, then, many philosophers think themselves obliged by reason to have recourse, on all occasions, to the same principle, which the vulgar never appeal to but in cases that appear miraculous and supernatural. They acknowledge mind and intelligence to be, not only the ultimate and original cause of all things, but the immediate and sole cause of every event which appears in nature. They pretend that those objects which are commonly denominated causes, are in reality nothing but occasions; and that the true and direct principle of every effect is not any power or force in nature, but a volition of the Supreme Being, who wills that such particular objects should for ever be conjoined with each other. Instead of saying that one billiard ball moves another by a force which it has derived from the author of nature, it is the Deity himself, they say, who, by a particular volition, moves the second ball, being determined to this operation by the impulse of the first ball, in consequence of those general laws which he has laid down to himself in the government of the universe. But philosophers advancing still in their enquiries, discover that, as we are totally ignorant of the power on which depends the mutual operation of bodies, we are no less ignorant of that power on which depends the operation of mind on body, or of body on mind, nor are we able, either from our senses or consciousness, to assign the ultimate principle in one case more than in the other. The same ignorance, therefore, reduces them to the same conclusion. They assert that the Deity is the immediate cause of the union between soul and body, and that they are not the organs of sense, which, being agitated by external objects, produce sensations in the mind, but that it is a particular volition of our omnipotent Maker, which excites such a sensation, in consequence of such a motion in the organ. In like manner, it is not any energy in the will that produces local motion in our members: it is God himself, who is pleased to second our will, in itself impotent, and to command that motion which we erroneously attribute to our own power and efficacy. Nor do philosophers stop at this conclusion. They sometimes extend the same inference to the mind itself, in its internal operations. Our mental vision or conception of ideas is nothing but a revelation made to us by our Maker. When we voluntarily turn our thoughts to any object, and raise up its image in the fancy, it is not the will which creates that idea. It is the universal Creator, who discovers it to the mind, and renders it present to us.

Thus, according to these philosophers, every thing is full of God. Not content with the principle, that nothing exists but by his will, that nothing possesses any power but by his concession, they rob nature, and all created beings, of every power, in order to render their dependence on the Deity still more sensible and immediate. They consider not that, by this theory, they diminish, instead of magnifying, the grandeur of those attributes, which they affect so much to celebrate. It argues surely more power in the Deity to delegate a certain degree of power to inferior creatures than to produce every thing by his own immediate volition. It argues more wisdom to contrive at first the fabric of the world with such perfect foresight that, of itself, and by its proper operation, it may serve all the purposes of providence, than if the great Creator were obliged every moment to adjust its parts, and animate by his breath all the wheels of that stupendous machine.

But if we would have a more philosophical confutation of this theory, perhaps the two following reflections may suffice.

First, it seems to me that this theory of the universal energy and operation of the Supreme Being is too bold ever to carry conviction with it to a man, sufficiently apprised of the weakness of human reason, and the narrow limits to which it is confined in all its operations. Though the chain of arguments which conduct to it were ever so logical, there must arise a strong suspicion, if not an absolute assurance, that it has carried us quite beyond the reach of our faculties, when it leads to conclusions so extraordinary, and so remote from common life and experience. We are got into fairy land, long ere we have reached the last steps of our theory; and there we have no reason to trust our common methods of argument, or to think that our usual analogies and probabilities have any authority. Our line is too short to fathom such immense abysses. And however we may flatter ourselves that we are guided, in every step which we take, by a kind of verisimilitude and experience, we may be assured that this fancied experience has no authority when we thus apply it to subjects that lie entirely out of the sphere of experience. But on this we shall have occasion to touch afterwards.[5]

Secondly, I cannot perceive any force in the arguments on which this theory is founded. We are ignorant, it is true, of the manner in which bodies operate on each other. Their force or energy is entirely incomprehensible. But are we not equally ignorant of the manner or force by which a mind, even the supreme mind, operates either on itself or on body? When, I beseech you, do we acquire any idea of it? We have no sentiment or consciousness of this power in ourselves. We have no idea of the Supreme Being but what we learn from reflection on our own faculties. Were our ignorance, therefore, a good reason for rejecting anything, we should be led into that principle of denying all energy in the Supreme Being as much as in the grossest matter. We surely comprehend as little the operations of one as of the other. Is it more difficult to conceive that motion may arise from impulse than that it may arise from volition? All we know is our profound ignorance in both cases.[6]

▮ Part II

But to hasten to a conclusion of this argument, which is already drawn out to too great a length: we have sought in vain for an idea of power or necessary connection in all the sources from which we could suppose it to be derived. It appears that, in single instances of the operation of bodies, we never can, by our utmost scrutiny, discover anything but one event following another, without being able to comprehend any force or power by which the cause operates, or any connection between it and its supposed effect. The same difficulty occurs in contemplating the operations of mind and body — where we observe the motion of the latter to follow upon the volition of the former, but are not able to observe or conceive the tie which binds together the motion and volition, or the energy by which the mind produces this effect. The authority of the will over its own faculties and ideas is not a whit more comprehensible. So that, upon the whole, there appears not, throughout all nature, any one instance of connection which is conceivable by us. All events seem entirely loose and separate. One event follows another; but we never can observe any tie between them. They seem conjoined, but never connected. And as we can have no idea of any thing which never appeared to our outward sense or inward sentiment, the necessary conclusion seems to be that we have no idea of connection or power at all, and that these words are absolutely without any meaning, when employed either in philosophical reasonings or common life.

But there still remains one method of avoiding this conclusion, and one source which we have not yet examined. When any natural object or event is presented, it is impossible for us, by any sagacity or penetration, to discover, or even conjecture, without experience, what event will result from it, or to carry out foresight beyond that object which is immediately present to the memory and senses. Even after one instance or experiment, where we have observed a particular event to follow upon another, we are not entitled to form a general rule, or foretell what will happen in like cases; it being justly esteemed an unpardonable temerity to judge of the whole course of nature from one single experiment, however accurate or certain. But when one particular species of event has always, in all instances, been conjoined with another, we make no longer any scruple of foretelling one upon the appearance of the other, and of employing that reasoning, which can alone assure us of any matter of fact or existence. We then call the one object, cause; the other, effect. We suppose that there is some connection between them, some power in the one, by which it infallibly produces the other, and operates with the greatest certainty and strongest necessity.

It appears, then, that this idea of a necessary connection among events arises from a number of similar instances which occur of the constant conjunction of these events; nor can that idea ever be suggested by any one of these instances, surveyed in all possible lights and positions. But there is nothing in a number of instances, different from every single instance, which is supposed to be exactly similar — except only, that after a repetition of similar instances the mind is carried by habit, upon the appearance of one event, to expect its usual attendant, and to believe that it will exist. This connection, therefore, which we feel in the mind, this customary transition of the imagination from one object to its usual attendant, is the sentiment or impression from which we form the idea of power or necessary connection. Nothing farther is in the case. Contemplate the subject on all sides; you will never find any other origin of that idea. This is the sole difference between one instance, from which we can never receive the idea of connection, and a number of similar instances, by which it is suggested. The first time a man saw the communication of motion by impulse, as by the shock of two billiard balls, he could not pronounce that the one event was connected, but only that it was conjoined with the other. After he has observed several instances of this nature, he then pronounces them to be connected. What alteration has happened to give rise to this new idea of connection? Nothing but that he now feels these events to be connected in his imagination, and can readily foretell the existence of one from the appearance of the other. When we say, therefore, that one object is connected with another, we mean only that they have acquired a connection in our thought, and give rise to this inference, by which they become proofs of each other's existence: a conclusion which is somewhat extraordinary, but which seems founded on sufficient evidence. Nor will its evidence be weakened by any general diffidence of the understanding, or sceptical suspicion concerning every conclusion which is new and extraordinary. No conclusions can be more agreeable to scepticism than such as make discoveries concerning the weakness and narrow limits of human reason and capacity.

And what stronger instance can be produced of the surprising ignorance and weakness of the understanding than the present? For surely, if there be any relation among objects which it imports to us to know perfectly, it is that of cause and effect. On this are founded all our reasonings concerning matter of fact or existence. By means of it alone we attain any assurance concerning objects which are removed from the present testimony of our memory and senses. The only immediate utility of all sciences, is to teach us, how to control and regulate future events by their causes. Our thoughts and enquiries are, therefore, every moment, employed about this relation, yet so imperfect are the ideas which we form concerning it, that it is impossible to give any just definition of cause, except what is drawn from something extraneous and foreign to it. Similar objects are always conjoined with similar. Of this we have experience. Suitably to this experience, therefore, we may define a cause to be *an object, followed by another, and where all the objects similar to the first are followed by objects similar to the second.* Or in other words *where, if the first object had not been, the second never had existed.* The appearance of a cause always conveys the mind, by a customary transition, to the idea of the effect. Of this also we have experience. We may, therefore, suitably to this experience, form another definition of cause, and call it, *an object followed by another, and whose appearance always conveys the thought to that other.* But though both these definitions be drawn from circumstances foreign to the cause, we cannot remedy this inconvenience, or attain any more perfect definition, which may point out that circumstance in the cause, which gives it a connection with its effect. We have no idea of this connection, nor even any distinct notion what it is we desire to know, when we endeavour at a conception of it. We say, for instance, that the vibration of this string is the cause of this particular sound. But what do we mean by that affirmation? We either mean that this vibration is followed by this sound, and that all similar vibrations have been followed by similar sounds; or, that this vibration is followed by this sound, and that upon the appearance of one the mind anticipates the senses, and forms immediately an idea of the other. We may consider the relation of cause and effect in either of these two lights; but beyond these, we have no idea of it.[7]

To recapitulate, therefore, the reasonings of this section: every idea is copied from some preceding impression or sentiment, and where we cannot find any impression, we may be certain that there is no idea. In all single instances of the operation of bodies or minds, there is nothing that produces any impression, nor consequently can suggest any idea, of power or necessary connection. But when many uniform instances appear, and the same object is always followed by the same event, we then begin to entertain the notion of cause and connection. We then feel a new sentiment or impression, to wit, a customary connection in the thought or imagination between one object and its usual attendant, and this sentiment is the original of that idea which we seek for. For as this idea arises from a number of similar instances, and not from any single instance, it must arise from that circumstance, in which the number of instances differ from every individual instance. But this customary connection or transition of the imagination is the only circumstance in which they differ. In every other particular they are alike. The first instance which we saw of motion communicated by the shock of two billiard balls (to return to this obvious illustration) is exactly similar to any instance that may, at present, occur to us; except only, that we could not, at first, infer one event from the other, which we are enabled to do at present, after so long a course of uniform experience. I know not whether the reader will readily apprehend this reasoning. I am afraid that, should I multiply words about it, or throw it into a greater variety of lights, it would only become more obscure and intricate. In all abstract reasonings there is one point of view which, if we can happily hit, we shall go farther towards illustrating the subject than by all the eloquence and copious expression in the world. This point of view we should endeavour to reach, and reserve the flowers of rhetoric for subjects which are more adapted to them.

| NOTES

1. Mr. Locke, in his chapter of power, says that, finding from experience, that there are several new productions in matter, and concluding that there must somewhere be a power capable of producing them, we arrive at last by this reasoning at the idea of power. But no reasoning can ever give us a new, original, simple idea; as this philosopher himself confesses. This, therefore, can never be the origin of that idea.

2. Section II.

3. It may be pretended, that the resistance which we meet with in bodies, obliging us frequently to exert our force, and call up all our power, this gives us the idea of force and power. It is this nisus, or strong endeavour, of which we are conscious, that is the original impression from which this idea is copied. But, first, we attribute power to a vast number of objects, where we never can suppose this resistance or exertion of force to take place; to the Supreme Being, who never meets with any resistance; to the mind in its command over its ideas and limbs, in common thinking and motion, where the effect follows immediately upon the will, without any exertion or summoning up of force; to inanimate matter, which is not capable of this sentiment. Secondly, this sentiment of an endeavour to overcome resistance has no known connection with any event. What follows it, we know by experience, but could not know it *a priori*. It must, however, be confessed, that the animal nisus, which we experience, though it can afford no accurate precise idea of power, enters very much into that vulgar, inaccurate idea, which is formed of it.

4. God outside the mechanism.

5. Section XII.

6. I need not examine at length the *vis inertiae* which is so much talked of in the new philosophy, and which is ascribed to matter. We find by experience, that a body at rest or in motion continues for ever in its present state, till put from it by some new cause; and that a body impelled takes as much motion from the impelling body as it acquires itself. These are facts. When we call this a *vis inertiae,* we only mark these facts, without pretending to have any idea of the inert power; in the same manner as, when we talk of gravity, we mean certain effects, without comprehending that active power. It was never the meaning of Sir Isaac Newton to rob second causes of all force or energy, though some of his followers have endeavoured to establish that theory upon his authority. On the contrary, that great philosopher had recourse to an etherial active fluid to explain his universal attraction, though he was so cautious and modest as to allow, that it was a mere hypothesis, not to be insisted on, without more experiments. I must confess, that there is something in the fate of opinions a little extraordinary.

Descartes insinuated that doctrine of the universal and sole efficacy of the Deity, without insisting on it. Malebranche and other Cartesians made it the foundation of all their philosophy. It had, however, no authority in England. Locke, Clarke, and Cudworth, never so much as take notice of it, but suppose all along, that matter has a real, though subordinate and derived power. By what means has it become so prevalent among our modern metaphysicians?

7. According to these explications and definitions, the idea of power is relative as much as that of cause, and both have a reference to an effect, or some other event constantly conjoined with the former. When we consider the unknown circumstance of an object, by which the degree or quantity of its effect is fixed and determined, we call that its power, and accordingly, it is allowed by all philosophers, that the effect is the measure of the power. But if they had any idea of power, as it is in itself, why could not they measure it in itself? The dispute whether the force of a body in motion be as its velocity, or the square of its velocity; this dispute, I say, need not be decided by comparing its effects in equal or unequal times; but by a direct mensuration and comparison.

As to the frequent use of the words, force, power, energy, etc., which every where occur in common conversation, as well as in philosophy, that is no proof, that we are acquainted, in any instance, with the connecting principle between cause and effect, or can account ultimately for the production of one thing by another. These words, as commonly used, have very loose meanings annexed to them, and their ideas are very uncertain and confused. No animal can put external bodies in motion without the sentiment of a nisus or endeavour; and every animal has a sentiment or feeling from the stroke or blow of an external object, that is in motion. These sensations, which are merely animal, and from which we can a priori draw no inference, we are apt to transfer to inanimate objects, and to suppose, that they have some such feelings, whenever they transfer or receive motion. With regard to energies, which are exerted, without our annexing to them any idea of communicated motion, we consider only the constant experienced conjunction of the events; and as we feel a customary connection between the ideas, we transfer that feeling to the objects; as nothing is more usual than to apply to external bodies every internal sensation, which they occasion.

I *Commentary*

Hume's treatment of causality is the most celebrated and influential part of his philosophy, and his presentation of it in the *Enquiry* is one of the most elegant of all his writings. Yet his exact purposes are still a matter of controversy. I shall try to make the nature of the scholarly debates clear without detracting from the clarity and grace of Hume's own profound and disturbing arguments.

Sections IV to VII of the *Enquiry* are a careful recasting of the much longer part iii of book I of the *Treatise* ("Of Knowledge and Probability"). In the main, section IV and part i of section V in the

Enquiry correspond to *Treatise* I iii 2 and 4–5; part ii of section V in the *Enquiry* corresponds to *Treatise* I iii 8–10; section vi in the *Enquiry* (omitted here) corresponds to *Treatise* I iii 11–13; and section vii is the counterpart of *Treatise* I iii 14. When points of detailed interpretation are being considered, there is no substitute for detailed comparisons between these texts. There is one important part of the *Treatise* that has no counterpart in the *Enquiry,* namely *Treatise* I iii 3 ("Why a Cause is Always Necessary"). In addition to these two lengthy treatments of causality, Hume gives an important summary of the *Treatise* discussion in the *Abstract,* although this says little of the matters dealt with in part i of section IV in the *Enquiry,* or those in section VII.

Hume's argument treats two related but distinguishable issues: the nature of our reasoning from experience (now commonly called induction) and the nature of the causal relationship between objects or events. In the course of this, he makes observations of the greatest importance on other matters: the nature of a priori knowledge, the nature of belief, and the phenomenology of the will. Even if all his contentions are mistaken, as some believe, there is a revelatory quality to his writing that makes these short consecutive essays a philosophical education in themselves. I shall begin here with a short summary of the whole argument, and then, with some regret, start to muddy the waters with the difficult questions of interpretation.

| *An Interpretive Summary*

Hume starts secton IV by setting up a division commonly known as "Hume's Fork." It is a crisp summary of what has since become the standard empiricist view of the nature and limits of knowledge. The empiricist tradition, which insists that all knowledge must come from experience, has always had to account for the special status of the truths of logic and mathematics, which, ever since the time of Plato and before, have been the prize exhibits of rationalism. Mathematical knowledge appears to be immune to refutation by experience (to be a priori) and therefore to be exempt from the empiricists' requirement. Attempts to explain mathematical truths as dependent on experience, after all, are manifestly implausible. The enormous influence of Descartes, combined with the prestige of Newtonian physics, in which mathematical formulae were applied with overwhelming success to the understanding of the physical universe, placed those, like Hume, who wished to stress the importance of experiment and observation in our knowledge of the world in a position where this emphasis had to be made consistent with the *non*observational character of mathematics itself. Hume's Fork is the modern empiricist answer, even though the language in which Hume expresses it is out of favor.

Hume's statement is a brief and entirely dogmatic one, although it has a strong and immediate intuitive appeal. He divides "the objects of human reason or enquiry" into two classes: relations of ideas and matters of fact. The first class contains the truths of mathematics and any other truths that are "intuitively or demonstrably certain." Their certainty is as real as any rationalist has ever claimed. But it comes at a very high price. The certainty of a statement like "Three times five is equal to the half of thirty" comes in part from its immunity to refutation by anything that exists or happens in "nature" or "the universe." But this immunity is the result of the fact that such statements are not *about* nature or the universe. As Hume sees it, the reason why such statements can be known for certain by "the mere operation of thought" is the fact that they are only *about our thoughts,* namely our ideas, and not about the world.

In maintaining this, Hume clearly does not mean to say that mathematics is a science based on introspection; that would make its assertions as vulnerable to the changes in our lives as any others. His view seems rather to be that the ideas we form (after deriving them from impressions) include some, such as those of numbers or geometrical figures, which we can then use according to rules of our own devising in ways that are not vulnerable to changes in our experience. Mathematics is a purely conceptual or stipulative discipline. This raises a host of questions, not the least of which is the question of how a discipline that is not about the changing world can nevertheless enable us to understand and control that world. But these are questions Hume is not concerned with here. He is merely concerned to show that there *is* a way to deal with a priori knowledge in an empiricist system, not to develop that way himself. What he wishes to do is to explore the character of our knowledge (or apparent knowledge) of the other class of objects of enquiry: matters of fact. Here, too, our ability to make assertions carries a price that rationalists and half-hearted empiricists have never completely recognized. The price can be stated, but not fully understood, by saying that no matter of fact can be demonstrated.

Matters of fact cannot be demonstrated because the "contrary" (he clearly means the *contradictory*) of any matter of fact is always possible, since it never implies a contradiction. Mathematical

errors generate contradictions, but the denial of a matter of fact
does not and can always be "conceived by the mind" with "facility
and distinctness." His example: "The sun will not rise tomorrow."
Hence no matter of fact can be demonstrated.

Some matters of fact, though not demonstrated, are matters
on which we can have easy assurance. These are "the present
testimony of our senses, or the records of our memory. " We feel
assured, however, of many more matters of fact than these. He
sets out to inquire about the way we become assured of these more
wide-ranging matters of fact, noting that this investigation has
been "little cultivated" by other philosophers. His answer is that
we acquire the assurance we have through "reasonings" founded
on the relation of cause and effect. Whenever someone claims to
know about some matter of fact that is "absent," this is because it
is the cause or the effect of some other, "present" one. But how do
we come to learn about causes and effects? He gives this a two-part
answer in the remainder of part i of the section: (a) We do not
learn of causes and effects by "reasonings *a priori.*" This is a
negative, antirationalist claim. (b) We learn of causes and effects
from experience. This is a positive, empiricist claim. It leads to
another inquiry, "What is the foundation of all conclusions from
experience?" which he says "implies a new question." In part ii of
the section, he gives a negative answer to it, leaving positive
responses to section V. The negative response has to be the reason
for his calling section IV one that raises "sceptical doubts." It is (c)
that conclusions from experience are not "founded on reasoning, or
on any process of the understanding."

There is little controversy about the nature of Hume's arguments for (a) and (b). He tells us that everyone will agree readily
enough that our knowledge of causal connections that used to be
unfamiliar comes from experience, such as the fact that two
smooth pieces of marble are hard to separate or that certain
chemical combinations lead to explosions. We need to be reminded,
however, that the same is true for very familiar causal connections. (This points to Hume's final conclusion that familiarity is the
essence of necessary connection.) Even in the most familiar cases,
of which his paradigm is the communication of motion between
two billiard balls, we should reflect that the cause and the effect
are distinct events, "nor is there anything in the one to suggest the
smallest hint of the other." We can always, easily, imagine some
unfamiliar outcome, such as the rebounding of the first billiard
ball. This is enough to show that there is no inconsistency in
supposing the cause to occur but the effect not to follow. Hence it is

only experience that makes the supposition of the familiar effect anything other than "arbitrary," and the supposition could never be derived from a priori reasoning.

There is much more controversy about the nature and intent of Hume's argument for (c). I shall state a reading here, and discuss the controversies below.

When Hume says that our conclusions from experience are not due to reasoning, he clearly cannot mean that we do not perform inferences expressed (or expressible) in words, for he says in his explanation that we do just this. He explains himself by saying it is not "drawn by reasoning and argument," and this is because there is no "medium" to enable it to be so drawn. He expresses what I take to be the same point by saying he wants to know "the foundation" of the inference that we make. What is it that joins propositions about past experience to conclusions that are about or include the future? If we search for it, there are only two places to look. First, we could try to represent the inference as a valid demonstration, on the pattern of those disciplines that deal with the relations of ideas, but this is clearly fruitless, since "it implies no contradiction that the course of nature may change, and that an object, seemingly like those which we have experienced, may be attended with different or contrary effects." Second, we can engage in "moral reasoning," that is, inductive reasoning, and say, in effect, that since we have regularly encountered this sort of sequence in the past, we can be confident it will be repeated — but this is "evidently going in a circle." The inference, then, is neither intuitive nor demonstrative, and it is "begging the question" to suggest it is experimental, since that is merely to assume that "the future will resemble the past." Anyone who concedes all this must therefore "confess that it is not reasoning which engages us to suppose the past resembling the future, and to expect similar effects from causes which are, to experience, similar." This conclusion, expressed throughout in psychological language, clearly involves the insistence that inferences from past experience to the future, although performed by all of us, have neither deductive nor inductive justification, and that philosophical attempts to provide either of these would be futile. Hume's readers have generally taken this to mean that this continual and indispensable inference has no intellectual basis in our psychological makeup and cannot be given rational justification. The "problem of induction," as it is commonly known to philosophers, is usually taken to be the problem of answering Hume's challenge and producing some sort of justification where he says there is none. Thus read, Hume's position is clearly a skeptical one and has generally been interpreted as a modern paradigm of a skeptical position in epistemology.

In section V Hume offers his "sceptical solution" in the form of an account, couched in tolerant but unflattering terms, of how everyone manages to acquire the practice of inferring from the past to the future in the absence of reasoning to justify it. He has already hinted at his account by stressing how important familiarity seems to be in making our inferences seem obvious to us. What the skeptic shows we cannot do by reasoning, Hume shows we do through habit, or "custom." Someone brought "on a sudden" into our world, however clever, could never interpret sequences of objects as causes and effects or infer the latter from the former until he had observed a good many of them. Since the repetition of sequences adds nothing new to any given sequence, something not observed in the sequences themselves must be the cause of the inferences such a person would certainly come to make. So all the inferences from experience are "effects of custom, not of reasoning." Custom is "the great guide of human life."

But custom guides human life by prompting us to make inferences from facts "'present to the senses." If this were not so, our reasonings would be "merely hypothetical." So beliefs about matters of fact arise from the presence to our senses of some object, plus a "customary conjunction between it and some other. Because of many past instances of such a conjunction, when the first object in it appears to the mind, it believes the second is to follow. To repeat Hume's conclusion and summation: "This belief is the necessary result of placing the mind in such circumstances. It is an operation of the soul, when we are so situated, as unavoidable as to feel the passion of love, when we receive benefits, or hatred, when we meet with injuries. All these operations are a species of natural instincts, which no reasoning or process of the thought and understanding is able either to produce or to prevent." This summation draws an explicit analogy between causal inference and our emotional responses to outer events and declares both to be forms of instinct that cannot be produced or prevented by intellectual processes. The power of such instincts makes skeptical doubts irrelevant to life, and the recognition of their power provides an antidote to those doubts — but *not* a refutation of them.

In part ii of section V, which corresponds to I iii 5–7 in the *Treatise,* Hume deals with a question he says is subsidiary, namely the nature of the phenomenon of *belief* that is the part of the introspectible sequence of causal judgment arising from custom. Given his doctrine of impressions and ideas, he has a problem accounting for it. Custom makes the imagination call up the idea

of the effect when the cause occurs. But there is a difference
between merely having the idea of some object and *believing* the
object so conceived will come to pass. In the *Enquiry* version of his
theory, Hume expresses the problem as that of distinguishing
between fiction and belief, and he says the difference between
them lies in a "sentiment or feeling" attached to the latter. This he
describes as "a more vivid, lively, forcible, firm, steady conception
of an object than what the imagination alone is ever able to
attain." He admits to being at a loss to describe it better; hence the
pileup of adjectives. He is quite clear that belief does not depend on
the will, and cannot be "commanded at pleasure." (This position
follows in any case from his Newtonian conception of mental
science.)

I defer comment on this theory here and draw attention to
Hume's important concluding remark that his account of beliefs in
matters of fact and their generation by custom shows there is "a
kind of pre-established harmony between the course of nature and
the succession of our ideas." His tone is ironic, but if his theory is
correct, the statement is literally true. The doctrine of pre-
established harmony was held by Leibniz, who used it to explain
the coincidence between the perceptions of numerically different
minds when his system excluded the possibility that they could
cause perceptions in each other.[1] The correspondence was due, he
argued, to the fact that God preordained the sequence of perceptions in each so that each of them had the perceptions they would
have had if there *were* such interaction between them. The fact
that this theory of perception and communication requires the
constant working of divine providence was considered by Leibniz
to be a theological merit in his metaphysics. Hume has no such
motive, of course, and has no share of the wish to find final causes
or purposes behind our daily experience. But in spite of this, he
does tell us that we are provided by nature with a mechanism for
belief formation that serves our biological needs by supplying
beliefs that fit the course of nature well enough to enable us to
function in our world. Hume holds, in effect, a Darwinian view of
the way our beliefs arise: they arise by convenient, law-governed
coincidence.

Section V has been concerned with reasoning from experience,
or induction. Section VII returns to the specific relation of causation. He here makes more explicit use of his doctrine of impressions and ideas instead of the noncommittal language of "objects."
He has accounted for our casual inferences as mental transitions
that are rooted in constant conjunctions. But our common notion of
cause contains more than this, and Hume never denies that it

does: after all, conjunction is a form of contiguity, and he has throughout distinguished cause and effect from it. He has also said that our causal inferences often take place in circumstances where we may not believe that the conjunctions we observe are ultimate, but may think they are due to secret powers or connections in objects that we do not know about. This may suggest that some awareness or intuition of secret powers like this is behind the origin of the idea of a cause. Locke seems to have held some such view in his account of powers or tertiary qualities.[2] Hume wants to deny this and to argue that it is custom that generates the distinctive element in the idea of a cause. (This, it is to be noted for future reference, is not identical with a denial of the reality of such secret powers; we are here dealing only with a supposed psychological explanation of the *origin* of this distinctive element in our idea.)

As we would expect after his comparison with love and hatred, Hume wants to account for our idea of cause in part by tracing its special features to inner sources. But this immediately forces him to confront a seductive thesis that many rationalists espouse. This is the thesis that our idea of causation is due to an impression of power within ourselves. This is seductive because the distinctive element in our idea of causation that needs to be accounted for is indeed that of power, or necessary connection. And Hume has already been at great pains to argue that we cannot find the impression of any such thing when we look outwards at such events as the paradigm sequence of billiard balls: here we only have impressions of solidity and motion. If we *did* find an impression of power or necessity in the first billiard ball, this would, of course, enable us to deduce from its presence that the second one would move, and it is the essence of Hume's argument that we cannot do this. So the suggestion that we can detect such power or necessity in sequences within ourselves is a real threat to his system.

But the very fact that would make such a theory a threat enables him to make short work of it. He considers two versions of the theory: that we can detect power within ourselves by reflecting on the "influence of volition over the organs of the body," and that we can detect it in our direct control over the "faculties of our mind." Hume in no way denies the familiarity of these experiences but denies they show what is required. In the first case, the reason is the simple one that some of the time volitions (whose occurrence he does not deny[3]) do *not* lead to bodily movements, and that even when they do, we often do not know which bodily movements are actually occasioned by them. In the second case, even though we do control many mental processes, no scrutiny of them will reveal any impression of power or force between the volition and its mental effects.

In part ii of the section, Hume identifies the impression from which our idea of necessary connection arises. When we observe a sequence of two events that has not taken place before, we say we have observed conjunction but do not talk of connection. We do this when the conjunction between two events has been observed frequently and with no exceptions. It is only then that we speak of the two as cause and effect. Since, once again, nothing new has been added to the observed sequence by the past repetitions, the addition must come from a change in the way the sequence has come to affect us. After many repetitions, custom or habit makes us expect the second event on the occurrence of the first. The connection is not some new feature in the objects but a feature of the workings of our imagination. Only when this occurs do we make causal inferences. The element of necessity in our idea of causation is the ideal counterpart of the internal impression we have when we feel the habitual transition from the first event's *actual* occurrence to the second event's *anticipated* occurrence — which is something we feel at the time of our perception of the first event. When we ascribe power to the first object in the sequence, we are, in today's parlance, projecting our own felt expectancy on to that part of the world we are observing.

Having given this account of how the idea of necessary connection comes to be, Hume concludes with two "definitions" of what a cause is. I shall quote them, adding numbers to them and noting that the first definition is, as Hume sees it, also put into "other words." *Definition (1)* "An object, followed by another, and where all the objects similar to the first are followed by objects similar to the second." *(1a)* "Or, in other words, where, if the first object had not been, the second never had existed." In the corresponding passage in *Treatise* I iii 14, we have "[a]n object precedent and contiguous to another, and when all the objects resembling the former are placed in like relations of precedency and contiguity to those objects that resemble the latter." There is nothing corresponding to (1a). *Definition (2)* reads: "An object followed by another, and whose appearance always conveys the thought to that other." In the *Treatise,* Hume's definition is more elaborate: "an object precedent and contiguous to another, and so united with it, that the idea of the one determines the mind to form the idea of the other, and the impression of the one to form a more lively idea of the other."

Hume has made it clear that, as he puts it in the *Treatise,* "necessity is something that exists in the mind, not in objects, nor is it possible for us ever to form the most distant idea of it, considered as a quality in bodies." Hence the two definitions must be read as telling us (1) what we observe in the objects that we call causes, and (2) how those objects affect the mind to make us so describe them. (In the *Treatise* Hume expresses this by saying that the first definition is of cause as a philosophical relation, and the second is of cause as a natural relation; the *Enquiry* is free from this technicality.[4]) Neither is intended to qualify as an analysis of, or synonym for, the common use of the *word* "cause," since, if Hume's story is true, the first definition leaves out an essential element in that use, and the second, while identifying it, makes its psychological character explicit, whereas this goes unrecognized in the use being explained.

It is clear that definition (1a) is not a mere rewording of definition (1). (1) is a definition of cause as a sufficient condition (if c, then e); (1a) is of cause as a necessary condition (if not-c, then not-e). The elementary character of this apparent error needs some explanation, and I shall hazard one below.

| *The Problem of Induction*

In his well-known essay, "The Permanent Significance of Hume's Philosophy," H. H. Price says that the greatest service Hume rendered to philosophy was his discovery of the problem of induction. He describes this as "one of the most important advances in the whole history of thought."[5] This is a common view. It is also common to think that Hume did not believe the problem of induction had an answer, and that this opinion is the most important example of his epistemological skepticism. I have attempted to argue that Kemp Smith's view that Hume is best understood as a naturalist can be reconciled readily enough with the earlier tradition that viewed him as a skeptic, and that these two features of his system reinforce one another. If this is true, it suggests in the present case that Hume's skepticism does indeed show itself in the negative view that the problem of induction has no answer, and his naturalism shows itself in his account of how our natures make us practice inductive thinking in spite of this. I think this view fits the text I have just paraphrased and is the true one. But there is a very significant trend in contemporary Hume scholarship that questions whether Hume was a skeptic about induction, and even whether it is accurate to say he raises a problem of induction at all. This view is most fully argued in the work of Tom Beauchamp and Alexander Rosenberg and is also found in that of Nicholas Capaldi and Fred Wilson.[6] I shall try, within the limits of

a work of this kind, to make the nature of their case clear, and
even to attempt a partial reconciliation of some aspects of it with
the more traditional interpretation I have myself adopted.

What, first, is the problem of induction thought to be? The
problem is thought to lie in finding a justification for the practice
of drawing inferences from experience. Hume is generally taken to
have asked for this when he asked, "What is the foundation of all
conclusions from experience?"; and he is also usually understood to
have said that we cannot find any such foundation, if "foundation"
means "justification," although we can indeed find a foundation
(viz. custom) if by "foundation" we merely mean "origin in human
nature."

Beauchamp and Rosenberg call the problem, thus identified,
the "external problem," indicating by this that it is a supposed
problem of the high generality typical of philosophical questions
and not a problem about this or that particular inductive inference, which we would all settle by applying the very inductive
standards whose application is here being scrutinized. They hold
that Hume does not raise the external problem, and that he is not
a skeptic about induction, even if he is a skeptic (which they
clearly doubt) about other matters.

This raises the question of what Hume is about in his discussion of induction, if it is not what so many readers have supposed.
Their answer is that he is concerned to attack rationalist interpretations of our reasonings from experience, not to put such reasonings themselves into question; and that Hume does not hold, as
those who read him as a skeptic think he does, that inductive
inferences are not rational, but merely that they are not rational in
the rationalists' sense — that is, they are not deductive and are
not justifiable by deductive demonstrations. In this view, Hume's
account of induction and causation does not show we are not
rational creatures, but that there is a form of rationality that is
quite different from that proclaimed by the rationalist tradition —
one that relies on regularities and probabilities, and in which we
are taught by experience and do not legislate for nature a priori.

What makes this rather bland reading of Hume attractive is
not, in my view, those parts of the texts of the *Treatise* and *Enquiry* that deal with the general character of induction and causation, but the fact that Hume is, indeed, anxious to recommend
good inductive procedures to us and to contrast them with other
ways in which beliefs can arise, particularly religious ones. One
example of this is to be found in *Treatise* I iii 15, the section
entitled "Rules by which to Judge of Causes and Effects." Having
told us that "[a]ny thing may produce any thing," he gives us rules

to help us determine when particular sequences are causal ones
and when they are not. Another example is to be found in the
whole argument of the *Dialogues,* which are partly prefigured in
section XI of the first *Enquiry,* which will concern us in Chapter
Six. Here Hume is anxious to show that the received view of his
age, that belief in God is good science and is well-based in evidence, is mistaken. These prominent features of his system make
it very clear that he sets great store by following inductive standards and sees them as normative for us. If, when he discusses
their "foundation," he is skeptical about them, it is natural to
suppose his system to be deeply inconsistent and to involve him in
making use in one place of standards he has argued in another to
be baseless.

It is, of course, a common opinion that Hume *is* inconsistent in
this way. Any interpretation that has this result has to be well-
based in the texts and at the very least must have some way of
reconciling the apparently conflicting elements that is not patently
feeble. I shall attempt to suggest one.

Let us look again at Hume's argument that our conclusions
from experience are not founded on reasoning, that is, at section
IV, part ii. Since Hume is clearly hostile to rationalism, and since
he is not careful to be consistent in his use of the term "reason," it
is tempting to think that he is here only making an antirationalist
point and means by "reason" something like "deductive or a priori
reasoning," or demonstration. Rationalists did believe that we
could learn about the realities of nature through a priori reasoning, and Hume denies this unambiguously. And when he tells us
elsewhere that moral distinctions are not derived from reason, he
clearly includes within the scope of "reason" the very procedures
he says in our present passages are not founded on reasoning.[7] I
am not as sure as some are that this shows he is confining the
notion of reason to deduction in our present passages. But I submit
we do not need to decide that in practice. For Hume merely argues,
I further submit, that if we seek to offer a justification for our
actual practice of making inferences from experience, such justification has only two possible forms. One is that of misrepresenting
such inferences as examples of deduction, which they are not. The
other is by underwriting them through an appeal to the principle
that the future will resemble the past, which is "circular" because
it must make use of the very practice it is designed to justify. I
think that the rejection of this second way of justifying induction
does not require Hume to identify reason with deductive reason,
whether or not he does tacitly so identify it here; for it is equivalent to saying that the only form of argument available to us when

we concede that induction is not deductive is an argument form that requires appeal to induction itself. One can say this without being definite about whether or not inductive inference is irrational in consequence of this.

I think Hume's argument here is intended to be (and is) a demonstration that the "external problem" of induction can have no answer; that he does raise that problem in his question, "What is the foundation of all conclusions from experience?" and then makes it clear that no justification of these conclusions can be had. Is this, however, a skeptical result? Slightly more clearly, does Hume think this means that we have no good reason to think we can arrive at truth through the practice of inductive inferences?

When Hume tells us that the actual origin of our inductive inferences is to be found in custom or habit, he reinforces his point with an argument that helps us answer this question. He also repeats the point when analyzing the origin of the belief in necessary connection: the repetition of a particular sequence does not uncover any new evidence, only more of the same. ("There is nothing in a number of instances, different from any single instance, which is supposed to be exactly similar.") All that the repetition contributes is a mental habit and concomitant feeling. I feel this argument can be interpreted in only one way: although repetition without contrary instances does indeed *make* us infer inductively without doubt or hesitation, it shows us nothing that underwrites inference to the unexperienced. It could only do this if, per impossible, sheer quantity of experience gave us knowledge of the "secret power" by which one object produces another. Now, it is of the essence of our inductive practice that we offer frequent repetition without contrary instances as the best of inductive reasons for our inferences, and think that the wise person is the one who proportions the strength of his beliefs to the amount of such evidence he has — a point Hume is very ready to make himself elsewhere.[8] I think the two facts together indicate strongly that Hume's argument about custom is that our universal inductive practice cannot be shown to be one that we have any good ground to expect will yield truth to us. This *is* a skeptical conclusion, and I have to agree with D. C. Stove and others that it is the natural reading of what Hume says.[9]

But the fact that, contrary to Beauchamp and Rosenberg, it is made in the context of a question about the "external" problem of induction allows us, I think, to interpret the form of skepticism Hume adopts as not being the mere negation it appears to be. For Hume thinks we should not take skeptical conclusions too seriously. Here we must recall his slightly irritating comment about the preestablished harmony between the course of nature and the succession of our ideas. In the succession of our ideas, the effect of custom is to make us follow inductive practices. The very fact that these practices are the result of habit insures that we feel total confidence in the outcome of frequent and unvarying sequences and less confidence in less frequent conjunctions, and that our degree of confidence varies directly with the proportion of positive to negative instances. We codify all this, once the practice of inductive inference is established, so that frequent and unvarying sequences appear as a norm against which other varieties of experience are judged. But we cannot give general grounds for maintaining that the practice that custom establishes is one that will lead to truth. This is just a fact; but it is one that seems absurd or paradoxical only from within daily life, where the inductive practices are applied. (Hence Hume would have to say that refutations of inductive skepticism, like that of Stove, represent applications to it of the very standards it evaluates negatively.[10]) It is a fact that only seems disturbing if we make the rationalist assumption that we can only act if we can give a general justification for the practices we follow. Since these practices are based upon instinct, we know that this is not so: indeed, the science of human nature shows that we cannot *refrain* from the forms of inference that custom establishes in us.

Does this skeptical outcome show it to be irrational to make inductive inferences? I think here that even the skeptical reading of Hume allows us to answer no to this question, and that Hume's remarks about preestablished harmony show this to be the right answer. Here much is to be learned from Fred Wilson.[11] He offers us as Hume's argument the principle that "*must* implies *ought*." Something at least close to this principle seems to me to be Hume's answer, good or bad, to the charge that he himself follows, and makes a virtue of following, practices that he has undermined. Its likeness to the resolution of the Academic Skeptics reported by Cicero is beyond question.

Both the Pyrrhonian and the Academic Skeptic were faced with the need to act. The Pyrrhonian met this need by acquiescing belieflessly in the conventional practices of his fellows. The Academic met it by following the appearances that seemed probable, while yet denying that any guaranteed truth.[12] Hume's naturalism makes him hold that belieflessness is impossible for us; and his account of how custom is not something external to each of us, but rather determines the very course of our mental lives through association, tells us how our natural beliefs come about. This determines that any accommodation to practice that Hume makes in the face of his skepticism will have to follow the Academic way, not the Pyrrhonian. Hume reinforces this by his recognition that suspense of judgment is impossible in the long term and productive of anxiety and melancholia in the short term. This means that we have to make inferences of some kind to live and that nature dictates to us that they be the ones it generates and not some others. (Its dictating this is equivalent to its making us anxious and disoriented if we attempt any others.) As it happens, this dictation by nature turns out to give us no unpleasant surprises because "our thoughts and conceptions have gone on in the same train as the other works of nature." So even if we had had a real choice in the matter, we would have found that it is "the best means for getting on with the task of living" (as Wilson describes the judgment of Cicero's Academic). Of course, custom is not the only source of beliefs. Religious fears and indoctrination are another, and Hume thinks that the inner turmoil *they* generate is a sign that they are not a good means for getting on with the business of living and that the inductive practices generated by custom are to be preferred.

I must admit that I find it difficult to see this as adding up to *"must* implies *ought,"* rather than that *"must* implies *unwise to resist."* Hume's general skepticism does not seem to me to admit of the degree of confidence in scientific procedures as a road to truth that his Newtonianism, and his secularism, require. So I do think he has, and knows that he has,[13] a problem of consistency in his system. But I think that the skepticism — which I agree with tradition in finding in his central epistemological arguments — is not of a kind that makes it self-evidently impossible for these two basic thrusts in his system to be reconciled with one another.

I have attempted to deal here with the major question of interpretation that contemporary debate has raised, and I conclude that Hume does raise the problem of induction as most readers have thought, and argues that it can have no answer. I have also tried to make a case for saying that he thinks the fact that we are naturally programmed, through association, to make inductive inferences is something that is not a mere brute fact about us but is a blessing; and that we should, therefore, not treat custom as a mere cause of our common practice but should gratefully allow it to become a norm for us in dealing with other forces working upon us.

If we do this, we shall find that our confidence in inferences we make from experience will be guided by the quantity of evidence we have and lessened by changes in it. Being guided by custom in this sense does not mean ignoring experience but changing our inferences if experience so indicates. Intellectual rigidity is the natural outcome of believing that one can learn about nature a priori or can demonstrate that the future will be like the past; and the kind of customary inference that is generated by repeated experience, rather than indoctrination, can accommodate the fact that such guarantees are not available to us. Hume is, therefore, an inductive fallibilist, in Stove's language: someone who recognizes that a science based on experience can never be seen as immune to error in the way the rationalist ideal of science pretended. Yet he manages (or seeks) to combine the view that experimental reasoning is the best source of belief formation with inductive skepticism: the view that the accumulation of similar instances does not show the practice of inferring similar outcomes to be one that leads to truth.

❙ *The Nature of Causes*

While not all inductive inference is causal,[14] Hume is clearly right to suppose that it is causal reasoning that we depend upon for most of our practical decisions. And while not all inductive reasonings are generalizations, Beauchamp and Rosenberg are clearly right to say that the "Copernican shift" that Hume achieved in the discussion of causation was to center it henceforth on casual laws rather than causal instances.[15] Hume's definitions of cause relate the individual instances to the repeated sequences of which they are examples, and make it clear that we call them causes because of the existence of these sequences. So a cause is an event that instances a universal sequence, rather than an event or object that contains innate powers that hold the future within them.

This shift of emphasis indicates that Hume's concern in providing his definitions is not that of encapsulating the common use of the word "cause." For although it may be true that when we search for causes, we search for events that can be conjoined with others in lawlike sequences, this is not encapsulated in the concept of a cause but merely implied by the ascription of causality to some object; and although Hume may be right in supposing that we ascribe causality when our mind is conveyed from some event to its regular result, he makes it clear he thinks that in calling it a cause we ascribe some necessity to the object itself, while this definition emphasizes the inner process leading to this ascription. Hume's definitions are at most extensional rather than intensional accounts of the meaning of "cause." He confirms this himself when he says that his definitions of cause both require the inclusion of something "extraneous and foreign to it."

This Copernican shift has been of immense consequence in philosophical discussions of explanation. Hume was convinced that it should be, as we can see from a glance at the list of "corollaries" he draws from his account in *Treatise* I iii 14. These are (1) that all causes are of the same kind, namely what Aristotle called "efficient" causes; (2) that there is only one kind of necessity, that is, no difference between physical necessity and moral necessity, so that events either happen from efficient causation or by chance, and that there is no foundation for our common distinction between power and its exercise (so that there is nothing I could ever have done that I did not do); (3) that our belief that everything has a cause does not arise from any a priori demonstration; and (4) that we can have no reason to believe in the existence of any "object" of which we have not formed an idea from experience.

Whether these corollaries do all follow from Hume's account of what a cause is and whether, even if they do, they are true are huge subjects that would take us far beyond the possible scope of this book. But we can see from them that Hume himself was well aware of the deep implications of his discoveries and would not have been surprised by the vast extent of his later influence. We can also see why he was so disappointed that these discoveries passed largely unnoticed when the *Treatise* appeared. The first corollary is the proclamation of the death knell of Aristotelian natural philosophy. The second requires, and has generated, a radical reorientation of the discussion of the freedom of the will, which Hume himself began in *Treatise* II iii 1–3 and section VIII of the first *Enquiry*.[16] The third raises the central question Kant tried to answer differently in the *Critique of Pure Reason*. The fourth expresses, in the language of Hume's psychology, the claim that all explanatory concepts have to be defined observationally, thus raising the deepest of questions in the philosophy of science.

Perhaps the most widespread debates about the Humean analysis of causation have been related to two issues: first, how far Hume's understanding of causation can accommodate the very varied examples of causal explanation we seem to offer in daily life and in many explanatory disciplines; second, how far Hume's emphasis on the origin of our idea of cause in sheer given sequence can provide for the lawlike character of scientific explanation. With regard to the first issue, a Humean understanding seems to have difficulty with mental causation and other occasions where we seem to ascribe causation without any reference to implied sequences, e.g., in history (a serious exception for Hume, if it is one).[17] The second issue is that of the difference between natural laws and accidental generalizations.[18] There does not seem much doubt, in view of the first of Hume's corollaries and his inclusion of definition (1a) in the *Enquiry,* that he would have claimed to have provided actual or possible answers to both, but these are not matters we can explore here.[19] I turn instead to two subsidiary questions of interpretation that need to be addressed as we seek to understand what he actually says in the texts.

▌ *Secret Powers*

On as many as six occasions in the three sections we have been considering, Hume concedes, or laments, that we are "ignorant . . . of the manner in which bodies operate on each other," and that their "force or energy is entirely incomprehensible." An individual instance of such a comment, especially in a quasi-theological connection, could be disregarded as due to irony. But when the comment is made so frequently, we must take it more seriously than this. There can be no doubt that Hume means what he says when he tells us that all our knowledge of unobserved matters of fact has to come from experience and cannot be attained by a priori reasoning, especially when this is reinforced by a sketchy but powerful theory that the mathematical sciences, thought to provide such a priori knowledge of nature by rationalists, tell us only about the relations of ideas. Nor can there be any doubt that he means what he says when he argues that our ascription of necessity to objects is due to the transference of an inner impression that comes from custom and is not due to the discernment of power or force in the objects of our experience.

Given these clear elements of his philosophy, the remarks about nature's secrecy have to be read, in my view, as reinforcing a skeptical interpretation of Hume's epistemology in two ways. First, they reinforce the interpretation of his views on induction as implying that the inferences custom leads us to make from past to future are inferences we should, in strictness, judge to be *coincidentally* correct ones only, however much their pragmatic success and our custom-bound natures make us forget this. Second, they reinforce the sheer subjectivity of the necessity we ascribe to objects; it is not, of course, that we know there is no necessity in objects (for this would be dogmatism), but that we can recognize that our *ascription* of necessity is mere projection, hallowed by habit and not by right.

Such a reading of Hume renders these comments about nature's hiddenness fully predictable. It might also seem to be a traditional reading. But the traditional reading of Hume contains another element inconsistent with this. It is very commonly thought that Hume's theory of causation renders nature *less* mysterious than common sense and rationalist metaphysics do, not more, and that Hume presents us with a purely empiricist world in which there is nothing but sheer given sequences and wholly disconnected facts completely open to our gaze, with no logical relationships to one another — a world, in fact, identical to that of Russell's logical atomism and Wittgenstein's *Tractatus* (if its mystical coda is ignored). This is the world summed up in Passmore's dictum that intelligibility is no more than familiarity.[20]

If that tough-minded reading of Hume were correct, all his remarks about our ignorance of the inner springs of nature would be incomprehensible. In fact, however, Hume allows himself to speculate about those inner springs, though he does this undogmatically enough. John Wright has brought this out.[21] It would seem that Hume allowed himself to suppose that there might be inner mechanical powers in nature of which our ideas are wholly fortuitous and inadequate reflections. He does not think that our perceptual experience shows us the powers in physical causes. Nor does he think that our inner experience yields any impression of power or, therefore, an idea of it. And he says, in addition, that the apparent ability of mind and matter to affect each other is mysterious, though he rejects, of course, the occasionalist view of Malebranche, who argued that because we have no idea of real power in nature, all causation must be due to God's activity — a view applied to matter by Berkeley.[22]

If Hume were as tough-minded as he is often thought to be, he might well have insisted that the observed sequences of events in our world are to be taken as ultimate in themselves. Perhaps he ought to have done this, but although it is easy to see it as the natural outcome of the account of causal reasoning that he does give us, it does not seem to have been his view. Perhaps Wright is correct in seeing this as primarily a result of his antitheological wish to leave open the possibility that all ultimate explanations, were they available to us, would be mechanical, and that the springs of all natural happenings are material ones. One might object that this is incoherent. Wright seems willing to ascribe incoherence to Hume in this way, saying that he "clearly assumes the existence of what is contradictory and meaningless according to our human ideas."[23] But this is unnecessarily heroic. All we need assume is that Hume engages in what he would agree is unconfirmable speculation about ultimate causes, using the ideas he has traced back to experience, and that he would be satisfied to argue that although such speculations of a mechanistic universe are in that sense ideal ones, they are not absurd and are a possible mental corrective to theories like those of Malebranche that tell us we must resort to a spiritual cause to allow for the facts of observation. A position like this is more in accord with the skeptic tradition than any insistence that such ultimate causes cannot exist.

| *The Causal Principle*

There is an important section in the *Treatise,* viz. I iii 3, that has no matching passage in the discussion of causation in the *Enquiry* but should be treated briefly here because it deals with a theme fundamental to the estimation of Hume's achievement. It is entitled "Why a Cause is Always Necessary." In it Hume considers the "general maxim in philosophy" that "whatever begins to exist, must have a cause of existence." It becomes clear almost at once that he is not merely interested in the question of the causes of the being of things, but also that of every "new modification of existence," so that he is talking not only of the production of objects but also that of events. He argues very effectively that the principle is "neither intuitively nor demonstrably certain": so that it is not known a priori to be true. It is a commonplace of the history of thought that Kant tried to show that this principle, even though it is not in his terms analytic, is, nevertheless, known a priori, and that he was challenged to attempt the proof of this by reading quotations from Hume in a translation of James Beattie. Like Hume in this section, Kant says that although the statement "Every effect has a cause" is analytic, "Every event has a cause" is not; and if we do indeed know it, our knowledge of it needs special explanation.[24]

Hume's arguments depend on his claim that a scrutiny of our experience shows that a cause and its effect are distinct and do not imply one another: that there is no contradiction in asserting the occurrence of the one and the nonoccurrence of the other. This, however, works two ways. It means that there is no logical necessity for the so-called effect to follow when the customary cause appears as it always has, even though we confidently expect it to; and it also means that there is no logical necessity for the cause to have been there beforehand when we find the so-called effect to have taken place, even though we may well be just as confident that it will have done so. There is no doubt that Hume thought we believe that a cause always has the same effect and that we believe every event has a cause. Nor is there any doubt that he himself believes both principles, even though he denies either is demonstrable, and that he relies on both. It is striking, however, that the account he gives of the origins of our belief in causal reasoning is an account only of our belief in the first of these principles (that of "same cause-same effect"), and not of the second (that of "for every event a cause").

Many readers have noted that Hume applies the first principle while explaining its emergence among our beliefs: whenever we have repeated experience of a sequence, this sets up a habit of transition that is then projected onto nature to make us ascribe necessity to the causal sequence. It is less often noticed that he not only applies the second principle but appeals to it openly and asserts it with dogmatism. For example, in his discussion of liberty in section VIII of the *Enquiry* we find: "It is universally allowed that nothing exists without a cause of its existence, and that chance, when strictly examined, is a mere negative word, and means not any real power which has anywhere a being in nature."[25] Through appealing to this principle, Hume argues that the science of human nature precludes the reality of what he calls "liberty of indifference," that is, the power to perform actions that we in fact do not choose to perform. For such a power would amount to a capacity to do things that we are not caused to initiate.

Given this clear two-way character of our causal reasonings, it is strange that Hume does not attempt to explain how we come to believe every event has a cause. In the *Treatise,* he does acknowledge the need for such an account. In the last paragraph of I iii 3, he says: "The next question, then, should naturally be, how experience gives rise to such a principle? But as I find it will be more convenient to sink this question in the following, Why we conclude that such particular causes must necessarily have such particular effects, and why we form an inference from one to another? We shall make that the subject of our future enquiry. It will, perhaps, be found in the end, that the same answer will serve for both questions." He never returns to the question he defers here, and it does indeed "sink" without trace.

There is no reason to expect that answering the question that he does address would answer the one he defers. The beliefs, like the principles, are logically independent of each other. One could explain why we think that causes give rise to their effects with necessity without explaining why we believe, indeed without even believing, that every event has a cause. The world might be such that certain events have to have certain results without it being the case that these resulting events can only occur from these causes, or even without it being the case that they are unable to occur without one. And to explain why we ascribe necessity to the cause-effect sequence is not to explain why we ascribe universality to it.

Another way of making this point is to say that although
Hume accounts for the origin of our belief in causes as sufficient
and regular conditions, he does not account for our belief that
events have necessary conditions. This does seem to require
independent explanation. There are some signs, however, that
Hume did not think this or thought he had provided all that is
needed. One such sign is a gloss he gives in *Treatise* I iii 14, when
he states the first corollary of his doctrine of causation: that all
causes are of the same kind. He glosses it by saying there is "no
foundation for that distinction which we sometimes make between
efficient causes and cases *sine qua non.*" This seems to be an
outright denial of the distinction between necessary and sufficient
conditions! Another sign, in our own text, is the odd definition (1a)
in section VII ("Or, in other words, if the first object had not been,
the second had never existed"). This is manifestly not a mere
rewording of what precedes it but an introduction of the concept of
a necessary condition or a cause sine qua non. A condition that is
necessary need not be sufficient (access to air may be necessary for
life, but unfortunately it is not enough), and a sufficient condition
may not be necessary (suffocation is sufficient to ensure death, but
unfortunately so are many other things). We are interested in
causes in both senses because we want to be able to predict results,
and we want to be able to prevent undesirable effects.[26] The
unannounced appearance of (1a) may show that Hume is aware of
the many-faceted nature of our causal concerns and reasonings.
But it also seems to show that he believes he has explained both
the forward-looking ascription of inevitability to effects and the
backward-looking ascription of inevitability to causes. He has only
done the first.

There is a passage in section VIII of the *Enquiry* where Hume
seems to give us an argument in favor of the "causal principle."
It appears also in *Treatise* I iii 12. Hume is discussing the phenomenon of "contrariety" in our observations. He is concerned with
cases where a cause seems to occur, but its usual effect does not,
and he wants to account for them in a manner that does not
compromise our universal commitment to the connection between
causes and their effects. Experts, he says, will find an additional,
"contrary" cause at work that the layman will miss — when the
layman says the clock does not go right, the expert will find the
speck of dust that impedes the regular motion of the spring. So
when the cause seems not to be followed by its effect, there is
another cause present. D. G. C. MacNabb suggests this is the place
where we find Hume telling us why we believe in the causal

principle.[27] I do not think this is quite clear. For one thing, if it is, it divides us into those (the experts) who do believe in it and the rest (the nonexperts) who do not. For another, although Hume's overall intent in this section is to insist that all human actions have causes even when we do not perceive them, he still selects for the purpose an apparent case where a cause does not seem to be followed by its usual effect, so that the principle being impugned and defended appears to be that of "same cause-same effect," even though that is not the one he really needs for his purpose. And the argument, if it is intended to relate directly to the principle that every event has a cause, looks like an inductive one — that since we often find causes we have overlooked for effects that baffle us, there always are such causes. This would make it an argument that is effective only after we have come to practice inductive reasoning, not an account of how we come to have such a practice.

I *Belief*

An important part of section V deals with the question of how it is that when a cause appears, we infer unhesitatingly that its effect will follow. The account Hume gives here involves his taking note of the fact that when the impression of the cause occurs, it is not merely followed by the appearance of the idea of the customary effect but by the belief that the effect will indeed happen. This is the key difference between cause and effect and contiguity as a principle of association. Hume is hard put to give an account of what this belief consists in. The nature and extent of Hume's obvious and candid perplexity over this can be seen even more clearly if we compare what he says here with the corresponding discussions in the *Treatise*. These are found in I iii 7 and 8. (There are relevant comments also in I iii 5, where Hume deals with the difference between imagination and memory, and in the appendix to the Treatise.) The most sympathetic discussion of Hume's account is that of H. H. Price,[28] who points out that we can find elements of a quite different sort of theory of belief elsewhere in Hume in *Treatise* I iii 9 and 10.

As the problem arises in the context of the discussion of custom and causation, it assumes a form that Hume's doctrine of impressions and ideas makes it virtually impossible to answer. To Hume it is the problem of saying what the difference is between what the imagination does when we *imagine* (what he calls "fiction") and what it does when we call up the idea of the effect and *believe* it will follow. The essence of Hume's account of the role of custom is that no new impression, and no new idea, comes to us when we infer the effect from the cause, and that what is before the mind is, therefore, the same as in the earlier sequences that we have not (he thinks) judged previously to be causal ones.

This consideration is reinforced in the *Treatise* by another argument of considerable independent importance, stated in I iii 7 but anticipated in I ii 6. It is an argument that "the idea of existence is nothing different from the idea of any object, and that when after the simple conception of any thing we would conceive it as existent, we in reality make no addition to or alteration on our first idea."[29] To think of an object and to think of its really existing may well be different, but the content of "the idea of the object" is the same in the latter as in the former. This is Hume's view on one of the deepest and most difficult of philosophical questions, a view that anticipates Kant's famous dictum that "being is not a real predicate."[30] I do not offer any interpretation of Kant's dictum here, and I do not offer any view of what the implications of Hume's claim are, except to note that it is a claim that prevents his answering his question about belief by saying that it is a new idea that enters the mind as a result of the customary transition. But if that route is closed, how is Hume to answer his question? His mental science only allows for the occurrence of impressions and ideas, and even if it does allow for the ascription of capacities and tendencies to the mind, Hume appears convinced that there is an introspectively recognizable fact about the actual events taking place during our causal inferences that such an ascription would not cover. (In this he seems to be reflecting the fact that we all seem able to answer the question of whether we believe something in an immediate way without recourse to a review of our own behavior.)

So the belief that is part of our experience when the impression of the cause gives rise to the idea of the effect cannot be another idea; and since the effect that the belief is belief *in* is not yet present, it cannot be an impression either. Hume can therefore only resort to the thesis that having a belief is having an idea, but having it in a special way: "I conclude upon the whole, that belief is a more vivid and intense conception of an idea."[31] He also refers to the special character of the "conception" of the idea as "lively, forcible, firm, steady." The introduction of the last two adjectives suggests the notion of *confidence,* which in turn confirms the view of most contemporary philosophers that we cannot understand what a belief is without relating its presence to the actions and policies of the person who has it.[32] Hume has chosen to confine himself here to the purely phenomenological aspects of belief as it arises in causal inferences, and his resources for interpreting those confined aspects are in turn limited by the constraints of his doctrine of impressions and ideas. His interpretation is made even more unattractive by the fact that he elects to use the language of liveliness and vividness to characterize the relevant idea, when these characteristics are definitive of what an impression is. This has the immediate benefit, in the *Treatise,* of enabling him to suggest that the liveliness of the believed idea is somehow borrowed from the impression that occasions the idea's appearance. This is ingenious, and from Hume we would expect no less; but an analysis of belief demands much more.

But however unsatisfactory the theory of belief is in its details, its most important feature is that Hume offers an account that makes belief an involuntary product of our instincts, not something that is under the control of the will. His view of it stands in sharp contrast to that of Descartes in the *Fourth Medita-tion.* Descartes is attempting to offer a doctrine that will allow him to escape from a predicament he, in his turn, has manufactured for himself. He has demonstrated in the *Third Meditation* that there is an all-good God; and he infers from this that we can be confident in the power of our reason to lead us to truth, since such a God would not endow us with a deceptive faculty. He is now faced with the question of why we ever make mistakes. He answers it by distinguishing between the role of the intellect in the formation of beliefs and that of the will. When dealing with matters on which we do not have the clarity and distinctness that guarantee truth, that is, what Hume was later to call matters of fact, we are able to withhold assent when the intellect suggests a proposition to us. This ability to suspend judgment, which Descartes has himself used, he thinks, in the *First Meditation,* is an ability we should always use to avoid error on those matters where the senses tempt us to draw conclusions without warrant. If we do this, we shall be making good use of the epistemic capacities God has given to us. If we do not, the resulting error will be our fault and not the fault of God.[33] Hume's account of belief is designed to show that we do not have the liberty that Descartes claims we have, and that belief is formed in us by our instincts. "Belief," he says, "is more properly an act of the sensitive, than of the cogitative part of our natures."[34] Its particular origin in custom is Hume's account of how our natures generate it. It is also, indirectly, an account of why the reasonings of the skeptic cannot dislodge it for more than brief moments. It is important to bear in mind that the inadequacy of

Hume's attempt to describe what belief is like does not itself show that he is wrong about its involuntariness or its essentially instinctive origin — though of course he may be wrong for other reasons.

❘ *NOTES*

1. See *The Monadology,* 51–58; *Principles of Nature and Grace* 4, 10–15; both in Leibniz 1898.
2. Locke 1959, book 2, chap. 21; Mabbott 1973, chap. 4.
3. Nowadays some would. For further comment on Hume's view, see Penelhum 1975a, 111–17; Bricke 1984.
4. See the debate between J. A. Robinson and Thomas J. Richards, with final comment by Robinson, in Chappell 1966, 129–86; also Penelhum 1975a, 53–57.
5. Price 1940b, reprinted in Sesonske and Fleming 1965.
6. Beauchamp and Rosenberg 1981, chap. 2; Capaldi 1975, chap. 5; Wilson 1983, 1985, and 1986a.
7. Winters 1979.
8. Most famously in his discussion of miracles in *EU* X. See Chapter Six.
9. Stove 1976.
10. Stove 1973.
11. Wilson 1983, 1985, and 1986a.
12. Cicero 1933, 595; and see Chapter One above.
13. Penelhum 1983a, chap. 6.
14. Price 1940.
15. Beauchamp and Rosenberg 1981, chap. 3.
16. Penelhum 1975a, chap. 6.
17. Anscombe 1971, 1973; Dray 1957.
18. Kneale 1949, Flew 1961, chaps. 4–6; Beauchamp and Rosenberg 1981, chap. 4.
19. But on the second corollary, see the next section.
20. Passmore 1952, 154.
21. Wright 1983, chaps. 3 and 4; also Wilson 1986b, Árdal 1986.
22. Berkeley 1929.
23. Wright 1983, 133.
24. Kant 1929, introduction.
25. *EU* VIII (SB 95).
26. Flew 1961, chap. 6. See also Anscombe 1974.
27. MacNabb 1951, 56–57. On Hume's failure to explain the causal principle, see also Penelhum 1975a, 53–60, and Beck 1978, 111–29.
28. H. H. Price 1969, lecture 7, series 1.
29. *T* I iii 7 (SB 94/EL I 96).
30. Kant 1929, A598/B626.
31. *T* I iii 8 (SB 103/EL I 105).
32. See Price 1969, lectures 1–3, series 2; Swinburne 1981, chap. 1.
33. Descartes 1954, 92–100; Kenny 1973, 81–112; Williams 1978, chap. 6.
34. *T* I iv 1 (SB 183/EL I 179).

 | **Morality and Justice**

Text
Enquiry Concerning
the Principles of Morals

Appendix I
Concerning Moral Sentiment

If the foregoing hypothesis be received, it will now be easy for us to determine the question first started,[1] concerning the general principles of morals; and though we postponed the decision of that question, lest it should then involve us in intricate speculations, which are unfit for moral discourses, we may resume it at present, and examine how far either *reason* or *sentiment* enters into all decisions of praise or censure.

One principal foundation of moral praise being supposed to lie in the usefulness of any quality or action, it is evident that *reason* must enter for a considerable share in all decisions of this kind; since nothing but that faculty can instruct us in the tendency of qualities and actions, and point out their beneficial consequences to society and to their possessor. In many cases this is an affair liable to great controversy: doubts may arise; opposite interests may occur; and a preference must be given to one side, from very nice views, and a small overbalance of utility. This is particularly remarkable in questions with regard to justice; as is, indeed, natural to suppose, from that species of utility which attends this virtue.[2] Were every single instance of justice, like that of benevolence, useful to society; this would be a more simple state of the case, and seldom liable to great controversy. But as single instances of justice are often pernicious in their first and immediate tendency, and as the advantage to society results only from the observance of the general rule, and from the concurrence and combination of several persons in the same equitable conduct, the case here becomes more intricate and involved. The various circumstances of society; the various consequences of any practice; the various interests which may be proposed; these, on many occasions, are doubtful, and subject to great discussion and enquiry. The object of municipal laws is to fix all the questions with regard to justice: the debates of civilians, the reflections of politicians, the precedents of history and public records, are all directed to the same purpose. And a very accurate *reason* or *judgement* is often requisite, to give the true determination, amidst such intricate doubts arising from obscure or opposite utilities.

But though reason, when fully assisted and improved, be sufficient to instruct us in the pernicious or useful tendency or qualities and actions; it is not alone sufficient to produce any moral blame or approbation. Utility is only a tendency to a certain end; and were the end totally indifferent to us, we should feel the same indifference towards the means. It is requisite a *sentiment* should here display itself, in order to give a preference to the useful above the pernicious tendencies. This sentiment can be no other than a feeling for the happiness of mankind, and a resentment of their misery; since these are the different ends which virtue and vice have a tendency to promote. Here, therefore, *reason* instructs us in the several tendencies of actions, and *humanity* makes a distinction in favour of those which are useful and beneficial.

This partition between the faculties of understanding and sentiment, in all moral decisions, seems clear from the preceding hypothesis. But I shall suppose that hypothesis false: it will then be requisite to look out for some other theory that may be satisfactory; and I dare venture to affirm that none such will ever be found, so long as we suppose reason to be the sole source of morals. To prove this, it will be proper to weigh the five following considerations.

I. It is easy for a false hypothesis to maintain some appearance of truth, while it keeps wholly in generals, makes use of undefined terms, and employs comparisons, instead of instances. This is particularly remarkable in that philosophy, which ascribes the discernment of all moral distinctions to reason alone, without the concurrence of sentiment. It is impossible that, in any particular instance, this hypothesis can so much as be rendered intelligible, whatever specious figure it may make in general declamations and discourses. Examine the crime of *ingratitude,* for instance, which has place, wherever we observe good-will, expressed and known, together with good-offices performed, on the one side, and a return of ill-will or indifference, with ill-offices or neglect on the other. Anatomize all these circumstances, and examine, by your reason alone, in what consists the demerit or blame. You never will come to any issue or conclusion.

Reason judges either of *matter of fact or of relations.* Enquire then, first, where is that matter of fact which we here call *crime;* point it out; determine the time of its existence; describe its essence or nature; explain the sense or faculty to which it discovers itself. It resides in the mind of the person who is ungrateful. He must, therefore, feel it, and be conscious of it. But nothing is there, except the passion of ill-will or absolute indifference. You cannot say that these, of themselves, always, and in all circumstances, are crimes. No, they are only crimes when directed towards persons who have before expressed and displayed good-will towards us. Consequently, we may infer, that the crime of ingratitude is not any particular individual *fact,* but arises from a complication of circumstances, which, being presented to the spectator, excites the sentiment of blame, by the particular structure and fabric of his mind.

This representation, you say, is false. Crime indeed, consists not in a particular *fact,* of whose reality we are assured by *reason,* but it consists *in certain moral relations,* discovered by reason in the same manner as we discover by reason the truths of geometry or algebra. But what are the relations, I ask, of which you here talk? In the case stated above, I see first good-will and good-offices in one person; then ill-will and ill-offices in the other. Between these, there is a relation of *contrariety.* Does the crime consist in that relation? But suppose a person bore me ill-will or did me ill-offices; and I, in return, were indifferent towards him, or did him good-offices. Here is the same relation of *contrariety;* and yet my conduct is often highly laudable. Twist and turn this matter as much as you will, you can never rest the morality on relation; but must have recourse to the decisions of sentiment.

When it is affirmed that two and three are equal to the half of ten, this relation of equality I understand perfectly. I conceive, that if ten be divided into two parts, of which one has as many units as the other; and if any of these parts be compared to two added to three, it will contain as many units as that compound number. But when you draw thence a comparison to moral relations, I own that I am altogether at a loss to understand you. A moral action, a crime, such as ingratitude, is a complicated object. Does the morality consist in the relation of its parts to each other? How? After what manner? Specify the relation; be more particular and explicit in your propositions, and you will easily see their falsehood.

No, say you, the morality consists in the relation of actions to the rule of right; and they are denominated good or ill, according as they agree or disagree with it. What then is this rule of right? In what does it consist? How is it determined? By reason, you say, which examines the moral relations of actions. So that moral relations are determined by the comparison of action to a rule. And that rule is determined by considering the moral relations of objects. Is not this fine reasoning?

All this is metaphysics, you cry. That is enough; there needs nothing more to give a strong presumption of falsehood. Yes, reply I, here are metaphysics surely; but they are all on your side, who advance an abstruse hypothesis, which can never be made intelligible, nor quadrate with any particular instance or illustration. The hypothesis which we embrace is plain. It maintains that morality is determined by sentiment. It defines virtue to be *whatever mental action or quality gives to a spectator the pleasing sentiment of approbation;* and vice the contrary. We then proceed to examine a plain matter of fact, to wit, what actions have this influence. We consider all the circumstances in which these actions agree, and thence endeavour to extract some general observations with regard to these sentiments. If you call this metaphysics, and find anything abstruse here, you need only conclude that your turn of mind is not suited to the moral sciences.

II. When a man, at any time, deliberates concerning his own conduct (as, whether he had better, in a particular emergence, assist a brother or a benefactor), he must consider these separate relations, with all the circumstances and situations of the persons, in order to determine the superior duty and obligation; and in order to determine the proportion of lines in any triangle, it is necessary to examine the nature of that figure, and the relations which its several parts bear to each other. But notwithstanding this appearing similarity in the two cases, there is, at bottom, an extreme difference between them. A speculative reasoner concerning triangles or circles considers the several known and given relations of the parts of these figures, and thence infers some unknown relation, which is dependent on the former. But in moral deliberations we must be acquainted beforehand with all the objects, and all their relations to each other, and from a comparison of the whole, fix our choice or approbation. No new fact to be ascertained; no new relation to be discovered. All the circumstances of the case are supposed to be laid before us, ere we can fix any sentence of blame or approbation. If any material circumstance be yet unknown or doubtful, we must first employ our enquiry or intellectual faculties to assure us of it; and must suspend for a time all moral decision or sentiment. While we are ignorant whether a man were aggressor or not, how can we determine whether the person who killed him be criminal or innocent? But after every circumstance, every relation is known, the understanding has no further room to operate, nor any object on which it could employ itself. The approbation or blame which then ensues, cannot be the work of the judgement, but of the heart, and is not a speculative proposition or affirmation, but an active feeling or sentiment. In the disquisitions of the understanding, from known circumstances and relations, we infer some new and unknown. In moral decisions, all the circumstances and relations must be previously known, and the mind, from the contemplation of the whole, feels some new impression of affection or disgust, esteem or contempt, approbation or blame.

Hence the great difference between a mistake of *fact* and one of *right;* and hence the reason why the one is commonly criminal and not the other. When Oedipus killed Laius, he was ignorant of the relation, and from circumstances, innocent and involuntary, formed erroneous opinions concerning the action which he committed. But when Nero killed Agrippina, all the relations between himself and the person, and all the circumstances of the fact, were previously known to him, but the motive of revenge, or fear, or interest, prevailed in his savage heart over the sentiments of duty and humanity. And when we express that detestation against him to which he himself, in a little time, became insensible, it is not that we see any relations, of which he was ignorant, but that, from the rectitude of our disposition, we feel sentiments against which he was hardened from flattery and a long perseverance in the most enormous crimes. In these sentiments then, not in a discovery of relations of any kind, do all moral determinations consist. Before we can pretend to form any decision of this kind, everything must be known and ascertained on the side of the object or action. Nothing remains but to feel, on our part, some sentiment of blame or approbation, whence we pronounce the action criminal or virtuous.

III. This doctrine will become still more evident, if we compare moral beauty with natural, to which in many particulars it bears so near a resemblance. It is on the proportion, relation, and position of parts that all natural beauty depends, but it would be absurd thence to infer, that the perception of beauty, like that of truth in geometrical problems, consists wholly in the perception of relations, and was performed entirely by the understanding or intellectual faculties. In all the sciences, our mind from the known relations investigates the unknown. But in all decisions of taste or external beauty, all the relations are beforehand obvious to the eye; and we thence proceed to feel a sentiment of complacency or disgust, according to the nature of the object, and disposition of our organs.

Euclid has fully explained all the qualities of the circle; but has not in any proposition said a word of its beauty. The reason is evident. The beauty is not a quality of the circle. It lies not in any part of the line, whose parts are equally distant from a common centre. It is only the effect which that figure produces upon the mind, whose peculiar fabric or structure renders it susceptible of such sentiments. In vain would you look for it in the circle, or seek it, either by your senses or by mathematical reasonings, in all the properties of that figure.

Attend to Palladio and Perrault, while they explain all the parts and proportions of a pillar. They talk of the cornice, and frieze, and base, and entablature, and shaft and architrave, and give the description and position of each of these members. But should you ask the description and position of its beauty, they would readily reply, that the beauty is not in any of the parts or members of a pillar, but results from the whole, when that complicated figure is presented to an intelligent mind, susceptible to those finer sensations. Till such a spectator appear, there is nothing but a figure of such particular dimensions and proportions; from his sentiments alone arise its elegance and beauty.

Again, attend to Cicero, while he paints the crimes of a Verres or a Catiline. You must acknowledge that the moral turpitude results, in the same manner, from the contemplation of the whole, when presented to a being whose organs have such a particular structure and formation. The orator may paint rage, insolence, barbarity on the one side, meekness, suffering, sorrow, innocence on the other. But if you feel no indignation or compassion arise in you from this complication of circumstances, you would in vain ask him, in what consists the crime or villainy, which he so vehemently exclaims against? At what time, or on what subject it first began to exist? And what has a few months afterwards become of it, when every disposition and thought of all the actors is totally altered or annihilated? No satisfactory answer can be given to any of these questions, upon the abstract hypothesis of morals; and we must at last acknowledge, that the crime or immorality is no particular fact or relation, which can be the object of the understanding, but arises entirely from the sentiment of disapprobation, which, by the structure of human nature, we unavoidably feel on the apprehension of barbarity or treachery.

IV. Inanimate objects may bear to each other all the same relations which we observe in moral agents, though the former can never be the object of love or hatred, nor are consequently susceptible of merit or iniquity. A young tree, which over-tops and destroys its parent, stands in all the same relations with Nero, when he murdered Agrippina, and if morality consisted merely in relations, would no doubt be equally criminal.

V. It appears evident that the ultimate ends of human actions can never, in any case, be accounted for by reason, but recommend themselves entirely to the sentiments and affections of mankind, without any dependence on the intellectual faculties. Ask a man why he uses exercise; he will answer, because he desires to keep his health. If you then enquire, why he desires health, he will readily reply, because sickness is painful. If you push your enquiries farther, and desire a reason why he hates pain, it is impossible he can ever give any. This is an ultimate end, and is never referred to any other object.

Perhaps to your second question, why he desires health, he may also reply, that it is necessary for the exercise of his calling. If you ask, why he is anxious on that head, he will answer, because he desires to get money. If you demand why? It is the instrument of pleasure, says he. And beyond this it is an absurdity to ask for a reason. It is impossible there can be a progress *in infinitum,* and that one thing can always be a reason why another is desired. Something must be desirable on its own account, and because of its immediate accord or agreement with human sentiment and affection.

Now as virtue is an end, and is desirable on its own account, without fee or reward, merely for the immediate satisfaction which it conveys, it is requisite that there should be some sentiment which it touches, some internal taste or feeling or whatever you please to call it, which distinguishes moral good and evil, and which embraces the one and rejects the other.

Thus the distinct boundaries and offices of *reason* and of *taste* are easily ascertained. The former conveys the knowledge of truth and falsehood; the latter gives the sentiment of beauty and deformity, vice and virtue. The one discovers objects as they really stand in nature, without addition or diminution; the other has a productive faculty, and gilding or staining all natural objects with the colours, borrowed from internal sentiment, raises in a manner a new creation. Reason being cool and disengaged, is no motive to action, and directs only the impulse received from appetite or inclination, by showing us the means of attaining happiness or avoiding misery; taste, as it gives pleasure or pain, and thereby constitutes happiness or misery, becomes a motive to action, and is the first spring or impulse to desire and volition. From circumstances and relations, known or supposed, the former leads us to the discovery of the concealed and unknown; after all circumstances and relations are laid before us, the latter makes us feel from the whole a new sentiment of blame or approbation. The standard of the one, being founded on the nature of things, is eternal and inflexible, even by the will of the Supreme Being; the standard of the other, arising from the internal frame and constitution of animals, is ultimately derived from that Supreme Will, which bestowed on each being its peculiar nature, and arranged the several classes and orders of existence.

I NOTES

1. Section I
2. See Appendix II

Appendix II
Some Farther Considerations with Regard to Justice

The intention of this Appendix is to give some more particular explication of the origin and nature of justice, and to mark some differences between it and the other virtues.

The social virtues of humanity and benevolence exert their influence immediately by a direct tendency or instinct, which chiefly
keeps in view the simple object, moving the affections, and compre-
hends not any scheme or system, nor the consequences resulting
from the concurrence, imitation, or example of others. A parent flies
to the relief of his child, transported by that natural sympathy
which actuates him, and which affords no leisure to reflect on the
sentiments or conduct of the rest of mankind in like circumstances.
A generous man cheerfully embraces an opportunity of serving his
friend, because he then feels himself under the dominion of the beneficent affections, nor is he concerned whether any other person in
the universe were ever before actuated by such noble motives, or will
ever afterwards prove their influence. In all these cases the social
passions have in view a single individual object, and pursue the
safety or happiness alone of the person loved and esteemed. With
this they are satisfied, in this they acquiesce. And as the good, resulting from their benign influence, is in itself complete and entire,
it also excites the moral sentiment of approbation, without any reflection on farther consequences, and without any more enlarged
views of the concurrence or imitation of the other members of society. On the contrary, were the generous friend or disinterested pa-
triot to stand alone in the practice of beneficence, this would rather
enhance his value in our eyes, and join the praise of rarity and nov-
elty to his other more exalted merits.

The case is not the same with the social virtues of justice and
fidelity. They are highly useful, or indeed absolutely necessary to
the well-being of mankind; but the benefit resulting from them is not
the consequence of every individual single act, but arises from the
whole scheme or system concurred in by the whole, or the greater
part of the society. General peace and order are the attendants of
justice or a general abstinence from the possessions of others; but a
particular regard to the particular right of one individual citizen
may frequently, considered in itself, be productive of pernicious consequences. The result of the individual acts is here, in many instances, directly opposite to that of the whole system of actions; and
the former may be extremely hurtful, while the latter is, to the highest degree, advantageous. Riches, inherited from a parent, are, in a

bad man's hand, the instrument of mischief. The right of succession may, in one instance, be hurtful. Its benefit arises only from the observance of the general rule; and it is sufficient, if compensation be thereby made for all the ills and inconveniences which flow from particular characters and situations.

Cyrus, young and unexperienced, considered only the individual case before him, and reflected on a limited fitness and convenience, when he assigned the long coat to the tall boy, and the short coat to the other of smaller size. His governor instructed him better, while he pointed out more enlarged views and consequences, and informed his pupil of the general, inflexible rules, necessary to support general peace and order in society.

The happiness and prosperity of mankind, arising from the social virtue of benevolence and its subdivisions, may be compared to a wall, built by many hands, which still rises by each stone that is heaped upon it, and receives increase proportional to the diligence and care of each workman. The same happiness, raised by the social virtue of justice and its subdivisions, may be compared to the building of a vault, where each individual stone would, of itself, fall to the ground; nor is the whole fabric supported but by the mutual assistance and combination of its corresponding parts.

All the laws of nature, which regulate property, as well as all civil laws, are general, and regard alone some essential circumstances of the case, without taking into consideration the characters, situations, and connections of the person concerned, or any particular consequences which may result from the determination of these laws in any particular case which offers. They deprive, without scruple, a beneficent man of all his possessions, if acquired by mistake, without a good title; in order to bestow them on a selfish miser, who has already heaped up immense stores of superfluous riches. Public utility requires that property should be regulated by general inflexible rules; and though such rules are adopted as best serve the same end of public utility, it is impossible for them to prevent all particular hardships, or make beneficial consequences result from every individual case. It is sufficient, if the whole plan or scheme be necessary to the support of civil society, and if the balance of good, in the main, does thereby preponderate much above that of evil. Even the general laws of the universe, though planned by infinite wisdom, cannot exclude all evil or inconvenience in every particular operation.

It has been asserted by some, that justice arises from human conventions, and proceeds from the voluntary choice, consent, or combination of mankind. If by *convention* be here meant a *promise* (which is the most usual sense of the word) nothing can be more absurd than this position. The observance of promises is itself one of the most considerable parts of justice, and we are not surely bound to keep our word because we have given our word to keep it. But if by convention be meant a sense of common interest, which sense each man feels in his own breast, which he remarks in his fellows, and which carries him, in concurrence with others, into a general plan or system of actions, which tends to public utility; it must be owned, that, in this sense, justice arises from human conventions. For if it be allowed (what is, indeed, evident) that the particular consequences of a particular act of justice may be hurtful to the public as well as to individuals, it follows that every man, in embracing that virtue, must have an eye to the whole plan or system, and must expect the concurrence of his fellows in the same conduct and behaviour. Did all his views terminate in the consequences of each act of his own, his benevolence and humanity, as well as his self-love, might often prescribe to him measures of conduct very different from those which are agreeable to the strict rules of right and justice. Thus, two men pull the oars of a boat by common convention for common interest, without any promise of contract; thus gold and silver are made the measures of exchange; thus speech and words and language are fixed by human convention and agreement. Whatever is advantageous to two or more persons, if all perform their part, but what loses all advantage if only one perform, can arise from no other principle. There would otherwise be no motive for any one of them to enter into that scheme of conduct.

The word *natural* is commonly taken in so many senses and is of so loose a signification, that it seems vain to dispute whether justice be natural or not. If self-love, if benevolence be natural to man; if reason and forethought be also natural; then may the same epithet be applied to justice, order, fidelity, property, society. Men's inclination, their necessities, lead them to combine; their understanding and experience tell them that this combination is impossible where each governs himself by no rule, and pays no regard to the possessions of others; and from these passions and reflections conjoined, as soon as we observe like passions and reflections in others, the sentiment of justice, throughout all ages, has infallibly and certainly had place to some degree or other in every individual of the human species. In so sagacious an animal, what necessarily arises from the exertion of his intellectual faculties may justly be esteemed natural.[1]

Among all civilized nations it has been the constant endeavour to remove everything arbitrary and partial from the decision of property, and to fix the sentence of judges by such general views and considerations as may be equal to every member of the society. For besides, that nothing could be more dangerous than to accustom the bench, even in the smallest instance, to regard private friendship or enmity; it is certain, that men, where they imagine that there was no other reason for the preference of their adversary but personal favour, are apt to entertain the strongest ill-will against the magistrates and judges. When natural reason, therefore, points out no fixed view of public utility by which a controversy of property can be decided, positive laws are often framed to supply its place, and direct the procedure of all courts of judicature. Where these too fail, as often happens, precedents are called for; and a former decision, though given itself without any sufficient reason, justly becomes a sufficient reason for a new decision. If direct laws and precedents be wanting, imperfect and indirect ones are brought in aid; and the controverted case is ranged under them by analogical reasonings and comparisons, and similitudes, and correspondences, which are often more fanciful than real. In general, it may safely be affirmed that jurisprudence is, in this respect, different from all the sciences; and that in many of its nicer questions, there cannot properly be said to be truth or falsehood on either side. If one pleader bring the case under any former law or precedent, by a refined analogy or comparison; the opposite pleader is not at a loss to find an opposite analogy or comparison; and the preference given by the judge is often founded more on taste and imagination than on any solid argument. Public utility is the general object of all courts of judicature, and this utility too requires a stable rule in all controversies; but where several rules, nearly equal and indifferent, present themselves, it is a very slight turn of thought which fixes the decision in favour of either party.

We may just observe, before we conclude this subject, that after the laws of justice are fixed by views of general utility, the injury, the hardship, the harm, which result to any individual from a violation of them, enter very much into consideration, and are a great source of that universal blame which attends every wrong or iniquity. By the laws of society, this coat, this horse is mine, and *ought* to remain perpetually in my possession. I reckon on the secure enjoyment of it; by depriving me of it, you disappoint my expectations, and doubly displease me, and offend every bystander. It is a public wrong, so far as the rules of equity are violated; it is a private harm, so far as an individual is injured. And though the second consideration could have no place, were not the former previously established (for otherwise the distinction of *mine* and *thine* would be unknown in society) yet there is no question but the regard to general good is much enforced by the respect to particular. What injures the community, without hurting any individual, is often more lightly thought of. But where the greatest public wrong is also conjoined with a considerable private one, no wonder the highest disapprobation attends so iniquitous a behaviour.

| N O T E

1. Natural may be opposed, either to what is unusual, miraculous, or artificial. In the two former senses, justice and property are undoubtedly natural. But as they suppose reason, forethought, design, and a social union and confederacy among men, perhaps that epithet cannot strictly, in the last sense, be applied to them. Had men lived without society, property had never been known, and neither justice nor injustice had ever existed. But society among human creatures had been impossible without reason and forethought. Inferior animals, that unite, are guided by instinct, which supplies the place of reason. But all these disputes are merely verbal.

| *Commentary*

The first appendix to the *Enquiry Concerning the Principles of Morals* corresponds to the two sections of part i of the third book of the *Treatise*. The second appendix (which became the third in the 1777 edition), together with the relatively lengthy section III of this *Enquiry,* embodies arguments found throughout part ii of book III of the *Treatise*. The changes noticeable between the *Treatise* and the second *Enquiry* are rather greater than those between the relevant parts of the *Treatise* and the first *Enquiry*. Since I shall have recourse to the *Treatise,* as before, in discussing the doctrines Hume sets before us, I shall have occasion to mention these changes, but I shall not enter more than is necessary into scholarly disputes about how far they represent shifts in Hume's position.

These two appendices serve to introduce Hume's naturalistic theory of the nature of moral evaluation and his view of how we come to accept the obligations of membership in society. In both, we find Hume arguing for a shift from rationalist forms of ethics to a view of morals as a subject for the science of human nature and as a set of practices and institutions that such a science can reinforce.

It is well known that Hume pointed out the difference between "is"-judgments and "ought"-judgments: that is, he emphasized the importance of the change that takes place when we move from describing our nature and situation to judging it good or bad and from describing the nature and results of our actions to judging them right or wrong. At first sight, treating ethics as part of the science of human nature seems to reduce that emphasis and to imply that morality is no more than another social or biological phenomenon. It seems to some to be a short step from this to denying morals any special authority. Given Hume's notorious irreligiousness, we would not expect him to have any sympathy for attempts to found moral obligation on divine commands; but if morality is to become a mere human product, how can his account of it preserve the distinctiveness that he himself seems to emphasize?

Hume regards concerns of this sort as signs of a closet rationalism. Rationalist views of human nature see the ethical as the sphere where mankind's reason demonstrates its affinity with eternal verities that enable us to transcend our temporal embodiment and see the study of human nature in this world as the study of those desires and physical concerns that distract us from those verities and hinder us from modeling our conduct upon them. Hence we find Kant, for example, insisting on the sharpest of distinctions between ethics and psychology, and the wholly a priori character of the moral imperative.[1] But in Hume's view, rationalist ethical theories are less than fully intelligible, are unable to account for the influence of moral discriminations on our conduct, and distract the attention of philosophers from the real sources of moral stability that our natures and our social institutions provide. Using the arguments of these two appendices as a starting point, I shall attempt to outline Hume's ethical position on these themes. It has three main elements: first, the negative phase, which is an attack on ethical rationalism; second, the positive general theory of evaluation, which centers on Hume's particular version of the doctrine of "moral sense"; and third, his doctrine of justice and what he calls the artificial virtues.

I *The Attack on Ethical Rationalism*

Hume begins appendix I by saying he will resume a question raised, but not answered, in the first section of the *Enquiry:* the question of whether what he there called "moral distinctions" are due to reason or to sentiment. The latter term is used throughout the *Enquiry,* whereas the same issues are mostly discussed in the *Treatise* in terms of passion, feeling, or moral sense. This difference reflects the same lessening of emphasis on the details of the science of human nature that we find in the transition from the *Treatise* to the first *Enquiry,* although Hume's commitment to the naturalistic setting of morality is undiminished.

Hume has deferred this question until now because he claims that answering it is unnecessary for resolving the question that the *Enquiry* is most concerned with. He described *this* question as that of discovering "the true origin of morals."[2] This appears to consist in the discovery of what virtue, or "personal merit" is. He summarizes his answer at the close of part i of section IX as follows: "I cannot, at present, be more assured of any truth which I learn from reasoning and argument, than that personal merit consists entirely in the usefulness or agreeableness of qualities to the person himself possessed of them, or to others who have any intercourse with him."[3] Those whose characters we praise as virtuous or morally good, therefore, have qualities that are agreeable or useful — a broadly utilitarian understanding of virtue. Indeed, the word "utility" is very prominent in this *Enquiry,* which in many respects anticipates the later work of Bentham and Mill.

But although one can determine what sorts of character we praise or blame without deciding what capacities we use to do the praising or blaming, this deeper and more controversial question remains. The appendix addresses it, recycling arguments found first in the relevant portions of the *Treatise.*

Hume is widely recognized to be what is now called an emotivist in ethics. He holds, that is, that moral discriminations and the judgments that express them are due to emotion or sentiment. It is striking, in view of this, that he starts here with the conciliatory recognition that "reason must enter for a considerable share" in our moral discriminations. This is not just a manifestation of the tendency for the *Enquiry* to seek for smoothness and consensus, when the *Treatise* had failed to get attention by shocking its readers. It is also an attempt to provide a balance in exposition that shows that intellectual considerations are as necessary for our moral decisions as sentiment is. Hume says here that reason is necessary to determine whether a particular action or practice is useful to society or not and that such a determination has to be made before there can *be* any moral praise or blame. But the core of Hume's value theory is his insistence that it cannot be enough. There must, he says, be a sentiment, for without one the usefulness or harmfulness of the action contemplated would be a matter of indifference to us. The sentiment is needed for there to be "a preference."

Hume here identifies that sentiment as *humanity,* which he says is a feeling for the happiness of mankind. This is one place where many readers detect a difference between the second *Enquiry* and the *Treatise,* on which I shall comment briefly at the close of this chapter. Taken alone, this paragraph suggests merely that Hume is drawing our attention to the important difference between knowing the facts about an action and its consequences and *caring* about these things. He does indeed want to stress this difference, since he believes that it is our interpersonal relationships and the emotions that determine them that mark the distinction between factual and evaluative thinking. But his primary purpose in this appendix is with the phenomenon of evaluation itself, which is something that "humanity" prompts or leads to; and what he tells us about it is in most key respects the same as what he tells us in the *Treatise* — that approval and disapproval are themselves passions or sentiments, and that virtue and vice are those states of character that arouse them.

Views of this form have always drawn the fire of rationalist moral philosophers, and Hume attempts to counter their positions before elaborating his own. Most of the first appendix is taken up with his antirationalist arguments. His criticism of them is very radical. He says that the hypothesis of moral discrimination being due to reason alone is unintelligible. For if moral discrimination were due only to reason, then it would consist in the discovery of moral facts or moral relations, and both these notions are devoid of meaning.

Hume's argument depends, in the first place, on the understanding of the word "reason." He uses it here and in the corresponding passages in the *Treatise* in a sense broader than that to which he has been said to confine it in sections IV and V of the first *Enquiry*, although in our previous chapter, I have expressed some doubt on whether his argument there does confine it as radically as is commonly supposed. Here he broadens it to include both judgments of matters of fact and those of relations of ideas. The relevant sentences in *Treatise* III i 1 are these: "Reason is the discovery of truth or falsehood. Truth or falsehood consist in an agreement or disagreement either to the real relations of ideas, or to real existence and matter of fact."[4] If reason is taken to be the power to do these things and these things only, then two consequences follow. The first is that if morality is a matter of reason, there must be moral facts that we discover when we make our moral discriminations or moral relations that we can demonstrate to hold by a priori argument. These opinions were held by predecessors and contemporaries of Hume, including Locke, Cudworth, and Clarke.[5] The second consequence is that if such facts or relations do not exist, or if the very idea of their existence is incoherent, then the claim that moral choices are more reasonable than their opposites must be false. Hume has embraced the latter view, almost stridently, in the *Treatise* (in section 3 of part iii of book II), although he glides past it in the *Enquiry*.

He takes the example of the "crime of ingratitude." This consists of a person responding with ill will to someone who has treated him with good will. The wickedness or criminality of this is presumably the object of the supposedly rational discernment. What sort of fact is this criminality, if it is a fact? What sort of relation is it if it is a relation? However we assess Hume's position here, the questions he raises are urgent for the theories he is attacking. If ingratitude is a fact, it will be a mental one, to be found in the consciousness of the ungrateful person. But the only relevant facts discernible there are indifference or hostility. These are not intrinsically criminal, since they only become criminal if their object is someone who has done us good, so their presence in the ingrate's mind is not the moral fact the rationalist requires. Hume concludes that the criminality "is not any particular individual fact, but arises from a complication of circumstances, which, being presented to the spectator, excites the sentiment of blame." (It is interesting to notice that there is a well-known twentieth-century theory to the effect that evaluation is indeed a matter of the discernment of a special quality, namely that of G. E. Moore in *Principia Ethica*.[6] Although Moore does not direct his argument against Hume, he insists that the quality discerned (goodness) is simple, indefinable, and non-natural — a combination that Hume would have found unintelligible. Moore also has to maintain that this non-natural quality is discerned in organic wholes rather than their parts: an attempt, perhaps, to deal with the problem Hume raises.)

Hume argues at greater length, both here and in the *Treatise*, against the theory that moral discernment is a matter of recognizing relations. Samuel Clarke had maintained that reason is able to recognize the fitness or obligatoriness of actions of certain kinds and that this fitness is an eternal truth comparable in its status and its clarity to the truths of mathematics.[7] This theory is tailor-made to fit Hume's doctrine of relations of ideas — except that Hume fails to find any analogy between actual moral judgments and mathematical ones. It is possible, he says, to spell out in detail what mathematical relations consist in, but no comparable explanation is available in the moral case. The only relationship he can himself discern in the case of ingratitude is that of "contrariety" — responding to someone in a manner opposite to that in which he has dealt with me. But in some circumstances (namely when I am returning good for evil), this is meritorious and not criminal, so this cannot be what the crime consists in. Hume then dismisses as circular the claim that the relationship we discern in moral evaluation is that between actions and moral rules; for if this is supposed to found moral discernment on the perception of relations, the rules themselves then need to be founded on these relations, and the argument turns back on itself. The only note-worthy feature of this argument is that it shows Hume is not unaware of the role of rules in moral decisions, as we shall see below. He is merely concerned here to point out that the recognition of the importance rules have in our choices does not show that the approval and disapproval we direct toward actions or rules is itself due to reason rather than feeling.

The antirationalist argument continues through subsections II, III, and IV of the appendix. The common theme is the emphasis on the distinction between fact and value. In subsection II, this is emphasized by another contrast between mathematical and moral reasoning. In geometry we infer previously unknown relations from the known relationships of the parts of a figure to one another, but in morality we have to know all the facts and relations before approval or disapproval are in order. If there are facts we do not yet know (and, it has to be added, if we are aware of this), we must suspend moral approval and disapproval until the required facts are in; then, and not until then, we can have "some new impression of affection or disgust, esteem or contempt, approbation or blame." This argument may well seem compelling to many contemporary readers, but it is in fact quite dogmatic, since the premise — that in moral reflection all the facts have to be in before evaluation is appropriate — is only acceptable if one assumes that there are no evaluative facts, which is, of course, the conclusion. If we accept it, however, we can go on to follow Hume in what he says about our disapproval of Nero's murder of his mother. He says the difference between us and Nero is not that we are aware of some relation of which he was ignorant, but that we have sentiments that his debauched life had drained away from his personality. The case is an interesting test of Hume's thesis, for although we do feel indignation at the crime of matricide, we are as likely to express this in the language of fact as that of feeling: we are as likely to wonder how Nero could not see the enormity of his action as that he could not feel it.

The same plausibility, and the same tendency to provoke second thoughts, attends Hume's analogy with aesthetic value in subsection III. For whatever reason, subjectivist theories have always had easier acceptance in aesthetics than in ethics; but this very fact is troubling when Hume, or anyone, leans on the likenesses between aesthetic and moral value to press subjectivism in moral theory. He argues that Euclid and the architects Palladio and Perrault can describe all the qualities of figures and buildings that combine to produce the result that we call beautiful; but the beauty of the objects they describe is something that supervenes and is not one of the qualities or relationships *in* the objects. The way it supervenes makes it clear, Hume thinks, that it is in fact a subjective sentiment in the observer, not an additional quality recognized by the observer's reason. He then argues by analogy that the same is true of the crimes of those politicians attacked by Cicero: the criminality of their acts depends on the effect of these acts and their circumstances on the sentiments of those to whom Cicero is speaking. While the analogy helps to make Hume's position even clearer than it was before, the rationalist can simply reject it, even though he does then incur the obligation of offering another account of moral judgments.

Likewise, one can readily reject Hume's analogy in response to the argument he uses in subsection IV, which repeats one he has used in *Treatise* III i 1. We condemn Nero's matricide, but we do not condemn the young tree that destroys its parents as it grows beside it. In the *Treatise,* Hume adds the example of incest, which repels us in humans but is not censured in animals. He claims that all the elements and relationships in the actions are the same in the nonhuman cases as they are in human life, so that any theory that claims moral qualities are discernible by reason ought to class plants and animals as criminal, too. The rationalist can easily say in reply that the presence of reason in the human agent makes a real difference to the nature of the actions and relationships involved.

Hume's final argument against rationalism in ethics is that human actions are always motivated by desire and not by reason. We justify our choices by reference to the desires they satisfy; either the objectives we pursue are desired as a means to others or for themselves. Virtue is desired for itself, he says (although such a comment sits uncomfortably with his emphasis on utility, just as the same assertion was a problem later on for John Stuart Mill[8]). Hence virtue must arouse an appropriate sentiment in us. This is a strange and muddled-looking argument. This is because the ones that have preceded it have been about moral discrimination, whereas this is clearly about what makes us *act*. These are not the same, since we can often approve of things without choosing to pursue them ourselves — something Hume himself makes clear when he says that virtue is whatever gives "the pleasing sentiment of approbation" to a *spectator*. He actually maintains two distinct theses: the thesis that reason cannot move us to action, and the thesis that reason cannot be the source of our moral distinctions. It is possible to hold either without the other, though it is no surprise to find someone as opposed to rationalism as Hume is maintaining both. In the *Treatise,* they are argued for separately (the first in part iii of book II and the second in part i of book III), whereas in the shorter space of the *Enquiry,* they are mingled together, so that the conclusion, which is a statement of the second thesis, is presented as though it followed from arguments that support the first.

One reason why Hume yields to the temptation to fuse them is that when he argues for them separately, he leans both times on the same central contention, which the repeats: that reason is confined to the determination of relations of ideas (a priori reasoning) and matters of fact (empirical, or inductive, reasoning). Although actions often follow on such rational processes, they cannot do so directly. Similarly, although approval and disapproval often follow on such processes, they are distinct from them. It is easy for a present-day reader to feel indifferent to the question of whether reason or the passions does this or that because this seems to be a question about the activities of two mythical human faculties. But Hume is too astute to care about issues of this sort for themselves, as indeed the rationalists he attacks, and Kant following them, also were. I have attempted in Chapter Two to connect Hume's treatment of this issue to his project of a science of human nature and his determination to naturalize the understanding of human action and morality. To do this he seeks to relate it at all times to human wants and satisfactions and not to realms of transcendent fact. He may, of course, be mistaken in supposing that this is only possible by tracing moral action and moral discrimination alike to the influence of passion or sentiment. I shall comment here briefly on his claim that only passion can motivate conduct and shall return to his positive account of moral discrimination below.

Hume states his main arguments in II iii 3 ("Of the influencing Motives of the Will"). After insisting that reason is confined to relations of ideas and matters of fact, he says that such reasoning does indeed have an effect on our choices when it reveals to us what will lead to the results we desire or what consequences the objects of our desires will have. But this does not show that reason determines our choices. It can only affect our choices if we already desire some object that reason investigates or come to have a desire for some object of which it informs us. Without this, the facts reason tells us of will have at most a detached intellectual interest for us. This seems plausible, but Hume goes on to say something less in accord with common sense: that reason and passion cannot even be "in contention." So reason is not only unable to create the desire for something; it cannot oppose such a desire, either. Hume has special reasons for maintaining this, derived from the particular analysis of the passions that he offers us in book II. Essentially he holds that passions are impressions, not ideas; I can only be in a state contrary to reason if I have *ideas* that are not in agreement with the objects of which they are supposedly copies — that is, if I have false beliefs about the world to which my ideas have reference. When I have a passion, I have an inner feeling that has no reference in this sense. So reason and the passions are not the sorts of mental entities that can oppose one another.

This is one of Hume's worst arguments, and unfortunately one of his most important. Since it makes no direct appearance in the *Enquiry*, I cannot discuss it at length here. To assess it fairly requires detailed attention to the theory of the passions in its entirety, which is beyond this work's scope; but some brief comments are in order. Hume is maintaining that reason is concerned with truth and falsity and that our choices and the passions that prompt them are not true or false. Stated with bald generality in this fashion, this view seems harmless. But as soon as its detailed meaning and consequences are spelled out, it becomes deeply controversial. If desires are passions, and passions are neither true nor false, and reason is only concerned with truth and falsity, then, Hume concludes, desires cannot be reasonable or unreasonable. He embraces this result with all the pride of paradox, telling us that it is not contrary to reason to prefer the destruction of the whole world to the scratching of my finger or to sacrifice my entire good to the minor betterment of a person wholly unknown to me or to prefer my lesser good to my greater.

In the sense to which he has confined "reason," this result is not even interesting, but trivially true, for none of these things are *false judgments*. But the reason this proclamation looks shocking is that we do not, in common usage, confine "reason" in this way. For we would call all these choices unreasonable, or irrational; and Hume's rhetoric depends for its effect on trading on this difference between his technical usage and ours. He reinforces his argument by maintaining, still under the rubric of his own view of reason, that our common ascription of irrationality to such choices is incorrect: for, he says, a passion cannot be called unreasonable unless it is accompanied by a false judgment, "and even then it is not the passion, properly speaking, which is unreasonable, but the judgment."[9] Here we run into a serious consequence of what might otherwise seem a trivial terminological restriction. For in calling a passion unreasonable, we commonly do *not* mean that it is based on a false judgment. If I am enraged at a supposed injury, my rage can be called reasonable if the injury I think has been done me is a major one, even if it turns out that I was wrong to think it *has* been done to me. My rage would vanish in the face of this discovery, but that would not show it to have been unreasonable while I felt it. Its reasonableness or unreasonableness depends on what we consider to be appropriate to the amount of harm I think I have received. My rage is *mistaken,* but not for that reason irrational. Similarly, my rage can be irrational even if my judgment is true if the injury I correctly thought I suffered was a trivial one. My rage would be irrational because it is judged to be disproportionate. Hume's insistence that only falsehood entails irrationality eliminates a whole scale of moral judgment at one stroke.

A final unhappy consequence of Hume's argument is the inevitable misrepresentation of the passions and desires themselves that is required to maintain it. It requires him to stress that the passions are impressions, not ideas, and are therefore nonrepresentative and have no reference beyond themselves. He states his case as follows: "A passion is an original existence, or, if you will, modification of existence, and contains not any representative quality, which renders it a copy of any other existence or modification. When I am angry, I am actually possessed with the passion, and in that emotion have no more a reference to any other object, than when I am thirsty, or sick, or more than five foot high."[10]

The last sentence quoted is so clearly false that it is not surprising that Hume does not repeat it, or offer any substitute for it, in the *Enquiry*. The whole theory of the passions is conspicuously absent from it, in part because it, too, was recast in 1757 in the dissertation "Of the Passions," and because the main concern of the *Enquiry,* the mapping of the "principles" moral agents adhere to, does not require the presentation of its complexities. But Hume does not abandon it.

The best-known thing Hume says about the practical limitations of reason is, of course, that it is the slave of the passions. It is important, in view of what we must examine next, to say that this is not, as it seems (and as it gets its impact through seeming), a declaration of the practical *impotence* of reason, but a declaration of its *limits*. This fact enables Hume to recognize the essential role reason does play in moral reflection when he comes to write the *Enquiry*. Even in the *Treatise,* however, it is clear that reason has plenty to do, as slaves always have. For example, even though reason does not move us, it does *prompt* desires which do, and it calculates the means to satisfy the desires we have. (He says this quite explicitly in *Treatise* III i 1.[11]) This is important because it is paralleled by similar functions in moral evaluation. But here, as there, we must not overrate the importance of Hume's concession, for he still insists that there are no occasions when reason takes charge of our conduct. The doctrine of calm passions is designed primarily to head off this possibility, central to all rationalist theories. A passion is calm if it is not felt with great intensity, but it can still be strong, that is, effective in our conduct, although not violent. The cases where we do not yield to strong temptations that agitate us but choose a greater good instead may involve reason, since they will be occasions when we calculate consequences, but it is the calm passion, including even "the general appetite to good and aversion to evil, considered merely as such," that produces the choice.[12] Reason may be indispensable, but it is through passions that we act.

| *Approval and Disapproval*

Let us now look at Hume's positive account of our moral evaluations. In section 2 of part i of book III of the *Treatise,* he gives as the section heading the phrase "Moral distinctions derived from a moral sense." He wisely changes to talk of sentiments when he writes the *Enquiry.* Although his choice of "moral sense" was intended to place him in the tradition of Hutcheson and Shaftesbury, as distinct from that of Cudworth and Clarke, the term does carry suggestions of a moral intuition,[13] or a capacity to perceive moral qualities, and this suggestion runs counter to all the positive things Hume says about how our evaluations actually take place. He tries to set the matter straight in the *Treatise.*

> Thus the course of the argument leads us to conclude that since vice and virtue are not discoverable merely by reason, or the comparison of ideas, it must be by means of some impression or sentiment they occasion that we are able to mark the difference betwixt them. Our decisions concerning moral rectitude and depravity are evidently perceptions; and as all perceptions are either impressions or ideas, the exclusion of the one is a convincing argument for the other. Morality, therefore, is more properly felt than judged of; though this feeling or sentiment is commonly so soft and gentle that we are apt to confound it with an idea, according to our common custom of taking all things for the same, which have any near resemblance to each other.[14]

So the moral sense, or moral sentiment, is a kind of feeling. There is more yet, in case we are unsure of Hume's intent: "To have the sense of virtue, is nothing but to *feel* a satisfaction of a peculiar kind from the contemplation of a character. The very *feeling* constitutes our praise or admiration. . . . We do not infer a character to be virtuous because it pleases, but in feeling that it pleases

after such a particular manner, we in effect feel that it is virtuous."[15] The feeling has a name: approbation. It is described as a
"pleasing sentiment" in the *Enquiry*. To complete the picture, we
must include one more important quotation from the beginning of
Treatise III iii 5: "The pain or pleasure which arises from the
general survey or view of any action or quality of the mind, constitutes its vice or virtue, and gives rise to our approbation or blame,
which is nothing but a fainter and more imperceptible love or
hatred."[16] Approval and disapproval, then, are sentiments (passions, feelings) that arise from the "general survey" of agents and
their actions, and are to be classed as calm passions, the violent
counterparts of which are love and hatred. What is the theory of
moral evaluation that emerges from these passages and is expressed without these refinements and qualifications in the
Enquiry?

The passages quoted are a little difficult to square with one
another, if we stress their wording. For example, it does not seem
quite the same to hold that in having "a satisfaction of a peculiar
kind," we are feeling that a certain character is virtuous as it is to
hold that the pleasure this character gives us "constitutes" its
virtue; nor is it the same to say that this feeling *constitutes* our
praise or admiration as to say that it *gives rise* to it. But if we read
with charity, we can say that Hume holds that when we say a
certain character is virtuous, we are expressing a feeling that this
character brings about in us; that this feeling is an agreeable one;
and that the fact that this feeling is what we are expressing when
we say the character is virtuous is in some way essential to the
character's *being* virtuous. Virtue is not, then, something we
discern in the character we so describe; it is somehow shed upon it
by our contemplation of it. This last fact is what makes it correct to
call Hume's theory "subjectivist" if one is so inclined, though this is
in many ways a dangerous description, as we shall see shortly.

The theory already has two relatively minor ambiguities built
into it. First, Hume's language makes it unclear whether he thinks
the pleasure the sight of a virtuous character gives us *is* the feeling
of approval, or whether it gives rise to such a feeling, which is
distinct from it. He says virtue "pleases after such a particular
manner." He does not seem to have great sensitivity to the complexities of the concept of pleasure, here or elsewhere,[17] but we can
manage to interpret him without insisting upon it. He certainly
holds that the contemplation of the virtuous character pleases us
(causes us to feel, that is to *be,* pleased); what is unclear is whether
being pleased is the sort of state that has specific varieties, of
which moral approbation is one, and perhaps being selfishly

pleased could be another, or whether he thinks that being pleased is a single state, or perception, which leads on to another, namely approval. Whichever is the case, he holds that the utterance that the character is virtuous is an expression of the approval, and this leads to the second ambiguity, wrapped in the phrase "praise or approval." Praise is an outward, usually verbal, performance, whereas approval seems to be, in most contexts, something Hume considers internal. Hume's language is unclear between saying that the feeling causes the praise or is to be identified with it. Obviously the latter would leave us in a position of having to say that Hume thought virtue only existed when it was *said* to exist, whereas what he clearly wishes to maintain is that it could not exist without being *felt* to exist. So this ambiguity need not detain us. He thinks that when we say someone's character is virtuous and thus praise that person, we are expressing a feeling of approval, and that this feeling of approval is somehow constitutive of his being virtuous, not a consequence of our discerning his virtue independently. The language of the *Enquiry* (that virtue is "whatever mental action or quality gives to a spectator the pleasing sentiment of approbation") confirms these readings and incorporates the same ambiguities without drawing our attention to them.

A more substantial ambiguity is to be found in the phrases "character or quality" and "action or quality." In practice we seem to approve or disapprove of individual actions and the general dispositions they manifest (or are departures from). This is enough to explain why Hume mentions both. But his theory stresses the centrality of judgments about character. This comes out in his choice of "virtuous" as the paradigmatic term of approval and in his claim that approval and disapproval are calm forms of love and hatred, which are directed to persons. To approve of a character is to love, in a calm fashion, the person who *has* that character. This places approval and disapproval on the map of human passions that Hume draws for us in book II of the *Treatise*. The passions of love and hatred have other people as their *objects*.[18] Hume distinguishes between an emotion's object and its cause, although not in quite the same manner as some twentieth-century writers.[19] The object is the person toward whom an emotion is directed, and the cause is some property of that person or something belonging to that person that arouses the emotion. Hume's position on approval and disapproval, then, seems to be that they are always directed to the person who has a character, so that the person is their object, but they are aroused or caused by that person's actions. This coheres with his apparent opinion that the standard terms for expressing approval and disapproval are "virtuous" and "vicious" and with his strange view that actions are only relevant to our moral judgments when they are manifestations of a settled character and never otherwise: "Actions themselves, not proceeding from any constant principle, have no influence on love or hatred, pride or humility, and consequently are never considered in morality."[20]

The subsumption of approval and disapproval under the passions of love and hatred raises a question that leads us into another, very important part of Hume's theory of evaluation. At the commonsense level, we seem frequently to find ourselves approving of the characters of people whom we do not find it easy, or even possible, to love, and to find ourselves loving people of whose characters we disapprove. Part of the problem this raises for interpreting Hume comes from the fact that his de-Christianized perspective does not distinguish between love and admiration. (He even says in *Treatise* III iii 4 that "love and esteem are at bottom the same passions."[21]) But Hume is quite aware of the fact that approval and disapproval are often directed at people who have no personal connection with us. This is why he says that the sense of virtue comes from the *contemplation* of a character and from the *general survey or view* of an action or quality of the mind, and that virtue is whatever mental action or quality gives *to a spectator* the pleasing sentiment of approbation. Even if we take him with full seriousness when he tells us that approval is a mild form of love, and disapproval a mild form of hatred, we must take into account his much more emphatic statements about the need for objectivity in moral evaluations. Here Flew draws our attention to an important passage in section IX of the second *Enquiry,* where Hume says the following:

> When a man denominates another his enemy, his rival, his antagonist, his adversary, he is understood to speak the language of self-love, and to express sentiments peculiar to himself, and arising from his particular circumstances and situation. But when he bestows on any man the epithets of vicious or odious or depraved, he then speaks another language, and expresses sentiments, in which he expects all his audience are to concur with him. He must here, therefore, depart from his private and peculiar situation, and must choose a point of view, common to him with others.[22]

This passage combines two opinions held by Hume: that the language of virtue and vice is language used in contexts where agreement and disagreement are to be expected, and that it is language used in contexts where agreement depends on the speaker's abandoning his "private" viewpoint. These opinions are, of course, connected: it has often been pointed out in modern moral philosophy that if moral judgments merely report the occurrence of certain feelings within the speaker, someone reporting different feelings is not disagreeing with that speaker, even if the subject of comment is the same person or action. Hume does not fall into the trap of supposing that moral opinions are immune to rational dispute in this way. Instead, he holds that the feelings these opinions manifest arise only when the point of view adopted by the speaker is objective or detached; and he also maintains that although moral judgments express feelings, they are true or false in a publicly discernible way.

"It is only," Hume says, "when a character is considered in general, without reference to our particular interest, that it causes such a feeling or sentiment as denominates it morally good or evil."[23] He goes on to say that the sentiments that arise in us when we have a personal interest and those that arise in us when we do not "are apt to be confounded." In other words, we are likely to deceive ourselves into thinking we are disapproving of someone morally when we are merely vexed by his behaving in a way that does not suit our interests. We confuse disapproval and hostility and, of course, approval and personal liking. To say this is to cast some doubt on the view that approval and disapproval are merely calm forms of love and hatred, since the confusion would then be between different degrees of the same emotion. But if we leave this aside, we can see Hume maintains that when we use the language of moral approval and disapproval, we are implicitly claiming to be judging the person on whom we are commenting from a point of view that is detached from our own personal wants. He clearly thinks that the moral sentiments only arise when we view the person in question *disinterestedly.* (In this respect, his ethical views and his aesthetic views are the same: a condition of good taste is the capacity to view objects with appropriate detachment.[24]) They arise when I take up the stance of a *spectator.* The human ability to do this is explained by Hume in terms of the doctrine of sympathy, to which I shall turn below.

At present, however, it is important to add to the condition that moral judgments, to claim truth, must be based on disinterested appraisal that this appraisal must involve the discernment of real qualities and tendencies in the character appraised. The understanding of the exact nature of Hume's subjectivism depends on the correct interpretation of what he says about this.

In his important recent studies, David Norton has claimed that Hume should be called a moral realist: one who believes in the real existence of virtues and vices.[25] This stresses an important truth, but exaggerates it. In his account of our moral evaluations, Hume makes it clear that our moral sentiments are responses to states of character in our fellows and that these states of character generate these responses because we discern them to have certain results.[26] They may be immediately agreeable or disagreeable to the person who has them, or to others; and they may be agreeable or disagreeable to the person who has them, or to others, in an indirect or long-term way. The inevitable emphasis in ethical discourse is on the effects our personalities have on others, so that, in the *Enquiry* particularly, Hume makes much of the virtues' utility. When I recognize, through a disinterested investigation (or "survey") that some state of character has beneficial or harmful effects, my imagination engages with those effects through the psychological mechanism of sympathy (see later in this chapter), and this in turn generates the sentiment of approval or disapproval toward the person whose character leads to those effects. Just as my discernment of the effects involves the reason, so does my discernment of those character traits that lead to them. Since I call these virtues or vices, they must be real, settled features of the makeup of the persons I am judging; and the names of these character traits (such as generosity, benevolence, industry, cruelty, indolence, and irresolution) are therefore names of actual dispositions that people have. They also express the positive or negative evaluation I and my fellow language-users place upon them.

To speak of this view as moral realism, however, is to suggest that Hume thinks the positive or negative value of the character judged is some discerned fact over and above the character itself and the sentiment expressed in the face of it, and he does not think this but rather spends much time, as we have seen, arguing that such facts can *not* be discerned.[27] But we cannot leave the matter here. Norton is right to hold that Hume's analysis of moral judgments makes them true or false. In the first place, the subjects I judge either do have the character traits I say they have or not; and these either have the effects I think they have or not. I can be right or wrong about both these matters, and they are matters on which I depend for the truth on reason and on which I can be corrected by reason.

There is more yet; and it is this extra that makes Norton's analysis tempting. In an important sentence in *Treatise* III i 1, Hume says: "Vice and virtue, therefore, may be compared to sounds, colours, heat and cold, which according to modern philosophy, are not qualities in objects, but perceptions in the mind; and this discovery in morals, like that other in physics, is to be regarded as a considerable achievement of the speculative sciences, though like that, too, it has little or no influence on practice."[28] We can disregard the strictures that Hume has pronounced on primary and secondary qualities in *Treatise* I iv 4. Whatever his final view on the epistemology of perception, he clearly wishes us to find the allusion clarificatory here. And what it tells us is that virtuousness and viciousness are indeed like what the modern philosophers tell us colors and flavors are like. They are not features of the objects (or persons) to whom we verbally ascribe them, but they are aspects of our own experience of characteristics that *do* belong, wholly objectively, to those objects or persons. They would not emerge but for the action of those characteristics on observers, but their being observer-dependent does not mean that they are matters on which each observer is the final authority — as each observer would be if my saying someone is virtuous were merely a matter of saying that that person's character makes *me* feel approval or that an object's chemical properties made it taste sour to *me*. For one can be wrong about secondary qualities and know it: a fruit can taste sour when it is not if I have just been eating chocolate. What counts is what most people in normal circumstances say about it. In saying someone is vicious I do not only tell you that I feel disapproval of him, but that others who scrutinize his character and its effects detachedly, as I am claiming by implication to have done, would also feel the same sentiment. I think Capaldi is right to call this an *intersubjective* view rather than a form of moral realism.[29]

I am not quite so sure that Capaldi is right to reject J. L. Mackie's suggestion that Hume considers moral judgments to involve projection.[30] This is a contemporary name for what Hume says we do when we talk of causation: we have an idea based on an internal impression, which we apply to outer objects we observe. One could say that if moral qualities are secondary qualities, they, too, are based on the internal impressions of approval and disapproval and are ascribed to the characters that have generated those impressions. Mackie seems to think that this implies Hume believes we all make the false judgment that moral qualities are resident in objects, and overlook their subjective origin; and Capaldi says with some justice that no one speaks of judgments about color as always false in this way. This is true; but Hume, when likening moral qualities to the secondary qualities of perception, does say that the recognition of this is an achievement of speculative science that has no bearing on practice — in other words, that at the commonsense level, we are unaware of the way our ascription of the secondary qualities, and presumably also the moral ones, depends on our involvement as perceivers. There is indeed a clear sense in which commonsense judgments about secondary qualities, if the theory about them that Hume alludes to here is true, *are* partially false for this reason, even though no one notices this.

I suggest that both views contain an important element of the truth about Hume's position. He does think that the verbal ascription of moral qualities to characters is *philosophically* misleading, in that the impressions whose occurrence prompts moral utterances are internal, and this is disguised by the fact that they are ascribed to the characters being judged. Nor does he clearly commit himself to the view that at the commonsense level we are aware of their internal character. He clearly does think that moral judgments can be corrected by reason, since the sentiments they express arise from disinterested scrutiny of real personal characteristics and their consequences, which are either the way we consider them to be or are not. But he does not consider (as I have suggested earlier that he does in the case of causal judgments) that our natures prompt us to transfer our awareness of an inner impression outwards in a way that coincidentally aligns us with outer realities otherwise unknown to us.[31] In the case of moral judgments, Hume is most anxious to insist that the relevant realities, namely the characters we judge, their consequences, and the sentiments they occasion, are all open to our scrutiny. He is not, at least in this sense, a skeptic about morality.

If the above analysis is correct in its main features, however, there is one clear feature of Hume's position that leads to problems that haunt all moral philosophies centered on moral feeling. Those opposed to such positions often argue that they cannot preserve the truth or falsity of moral judgments. We have seen how Hume's analysis can respond to such charges. The moral sentiments he claims we express in our judgments arise, in his view, only after disinterested scrutiny of facts about the characters judged and their results, and when I call someone virtuous or vicious, I thereby imply that those who disagree are mistaken about those facts or have not been sufficiently disinterested in investigating them. The obvious question is, What if someone who does meet all these requirements assesses the person differently from the way I assess him or her? In common with other writers of his time, Hume assumes a general consensus among his readers about what sorts of character are properly judged virtuous or vicious. Given his utilitarian bent, this requires him also to assume consensus about what consequences of a person's character and actions are desirable ones and what not. He writes in a context where what is at issue is not what is good, but how its agreed goodness is to be interpreted philosophically. In the language of C. L. Stevenson, whose ethical analysis is very Humean, he assumes that disagreement in attitude is always the result of disagreement in belief.[32] But we can hardly take this for granted as does Hume. It seems that while Hume's analysis of the nature of moral judgments does indeed allow for rational dispute about them, it is not clear that it can provide for moral truth and falsity, as opposed to moral coincidence or dissonance within one social unit.

▎ *Sympathy and Humanity*

This account of Hume's moral theory has so far omitted its best-known doctrine: that of sympathy. Hume uses this term in a technical way to refer not to the emotion of compassion but to a psychic mechanism that plays a key role in the genesis of many phenomena of our emotional life, especially that of the moral sentiments.

Moral approval and disapproval arise when we assume the role of spectator and are disinterested or, as we sometimes express it, dispassionate. Yet it is also Hume's view that rationalist theories of morality do not relate our moral sentiments and judgments to the passions and so fail to explain how moral considerations motivate us. He is therefore at great pains to insure that his own theory can do this. The most important passions in our lives are those of pride, humility, love, and hatred; and although he says that love and esteem are essentially the same, there does seem to be some tension between saying that approval and disapproval are calm forms of love and hatred and saying that they arise when we are disinterested observers. How can morality both be the product of objectivity and be the manifestation of passion? The doctrine of sympathy is Hume's answer to this, at least in the *Treatise*. The mechanism of sympathy generates a special sort of emotional involvement with the experience of others that leads to the sentiments of approval and disapproval.

It might not seem as clear to everyone as it does to Hume that we need a special mechanism to account for this involvement. To assume we need it is to assume that we are naturally self-centered, and that the scruples of conscience are somehow alien to our makeup. In common with many thinkers of his time, Hume felt obliged to respond to the cynical theories of Thomas Hobbes, who had maintained just this and had gone on to say that the whole of morality was an imposition of the state and gained its hold upon us only because our self-interest made it clear we should submit to its institutions. Other answers to Hobbes included that of Shaftesbury, who stressed the importance of benevolence in human life, and that of Butler, who maintained that conscience was not merely part of human nature but supreme in it over self-love and benevolence.[33] Hume does not think we are wholly selfish, but he does think that our benevolence, though real enough, is naturally confined to those close to us — roughly, our friends and families: "In general it may be affirmed that there is no such passion in human minds as the love of mankind, merely as such, independent of personal qualities, of services, or of relation to ourself."[34]

As far as conscience is concerned, Hume agrees with Hobbes that it has a necessary connection with the social order, though not the simplistically conceived one that Hobbes postulates. His primary reason appears to be that it is absurd to suppose that the sense of right and wrong is an original source of motivation in our natures because it is manifested in the emotions of approval and disapproval, and these are necessarily reactive and directed at character traits and actions already in place for us to appraise. No one would suppose that the motivation for vicious conduct was the sense of vice (or moral disapproval); similarly, it is a mistake to suppose that, for more than some special cases, the sense of virtue (or approval) could be what motivates virtuous conduct. Hence: "In short, it may be established as an undoubted maxim, that no action can be virtuous, or morally good, unless there be in human nature some motive to produce it, distinct from the sense of its morality."[35] Hume does not deny that moral sense motivates conduct on its own from time to time, but he does deny it to be a basic feature of our makeup in the way that a passion like restricted benevolence is.

The sympathetic mechanism is introduced by Hume in section 11 of part i of book II of the *Treatise*.[36] It proceeds as follows: I become aware of the passion of another person through observation of the behavioral signs of it that are familiar in my own case. This gives me the idea of the other's emotion. This becomes enlivened in me to the point where it develops into an impression, that is, into a counterpart in me of the very emotion the other person is feeling. What communicates the vivacity necessary for this transformation is the "idea, or rather impression" of myself. (It is clear that Hume does not mean here the simple rationalist self, which he declares in book I to be something of which we have no impression or idea.[37]) The closer the person is to me and the more recognizably like me he or she is, the more intensely this vivacity is communicated, according to Hume's associative principles; but all human beings bear some significant resemblance to one another, so there is in principle no one for whom I cannot feel a passion sympathetically. Hume clearly thinks that his associative system here is based on common experience: "It is also evident, that the ideas of the affections of others are converted into the very impressions they represent, and that the passions arise in conformity to the images we form of them. All this is an object of the plainest experience, and depends not on any hypothesis of philosophy."[38]

When sympathy generates parallel emotions in me to the feelings of others not connected with me by more than general human resemblance, Hume calls it extensive sympathy.

Sympathy operates in the generation of the moral sentiments when I recognize the pleasing or displeasing effects that someone's character or conduct has on himself or on other persons. When I recognize these effects, the passions that arise in him or in those other persons as a result of his character and conduct are sympathetically paralleled in me. These give rise, again by association (here the association of impressions), to the moral sentiments of approval (if the sympathetically generated passion is pleasant) or disapproval (if it is painful). In feeling these moral sentiments, I am feeling a calm love or hate toward the person who has caused the effects with which I have sympathized (in this technical sense). I feel for them (that is, I have the very feelings they have) and thus feel love or hate toward the agent whose character affects them.

This is Hume's psychological explanation of the emotional commonality between members of the same society that enables them to share a common moral discourse. At least, this is the basis of the details of his analyses in the *Treatise.* By the time we come to the second *Enquiry,* however, the mechanism of sympathy drops out of sight. Whether Hume abandons it or not is a matter of controversy.[39] Capaldi suggests that it is not so much abandoned as it is dropped as an explanation of the moral sentiments, to be replaced by the sentiment of humanity. He maintains that Hume felt the need to invoke this sentiment (which bears more than a passing resemblance to the universal benevolence that he previously rejects) because extensive sympathy cannot account for our tendency to feel moral approval toward others even when they act against our interests, or when they belong to societies remote from ours in space or time. In such cases, Capaldi asserts, Hume thinks that the sympathetic mechanism, depending as it does on the enlivening power of the sense of self, cannot be powerful enough to generate sentiments that will counteract the negative effects of hostility or remoteness even though we still seem able to produce the positive moral judgments that would be the expression of such sentiments if they *were* felt. He claims Hume here invokes another sentiment in order to preserve the disinterestedness of our moral judgments on such occasions. I am at present unsure of the merits of this interpretation; if it is not accepted, one has to ascribe the absence of clear inclusion of sympathy in the second *Enquiry* to Hume's more limited concerns in that work, which made him confine the psychological underpinnings of his ethics to appendices. If this is true, then the reference to a sentiment of humanity has to be construed as a shorthand for the details of sympathy that are spelled out in the *Treatise*.

▮ *Justice*

We can clearly approve of actions without ourselves doing them. This is because our desires and fears motivate us to do other things. Sometimes we do things that we approve of but not *because* we think them morally good — a point much stressed later by Kant. Hume is not uncomfortable about this the way Kant was to be; his theory of morality demands it should be so. As we have seen, he emphasizes that moral approval and disapproval can only come about if we respond emotionally to patterns of human choice that are already in place in society. The problem about moral motivation that worries Hume most is that of explaining how it is that we do, in an important range of cases, perform actions of which we approve, but for which we do not seem to have any distinct motive other than that approval. There are two aspects to this question. First, how is it that we do sometimes perform actions from a mere sense of their rightness when we lack the motives that usually prompt them? Second, why do we ever perform such actions as the payment of taxes, to which no one *ever* has a spontaneous inclination? Both are examples of performances where the sense of duty motivates us by itself; or so it seems.

For the first question, Hume's answer, for which we have to turn to the *Treatise,* comes in two parts. The first is to be drawn from this quotation: "All morality depends upon our sentiments; and when any action, or quality of the mind, pleases us after a certain manner, we say it is virtuous; and when the neglect or non-performance of it, displeases us after a like manner, we say that we lie under an obligation to perform it."[40]

This seems to mean that saying an action is an obligation is saying that we are displeased at, or disapprove of, its *non*performance. The double negative here is something that shows Hume's insight into duty's lack of intrinsic charm. The second part of Hume's answer is to be found in a statement he makes in section 1 of part ii of book III.[41] He says that a person may perform an action without the motive that normally prompts it to avoid the displeasure that its absence causes. The point is that our approval and disapproval are here, as always, seen by Hume as directed to the character behind actions, and Hume says that someone who recognizes that he does not have the motive that would be approved of if the act were done from it might still do the action because he will otherwise "hate himself" on account of his motivational defect. He will thus do the action "from a certain sense of duty, in order to acquire, by practice, that virtuous principle, or at least to disguise to himself as much as possible his want of it." This sense of duty is, on this account, a substitute motive — almost, one supposes, a *conscious* substitute for the natural motive that would normally prompt such an action.

Briefly, then, doing something from duty is doing it from discomfort or disapproval at its neglect. This can, of course, only be the motive to action in a modest number of cases. This leads us to the very important question of how to explain that large class of actions we think of as duties for which there seems to be no natural motivation at all. For example, some people, at least, pay their taxes from a sense of duty; but this is not because they would usually expect to have a natural inclination to pay them. So the approval of paying them cannot be the consequence of discerning this inclination as their proper source. This is the problem of explaining the origin of *justice.* The practice on which our approval of just actions depends is, in Hume's view, an essentially social institution. Justice is, in the language of the *Treatise,* not a natural but an artificial virtue: that is, it is due to social artifice or convention.

Once the practice of justice is established, it is not puzzling that we approve of those who engage in it, and disapprove of those who do not. For justice has an obvious utility in promoting goods and averting evils. But this does not explain the existence of the general practice on which such approval depends. For this reason, Hume rejects the literal doctrine of social contract, according to which human beings originally met and promised one another to observe social rules for mutual benefit. Hume insists that promise keeping is itself one of the social institutions that manifest justice; so it cannot explain it. ("We are not surely bound to keep our word because we have given our word to keep it. ") The institution of promise keeping would not exist without a prior sense of obligation, and it is this sense of obligation that we have yet to account for.[42]

Hume's account is based on the value social institutions have for us and our incapacity to establish them from our natural motives. We do have some socially unifying motives in our natural benevolence and love of family. But these are restricted in scope and cannot be enough to establish a large social grouping. They also militate against the security of possessions, that is, against property. We are, however, able to see the advantages of a convention that would stabilize property rights and other social conveniences. Hume holds that the convention that establishes this practice is implicit, not explicit, and in both books he uses the analogy of oarsmen who row together without an explicit undertaking to do so because of their capacity to recognize their common interest. Social conventions, then, arise because of our self-interest and our awareness of the fact that this interest dictates conventions that habituate us to actions that confined benevolence cannot guarantee. We thus find ourselves upholding the conventions even when their applications are inconvenient for us. Impartiality comes, then, from convention or artifice. Convention depends for its existence on self-interest. This is the original motive behind justice and obligation, not in the sense that self-interest directly dictates each just act (because the very opposite may be true), but because self-interest dictates that each of us be protected by custom.

Once convention establishes just practices, sympathy (or humanity) accounts for the moral aspect the convention comes to wear. Each of us is able to be sensitive, through sympathy, to the unpleasant effects that unjust actions have on those who suffer from them. Indeed, we are sometimes ourselves the victims. It is this displeasure that we express by saying that just actions are our duty and that we avoid by doing our duty, encouraging our fellows to do theirs, and supporting the sanctions that society establishes to insure its conventions are followed.

Hume is not an egoist about human motives and fully recognizes that we act from benevolence and from duty. But he is an egoist in his account of the origin of justice and therefore about the original source of the sense of duty that attends the practice of the artificial virtues. To some extent, this is a consequence of his secularism. Butler, who believed in the natural supremacy of conscience and thought, like Hume, that we should do our duty even when it seemed contrary to benevolence to do so, thought that the correctness of this stance depended on God seeing to it that following the right was ultimately for the good of all, including oneself. Hume seeks no such providential assurance and has to explain the priority that we ascribe to the observance of the requirements of justice by our perception that the rule of law is in our interest.[43]

| *N O T E S*

1. Kant 1949.
2. *EM* I (SB 173).
3. SB 278.
4. *T* III i 1 (SB 458/EL III 167).
5. See Mackie 1980; Kemp 1964; Raphael 1947; Capaldi 1989; Hudson 1967.
6. Moore 1903.
7. Clarke 1738.
8. Mill 1897, chap. 4.
9. *T* II iii 3 (SB 416/EL II 128).
10. *T* II iii 2 (SB 415/EL II 127).
11. SB 459/EL III 168.
12. See again *T* II iii 3 and iii 4; also Árdal 1966, chap. 5.
13. Hudson 1967.
14. *T* III i 2 (SB 470/EL III 178).
15. *T* III i 2 (SB 471/EL III 179).
16. *T* III iii 5 (SB 614/EL III 307).
17. Sutherland 1977.
18. *T* II i 2 (SB 277/EL II 6–7).
19. Penelhum 1975a, 97.
20. *T* III iii 1 (SB 575/EL III 272).
21. *T* III iii 4 (SB 608 n/EL III 301 n).
22. *EM* IX (SB 272); the importance of this passage is noted by Flew 1986, 154.
23. *T* III i 2 (SB 472/EL III 180).
24. See his essay "Of the Standard of Taste," Green and Grose vol. 3, 266–84.
25. Norton 1975, 1982, and 1985.
26. *EM* V–VIII. *T* III iii 1–3.
27. Penelhum 1985b.
28. *T* III i 1 (SB 469/EL III 177).
29. Capaldi 1989, 151.
30. Capaldi 1989, 150; Mackie 1980, 71.
31. See chap. 4.
32. Stevenson 1944, esp. 273–76.
33. Mackie 1980, chap. 2; Capaldi 1989, chap. 1.
34. *T* III ii 1 (SB 481/EL 187–88).
35. *T* III ii 1 (SB 479/EL III 185). I do not think Butler would have contested this: see Penelhum 1985a, chap. 3; and 1988.
36. SB 316–24/EL II 40–46.
37. What he *does* mean is a contested question. See Mercer 1972; Penelhum 1976b; McIntyre 1979a and b; Capaldi 1989.
38. *T* II i 11 (SB 319–20/EL II 43).
39. Capaldi 1989; also J. B. Stewart 1963, 325–40; and the introduction to Selby-Bigge's edition of the *Enquiries*.
40. *T* III ii 5 (SB 517/EL III 220).
41. SB 479/EL III 185.
42. *T* III 5. See Gough 1936.
43. See Penelhum 1985a, 1988; Schneewind 1984; Gaskin 1979.

CHAPTER
S I X | **Religion**

> Text
> Enquiry Concerning
> Human Understanding
>
> Section XI
> Of a Particular Providence and
> of a Future State

I was lately engaged in conversation with a friend who loves sceptical paradoxes; where, though he advanced many principles, of which I can by no means approve, yet as they seem to be curious, and to bear some relation to the chain of reasoning carried on throughout this enquiry, I shall here copy them from my memory as accurately as I can, in order to submit them to the judgement of the reader.

Our conversation began with my admiring the singular good fortune of philosophy, which, as it requires entire liberty above all other privileges, and chiefly flourishes from the free opposition of sentiments and argumentation, received its first birth in an age and country of freedom and toleration, and was never cramped, even in its most extravagant principles, by any creeds, confessions or penal statutes. For, except the banishment of Protagoras, and the death of Socrates, which last event proceeded partly from other motives, there are scarcely any instances to be met with, in ancient history, of this bigoted jealousy, with which the present age is so much infested. Epicurus lived at Athens to an advanced age, in peace and tranquility. Epicureans[1] were even admitted to receive the sacerdotal character, and to officiate at the altar, in the most sacred rites of the established religion. And the public encouragement[2] of pensions and salaries was afforded equally, by the wisest of all the Roman emperors,[3] to the professors of every sect of philosophy. How requisite such kind of treatment was to philosophy, in her early youth, will easily be conceived, if we reflect, that, even at present, when she may be supposed more hardy and robust, she bears with much difficulty the inclemency of the seasons, and those harsh winds of calumny and persecution, which blow upon her.

You admire, says my friend, as the singular good fortune of philosophy, what seems to result from the natural course of things, and to be unavoidable in every age and nation. This pertinacious bigotry, of which you complain, as so fatal to philosophy, is really her off-spring, who, after allying with superstition, separates himself entirely from the interest of his parent, and becomes her most inveterate enemy and persecutor. Speculative dogmas of religion, the present occasions of such furious dispute, could not possibly be conceived or admitted in the early ages of the world, when mankind, being wholly illiterate, formed an idea of religion more suitable to their weak apprehension, and composed their sacred tenets of such tales chiefly as were the objects of traditional belief, more than of argument or disputation. After the first alarm, therefore, was over, which arose from the new paradoxes and principles of the philosophers, these teachers seem ever after, during the ages of antiquity, to have lived in great harmony with the established superstition, and to have made a fair partition of mankind between them; the former claiming all the learned and wise, the latter possessing all the vulgar and illiterate.

It seems then, say I, that you leave politics entirely out of the question, and never suppose, that a wise magistrate can justly be jealous of certain tenets of philosophy, such as those of Epicurus, which, denying a divine existence, and consequently a providence and a future state, seem to loosen, in a great measure, the ties of morality, and may be supposed, for that reason, pernicious to the peace of civil society.

I know, replied he, that in fact these persecutions never, in any age, proceeded from calm reason, or from experience of the pernicious consequences of philosophy, but arose entirely from passion and prejudice. But what if I should advance farther, and assert, that if Epicurus had been accused before the people, by any of the sycophants or informers of those days, he could easily have defended his cause, and proved his principles of philosophy to be as salutary as those of his adversaries, who endeavoured, with such zeal, to expose him to the public hatred and jealousy?

I wish, said I, you would try your eloquence upon so extraordinary a topic, and make a speech for Epicurus, which might satisfy, not the mob of Athens, if you will allow that ancient and polite city to have contained any mob, but the more philosophical part of his audience, such as might be supposed capable of comprehending his arguments.

The matter would not be difficult, upon such conditions, replied he, and if you please, I shall suppose myself Epicurus for a moment, and make you stand for the Athenian people, and shall deliver you such an harangue as will fill all the urn with white beans, and leave not a black one to gratify the malice of my adversaries.

Very well. Pray proceed upon these suppositions.

I come hither, O ye Athenians, to justify in your assembly what I maintained in my school, and I find myself impeached by furious antagonists, instead of reasoning with calm and dispassionate enquirers. Your deliberations, which of right should be directed to questions of public good, and the interest of the commonwealth, are diverted to the disquisitions of speculative philosophy; and these magnificent, but perhaps fruitless enquiries, take place of your more familiar but more useful occupations. But so far as in me lies, I will prevent this abuse. We shall not here dispute concerning the origin and government of worlds. We shall only enquire how far such questions concern the public interest. And if I can persuade you that they are entirely indifferent to the peace of society and security of government, I hope that you will presently send us back to our schools, there to examine, at leisure, the question the most sublime, but at the same time, the most speculative of all philosophy.

The religious philosophers, not satisfied with the tradition of your forefathers, and doctrine of your priests (in which I willingly acquiesce), indulge a rash curiosity, in trying how far they can establish religion upon the principles of reason; and they thereby excite, instead of satisfying, the doubts, which naturally arise from a diligent and scrutinous enquiry. They paint, in the most magnificent colours, the order, beauty, and wise arrangement of the universe; and then ask, if such a glorious display of intelligence could proceed from the fortuitous concourse of atoms, or if chance could produce what the greatest genius can never sufficiently admit. I shall not examine the justness of this argument. I shall allow it to be as solid as my antagonists and accusers can desire. It is sufficient, if I can prove, from this very reasoning, that the question is entirely speculative, and that, when, in my philosophical disquisitions, I deny a providence and a future state, I undermine not the foundations of society, but advance principles, which they themselves, upon their own topics, if they argue consistently, must allow to be solid and satisfactory.

You then, who are my accusers, have acknowledged, that the chief or sole argument for a divine existence (which I never questioned) is derived from the order of nature; where there appear such marks of intelligence and design, that you think it extravagant to assign for its cause either chance, or the blind and unguided force of matter. You allow that this is an argument drawn from effects to causes. From the order of the work, you infer that there must have been project and forethought in the workman. If you cannot make out this point, you allow that your conclusion fails; and you pretend not to establish the conclusion in a greater latitude than the phenomena of nature will justify. These are your concessions. I desire you to mark the consequences.

When we infer any particular cause from an effect, we must proportion the one to the other, and can never be allowed to ascribe to the cause any qualities, but what are exactly sufficient to produce the effect. A body of ten ounces raised in any scale may serve as a proof, that the counterbalancing weight exceeds ten ounces; but can never afford a reason that it exceeds a hundred. If the cause, assigned for any effect, be not sufficient to produce it, we must either reject that cause, or add to it such qualities as will give it a just proportion to the effect. But if we ascribe to it farther qualities, or affirm it capable of producing other effects, we can only indulge the licence of conjecture, and arbitrarily suppose the existence of qualities and energies, without reason or authority.

The same rule holds, whether the cause assigned be brute unconscious matter, or a rational intelligent being. If the cause be known only by the effect, we never ought to ascribe to it any qualities, beyond what are precisely requisite to produce the effect. Nor can we, by any rules of just reasoning, return back from the cause, and infer other effects from it, beyond those by which alone it is known to us. No one, merely from the sight of one of Zeuxis's pictures, could know that he was also a statuary or architect, and was an artist no less skillful in stone and marble than in colours. The talents and taste, displayed in the particular work before us: these we may safely conclude the workman to be possessed of. The cause must be proportioned to the effect, and if we exactly and precisely proportion it, we shall never find in it any qualities that point farther, or afford an inference concerning any other design or performance. Such qualities must be somewhat beyond what is merely requisite for producing the effect which we examine.

Allowing, therefore, the gods to be the authors of the existence or order of the universe; it follows, that they possess that precise degree of power, intelligence, and benevolence, which appears in their workmanship. But nothing farther can ever be proved, except we call in the assistance of exaggeration and flattery to supply the defects of argument and reasoning. So far as the traces of any attributes at present appear, so far we may conclude these attributes to exist. The supposition of farther attributes is mere hypothesis; much more the supposition that in distant regions of space or periods of time, there has been, or will be, a more magnificent display of these attributes, and a scheme of administration more suitable to such imaginary virtues. We can never be allowed to mount up from the universe, the effect, to Jupiter, the cause, and then descend downwards, to infer any new effect from that cause; as if the present effects alone were not entirely worthy of the glorious attributes which we ascribe to that deity. The knowledge of the cause being derived solely from the effect, they must be exactly adjusted to each other, and the one can never refer to anything farther, or be the foundation of any new inference and conclusion.

You find certain phenomena in nature. You seek a cause or author. You imagine that you have found him. You afterwards become so enamoured of this offspring of your brain, that you imagine it impossible, but he must produce something greater and the more perfect than the present scene of things, which is so full of ill and disorder. You forget, that this superlative intelligence and benevolence are entirely imaginary, or, at least, without any foundation in reason, and that you have no ground to ascribe to him any qualities, but what you see he has actually exerted and displayed in his productions. Let your gods, therefore, O philosophers, be suited to the present appearances of nature, and presume not to alter these appearances by arbitrary suppositions, in order to suit them to the attributes, which you so fondly ascribe to your deities.

When priests and poets, supported by your authority, O Athenians, talk of a golden or silver age, which preceded the present state of vice and misery, I hear them with attention and with reverence. But when philosophers, who pretend to neglect authority, and to cultivate reason, hold the same discourse, I pay them not, I own, the same obsequious submission and pious deference. I ask who carried them into the celestial regions, who admitted them into the councils of the gods, who opened to them the book of fate, that they thus rashly affirm that their deities have executed, or will execute, any purpose beyond what has actually appeared? If they tell me, that they have mounted on the steps or by the gradual ascent of reason, and by drawing inferences from effects to causes, I still insist, that they have aided the ascent of reason by the wings of imagination. Otherwise, they could not thus change their manner of inference, and argue from causes to effects, presuming that a more perfect production than the present world would be more suitable to such perfect beings as the gods, and forgetting that they have no reason to ascribe to these celestial beings any perfection of any attribute, but what can be found in the present world.

Hence all the fruitless industry to account for the ill appearances of nature, and save the honour of the gods, while we must acknowledge the reality of that evil and disorder, with which the world so much abounds. The obstinate and intractable qualities of matter, we are told, or the observance of general laws, or some such reason, is the sole cause, which controlled the power and benevolence of Jupiter, and obliged him to create mankind and every sensible creature so imperfect and so unhappy. These attributes then, are, it seems, beforehand, taken for granted, in their greatest latitude. And upon that supposition, I own that such conjectures may, perhaps, be admitted as plausible solutions of the ill phenomena. But still I ask, Why take these attributes for granted, or why ascribe to the cause any qualities but what actually appear in the effect? Why torture your brain to justify the course of nature upon suppositions, which, for aught you know, may be entirely imaginary, and of which there are to be found no traces in the course of nature?

The religious hypothesis, therefore, must be considered only as a particular method of accounting for the visible phenomena of the universe. But no just reasoner will ever presume to infer from it any single fact, and alter or add to the phenomena, in any single particular. If you think, that the appearances of things prove such causes, it is allowable for you to draw an inference concerning the existence of these causes. In such complicated and sublime subjects, every one should be indulged in the liberty of conjecture and argument. But here you ought to rest. If you come backward, and arguing from your inferred causes, conclude that any other fact has existed, or will exist, in the course of nature, which may serve as a fuller display of particular attributes, I must admonish you that you have departed from the method of reasoning attached to the present subject, and have certainly added something to the attributes of the cause, beyond what appears in the effect. Otherwise you could never, with tolerable sense or propriety, add anything to the effect, in order to render it more worthy of the cause.

Where, then, is the odiousness of that doctrine, which I teach in my school, or rather, which I examine in my gardens? Or what do you find in this whole question, wherein the security of good morals, or the peace and order of society, is in the least concerned?

I deny a providence, you say, and supreme governor of the world, who guides the course of events, and punishes the vicious with infamy and disappointment, and rewards the virtuous with honour and success, in all their undertakings. But surely, I deny not the course itself of events, which lies open to every one's inquiry and examination. I acknowledge that in the present order of things, virtue is attended with more peace of mind than vice, and meets with a more favourable reception from the world. I am sensible that according to the past experience of mankind, friendship is the chief joy of human life, and moderation the only source of tranquillity and happiness. I never balance between the virtuous and the vicious course of life; but am sensible that, to a well-disposed mind, every advantage is on the side of the former. And what can you say more, allowing all your suppositions and reasonings? You tell me, indeed, that this disposition of things proceeds from intelligence and design. But whatever it proceeds from, the disposition itself, on which depends our happiness or misery, and consequently our conduct and deportment in life is still the same. It is still open for me, as well as you, to regulate my behaviour by my experience of past events. And if you affirm, that, while a divine providence is allowed, and a supreme distributive justice in the universe, I ought to expect some more particular reward of the good, and punishment of the bad, beyond the ordinary course of events; I here find the same fallacy, which I have before endeavoured to detect. You persist in imagining that, if we grant that divine existence, for which you so earnestly contend, you may safely infer consequences from it, and add something to the experienced order of nature, by arguing from the attributes which you ascribe to your gods. You seem not to remember that all your reasonings on this subject can only be drawn from effects to causes, and that every argument, deduced from causes to effects, must of necessity be a gross sophism, since it is impossible for you to know anything of the cause, but what you have antecedently, not inferred, but discovered to the full, in the effect.

But what must a philosopher think of those vain reasoners, who, instead of regarding the present scene of things as the sole object of their contemplation, so far reverse the whole course of nature, as to render this life merely a passage to something farther — a porch, which leads to a greater, and vastly different building, a prologue, which serves only to introduce the piece, and give it more grace and propriety? Whence, do you think, can such philosophers derive their idea of the gods? From their own conceit and imagination surely. For if they derived it from the present phenomena, it would never point to anything farther, but must be exactly adjusted to them. That the divinity may possibly be endowed with attributes, which we have never seen exerted; may be governed by principles of action, which we cannot discover to be satisfied — all this will freely be allowed. But still this is mere possibility and hypothesis. We never can have reason to infer any attributes, or any principles of action in him, but so far as we know them to have been exerted and satisfied.

Are there any marks of a distributive justice in this world? If you answer in the affirmative, I conclude, that, since justice here exerts itself, it is satisfied. If you reply in the negative, I conclude that you have then no reason to ascribe justice, in our sense of it, to the gods. If you hold a medium between affirmation and negation, by saying that the justice of the gods, at present, exerts itself in part, but not in its full extent, I answer that you have no reason to give it any particular extent, but only so far as you see it, at present, exert itself.

Thus I bring the dispute, O Athenians, to a short issue with my antagonists. The course of nature lies open to my contemplation as well as to theirs. The experienced train of events is the great standard, by which we all regulate our conduct. Nothing else can be appealed to in the field, or in the senate. Nothing else ought ever to be heard of in the school, or in the closet. In vain would our limited understanding break through those boundaries, which are too narrow for our fond imagination. While we argue from the course of nature, and infer a particular intelligent cause, which first bestowed, and still preserves order in the universe, we embrace a principle, which is both uncertain and useless. It is uncertain, because the subject lies entirely beyond the reach of human experience. It is useless, because our knowledge of this cause being derived entirely from the course of nature, we can never, according to the rules of just reasoning, return back from the cause with any new inference, or making additions to the common and experienced course of nature, establish any new principles of conduct and behavior.

I observe (said I, finding he had finished his harangue) that you neglect not the artifice of the demagogues of old, and as you were pleased to make me stand for the people, you insinuate yourself into my favour by embracing those principles, to which, you know, I have always expressed a particular attachment. But allowing you to make experience (as indeed I think you ought) the only standard of our judgement concerning this and all other questions of fact, I doubt not but, from the very same experience to which you appeal, it may be possible to refute this reasoning which you have put into the mouth of Epicurus. If you saw, for instance, a half-finished building, surrounded with heaps of brick and stone and mortar, and all the instruments of masonry, could you not infer from the effect, that it was a work of design and contrivance? And could you not return again, from this inferred cause, to infer new additions to the effect, and conclude, that the building would soon be finished, and receive all the further improvements, which art could bestow upon it? If you saw upon the sea-shore the print of one human foot, you would conclude, that a man had passed that way, and that he had also left the traces of the other foot, though effaced by the rolling of the sands or inundation of the waters. Why then do you refuse to admit the same method of reasoning with regard to the order of nature? Consider the world and the present life only as an imperfect building, from which you can infer a superior intelligence, and arguing from that superior intelligence, which can leave nothing imperfect; why may you not infer a more finished scheme or plan, which will receive its completion in some distant point of space or time? Are not these methods of reasoning exactly similar? And under what pretence can you embrace the one, while you reject the other?

The infinite difference of the subjects, replied he, is a sufficient foundation for this difference in my conclusions. In works of *human* art and contrivance, it is allowable to advance from the effect to the cause, and returning back from the cause, to form new inferences concerning the effect, and examine the alterations, which it has probably undergone, or may still undergo. But what is the foundation of this method of reasoning? Plainly this — that man is a being whom we know by experience, whose motives and designs we are acquainted with, and whose projects and inclinations have a certain connection and coherence, according to the laws which nature has established for the government of such a creature. When, therefore, we find that any work has proceeded from the skill and industry of man; as we are otherwise acquainted with the nature of the animal, we can draw a hundred inferences concerning what may be expected from him, and these inferences will all be founded in experience and observation. But did we know man only from the single work or production which we examine, it were impossible for us to argue in this manner; because our knowledge of all the qualities, which we ascribe to him, being in that case derived from the production, it is impossible they could point to anything farther, or be the foundation of any new inference. The print of a foot in the sand can only prove, when considered alone, that there was some figure adapted to it, by which it was produced, but the print of a human foot proves likewise, from our other experience, that there was probably another foot, which also left its impression, though effaced by time or other accidents. Here we mount from the effect to the cause, and descending again from the cause, infer alterations in the effect; but this is not a continuation of the same simple chain of reasoning. We comprehend in this case a hundred other experiences and observations, concerning the usual figure and members of that species of animal, without which this method of argument must be considered as fallacious and sophistical.

The case is not the same with our reasonings from the works of nature. The Deity is known to us only by his productions, and is a single being in the universe, not comprehended under any species or genus, from whose experienced attributes or qualities, we can, by analogy, infer any attribute or quality in him. As the universe shows wisdom and goodness, we infer wisdom and goodness. As it shows a particular degree of these perfections, we infer a particular degree of them, precisely adapted to the effect which we examine. But farther attributes or farther degrees of the same attributes, we can never be authorised to infer or suppose, by any rules of just reasoning. Now, without some such licence of supposition, it is impossible for us to argue from the cause, or infer any alteration in the effect, beyond what has immediately fallen under our observation. Greater good produced by this Being must still prove a greater degree of goodness; a more impartial distribution of rewards and punishments must proceed from a greater regard to justice and equity. Every supposed addition to the works of nature makes an addition to the attributes of the Author of nature; and consequently, being entirely unsupported by any reason or argument, can never be admitted but as mere conjecture and hypothesis.[4]

The great source of our mistake in this subject, and of the unbounded licence of conjecture, which we indulge, is that we tacitly consider ourselves as in the place of the Supreme Being, and conclude that he will, on every occasion, observe the same conduct which we ourselves, in his situation, would have embraced as reasonable and eligible. But, besides that the ordinary course of nature may convince us, that almost everything is regulated by principles and maxims very different from ours — besides this, I say, it must evidently appear contrary to all rules of analogy to reason, from the intentions and projects of men, to those of a Being so different, and so much superior. In human nature, there is a certain experienced coherence of designs and inclinations; so that when, from any fact, we have discovered one intention of any man, it may often be reasonable, from experience, to infer another, and draw a long chain of conclusions concerning his past or future conduct. But this method of reasoning can never have place with regard to a Being so remote and incomprehensible, who bears much less analogy to any other being in the universe than the sun to a waxen taper, and who discovers himself only by some faint traces or outlines, beyond which we have no authority to ascribe to him any attribute or perfection. What we imagine to be a superior perfection, may really be a defect. Or were it ever so much a perfection, the ascribing of it to the Supreme Being, where it appears not to have been really exerted to the full in his works, savours more of flattery and panegyric, than of just reasoning and sound philosophy. All the philosophy, therefore, in the world, and all the religion, which is nothing but a species of philosophy, will never be able to carry us beyond the usual course of experience, or give us measures of conduct and behaviour different from those which are furnished by reflections on common life. No new fact can ever be inferred from the religious hypothesis; no event foreseen or foretold; no reward or punishment expected or dreaded, beyond what is already known by practice and observation. So that my apology for Epicurus will still appear solid and satisfactory; nor have the political interests of society any connection with the philosophical disputes concerning metaphysics and religion.

There is still one circumstance, replied I, which you seem to have overlooked. Though I should allow your premises, I must deny your conclusion. You conclude that religious doctrines and reasonings can have no influence on life, because they ought to have no influence; never considering, that men reason not in the same manner you do, but draw many consequences from the belief of a divine

Existence, and suppose that the Deity will inflict punishments on vice, and bestow rewards on virtue, beyond what appear in the ordinary course of nature. Whether this reasoning of theirs be just or not, is no matter. Its influence on their life and conduct must still be the same. And those who attempt to disabuse them of such prejudices, may, for aught I know, be good reasoners, but I cannot allow them to be good citizens and politicians; since they free men from one restraint upon their passions, and make the infringement of the laws of society, in one respect, more easy and secure.

After all, I may, perhaps, agree to your general conclusion in favour of liberty, though upon different premises from those on which you endeavour to found it. I think, that the state ought to tolerate every principle of philosophy; nor is there an instance that any government has suffered in its political interests by such indulgence. There is no enthusiasm among philosophers; their doctrines are not very alluring to the people; and no restraint can be put upon their reasonings, but what must be of dangerous consequence to the sciences, and even to the state, by paving the way for persecution and oppression in points where the generality of mankind are more deeply interested and concerned.

But there occurs to me (continued I) with regard to your main topic, a difficulty, which I shall just propose to you without insisting on it, lest it lead into reasonings of too nice and delicate a nature. In a word, I much doubt whether it be possible for a cause to be known only by its effect (as you have all along supposed) or to be of so singular and particular a nature as to have no parallel and no similarity with any other cause or object, that has ever fallen under our observation. It is only when two *species* of objects are found to be constantly conjoined, that we can infer the one from the other; and were an effect presented, which was entirely singular and could not be comprehended under any known *species,* I do not see that we could form any conjecture or inference at all concerning its cause. If experience and observation and analogy be, indeed, the only guides which we can reasonably follow in inferences of this nature, both the effect and cause must bear a similarity and resemblance to other effects and causes which we know, and which we have found, in many instances, to be conjoined with each other. I leave it to your own reflection to pursue the consequences of this principle. I shall just observe that, as the antagonists of Epicurus always suppose the universe, an effect quite singular and unparalleled, to be the proof of a Deity, a cause no less singular and unparalleled; your reasonings upon that supposition, seem, at least, to merit our attention. There is, I own, some difficulty how we can ever return from the cause to the effect, and, reasoning from our ideas of the former, infer any alteration on the latter, or any addition to it.

| NOTES

1. Lucian: The Carousal or the Lapiths.

2. Lucian: The Eunuch.

3. Lucian and Dio.

4. In general, it may, I think, be established as a maxim, that where any cause is known only by its particular effects, it must be impossible to infer any new effects from that cause; since the qualities which are requisite to produce these new effects along with the former, must either be different, or superior, or of more extensive operation, than those which simply produced the effect, whence alone the cause is supposed to be known to us. We can never, therefore, have any reason to suppose the existence of these qualities. To say, that the new effects proceed only from a continuation of the same energy which is already known from the first effects, will not remove the difficulty. For even granting this to be the case (which can seldom be supposed), the very continuation and exertion of a like energy (for it is impossible it can be absolutely the same), I say, this exertion of a like energy, in a different period of space and time, is a very arbitrary supposition, and what there cannot possibly be any traces of in the effects, from which all our knowledge of the cause is originally derived. Let the inferred cause be exactly proportioned (as it should be) to the known effect; and it is impossible that it can possess any qualities, from which new or different effects can be inferred.

| *Commentary*

Section XI of the first Enquiry is a relatively neglected text, especially if we compare it with the section "Of Miracles" that precedes it. But it contains many of the arguments that Hume later developed more fully in the *Dialogues Concerning Natural Religion,* and it is therefore a more informative introduction to his philosophy of religion than any other of his shorter writings. Since Hume excised from the *Treatise* the material on this subject he had originally intended to include, the references to other works that we shall require here will be to the *Dialogues* and the *Natural History of Religion.*

| *Revelation, Reason, and the Design Argument*

I shall first attempt to set this gently worded but intensely destructive essay in the setting of the *Enquiry* where it appears. Hume has completed the exposition of his revolutionary theories of causation and induction and has tried to show (in section VIII) that our everyday assumption of freedom is not under threat in the law-governed world in which we all believe. After a short discourse on the reason of animals, he turns in section X to the idea of the miraculous. His argument in this section is his most famous, though by general consent it is certainly not his best. The belief in miracles, especially those of the New Testament, was taken by most of Hume's contemporaries to be essential to Christian faith. Not only were the miracle stories of the Bible considered to be at the core of the content of Christian teaching; the historicity of the miracles was also considered to be a key reason for accepting the doctrinal authority of the New Testament itself. Revelation and miracle attested to each other. The Deists had indeed begun to question the authenticity of the biblical miracle stories, beginning from the premise that God was too rational and efficient a planner to have need of miraculous intervention. By 1736 they had an ingenious answer from Joseph Butler, who argued in his *Analogy of Religion* that anyone willing to concede that our world is governed by a divine intelligence should also concede that our knowledge of God's plans and purposes is too limited for us to be as sure as the Deists that miracles could have no rational place in those plans.[1] It was left to Hume to offer stronger arguments against the miraculous and to undermine the assumption of divine governance that Butler and the Deists shared. Hume addresses the first issue in section X, the second in section XI.

A brief summary, first, of the argument of section X. It is devoted to the question of how one ought to respond to testimony to miracles, not the question of what to think if one is a witness oneself to some event that seems miraculous. A wise man, says Hume, will proportion his belief to the evidence he has. When someone tells him a story of some alleged event, he must judge the evidence in two ways, both of which require him to depend on his experience. He must first of all consider whether the event reported is itself likely or unlikely. If it is the sort of event that happens frequently, according to his experience, then that is in the story's favor, especially if events of an opposite sort are rare. If it is a rare sort of event, this counts against it, though not, of course, conclusively. Experience alone can guide us. The same is true for the estimate we must make of the quality of the testimony available to us. Only experience can tell us how far the event reported is of a sort that only an educated or expert witness could recognize; only experience can tell us how often witnesses have been confused or deceived about events of this type in the past; and only experience can tell us how expert, or intelligent, or honest, the particular witness who is testifying is.

All this seems clear enough; but it can lead to conflicts. For we might find ourselves confronted with testimony to a likely enough event, given by a foolish or dishonest witness. Or, more to the present purpose, we might find ourselves confronted with testimony from an intelligent and honest witness who tells us of a very unlikely event. Then we have to weigh opposing considerations and make a judgment.

The case of miracles is an extreme example of the latter conflict. But it does not, in Hume's opinion, justify any prolonged hesitation, for a miracle is a violation of a law of nature. That entails, Hume thinks, that the event reported is not merely one that has only happened rarely in the past. Given that laws of nature are recognized only when we have *uniform* past experience, a miracle would have to be something that has *never* happened before. In such circumstances, it can never be wise to accept the miracle story; although if the quality of the testimony is impeccable, the wise man ought to suspend judgment. Even impeccable testimony can do no more than lead to such suspension. It can never justify acceptance. If we look at the testimony we actually have, says Hume, it is far from impeccable. The quality of the witnesses has always been low, and the reports always come from "ignorant and barbarous nations." The very wondrousness of the miracle stories makes many people more inclined to believe them, not less. (People are not wise as often as they should be.) And the miracle stories of one religious tradition have the effect of undermining those of opposed religious traditions. Hume's conclusion is "that no human testimony can have such force as to prove a miracle, and make it a just foundation for any such system of religion."[2]

Hume is here presenting the standards he thinks necessary for assessing the evidence of all historical claims, and in doing this he is consciously secularizing history. For secular history, the reliability of the testimony or documents is directly related to the likelihood of the events reported; and that is a matter on which experience has to be the only standard.

Needless to say, Hume's arguments have drawn repeated criticism, and the relevant literature is very extensive and grows continually.[3] For our present purpose, we must consider one particular response from the Christian side that leads us into the substance of the section now before us. William Paley made this response most clearly, in his *Evidences of Christianity,* in 1794. In the "Preparatory Considerations" with which this work begins, Paley says that Hume has no right to dismiss the evidences of miracles a priori. Hume can only do this because he confines his consideration to previous experience of events of the kind reported by the witnesses. But the whole case changes if one recognizes that miracles serve the theological purpose of attesting revelation. Revelation is claimed to be a source of knowledge specially vouchsafed by God to tell his creatures about his care for them, the future existence he has planned for them, and what they must do to inherit it. If one already has reason to suppose that the world is the creation of a God whose nature is such that he would care for his creatures, it becomes far less unlikely that he would make such revelatory knowledge available, and therefore far less unlikely that he would perform miracles to draw our attention to it and reinforce the authority of those who proclaim it. It is not, says Paley, that we can ever rationally dispense with the need for the best possible evidence that a miracle has occurred; but if we have reason to suppose that miracles *might* occur, we have reason to consider that evidence on its merits and not accept Hume's claim that even the best evidence must fail to convince the wise man. "In a word, once believe that there is a God, and miracles are not incredible."[4]

Paley himself attempted to provide detailed reasons for the independent belief in God that this argument demands. His arguments for God's existence, in his *Natural Theology,* and the detailed defenses of miracle and revelation that he offers in the *Evidences* still repay study and were very influential for generations after he wrote them. In responding to Hume in this way, he was trying to reinstate a long-standing tradition of apologetic argument that dates back at least to Thomas Aquinas in the thirteenth century.[5]

Aquinas held that although many believers adhere to the Christian faith solely because they have accepted the proclamations of the Church and the Scriptures, their doing so can be given rational support using the arguments of philosophers and the evidences of history. The philosopher can in fact demonstrate by reason some of the fundamental truths of the faith, in particular that God exists, that he is one, that he is perfect, that he governs the world providentially, and so on. The proofs of these truths constitute a body of philosophical knowledge known traditionally as natural theology. Once these things are accepted, which can be on philosophical grounds alone, it then becomes reasonable to inquire whether the God whose being and goodness are proved in this way has made any special revelation available to us, as he well might have done in view of our intellectual limitations and the natural preoccupation with other matters in the lives of most people. Once this inquiry is made, we find that there are many evidences that God has done so. These include the historical events recorded in the Scriptures, the remarkable fulfillments of prophecy that are found there, and the many miraculous events that have reinforced the claims his Church has made on his behalf down the centuries. In other words, the Church has historical credentials which, added to the proofs of God's reality that philosophy can provide, make a strong rational case for accepting the demands of faith. Faith and reason are distinct, and some of the claims of faith, such as the key claim that Christ was the son of God, cannot be proved by reason alone; but it is still more rational to accept these claims than not. In responding to Hume as he does, Paley is reasserting this apologetic tradition.

The irony of Paley's argument, however, is that by the time he wrote, Hume had not only attacked the historical credentials of Christian miracles but had also attacked the credentials of natural theology, on which the whole of Paley's argument depends. Paley's own work in natural theology, found in his book of that title, proceeds in total disregard of Hume's arguments against it, even though he chooses to respond to Hume's attack on miracles at some length. This is particularly striking in view of the fact that the mode of argument Paley practices is the very one that Hume attacks. Paley produces what became the best-known version of the argument from design, which was the target of Hume's *Dialogues Concerning Natural Religion.* The key arguments Hume marshals against it appear first in section XI of the first *Enquiry.*

Before we attend to the details of the section, some comments on the design argument itself are necessary. While there are many possible forms of attempted proof of the existence of God in natural theology, most philosophical texts concentrate attention on three: the ontological proof, the cosmological proof, and the teleological proof or design argument. The ontological proof, originated by Anselm and revived by Descartes in his fifth Meditation, attempts to prove that God must exist by consideration of the concept of God itself.[6] The cosmological proof, associated primarily with the first three of the Five Ways of Thomas Aquinas, attempts to show that God must exist to account for the fact that the world does. It was revived most particularly in Hume's day by Samuel Clarke.[7] The argument from design is found in the fifth of Aquinas' Five Ways and was used in Hume's time repeatedly by philosophers and theologians, but in a form importantly different from the one that Aquinas presented. Aquinas argued that there must be a divine creative mind to explain the fact that natural bodies, especially organic bodies, act for an end or purpose even though they are themselves unconscious of it; the phenomena of biological adaptation are the most natural examples that come to mind, but Aquinas is clearly assuming an Aristotelian natural philosophy in which all phenomena, including nonbiological ones, are teleological or purposive in character. By Hume's day, the influence of Descartes and Newton had changed the way the phenomena of the physical world were viewed. They were seen, physically speaking, as mechanical in operation. But the fact that their mechanics were so complex and the fact that (or so it was claimed) they are nevertheless biologically adaptive and suited in so many cases to human needs showed that their operation must have been planned by a divine intelligence for good purposes.

The most famous illustration of this, which Hume would have been happy to comment on directly if he had been able to read of it, is Paley's watch. If I find a watch on the ground, says Paley at the outset of his *Natural Theology*,[8] I do not suppose, as I would in the case of a stone, that it might have been there forever, but judge that someone must have dropped it there because an examination of it shows its inner workings to be something designed by a human mind. Similarly, the vast range of complex adaptive phenomena in the world of nature could not have arisen by accident but demand explanation by reference to a benign intelligence. Most of Paley's book consists of a detailed series of examples of such supposed design. (Darwin's key purpose was to offer an alternative, naturalistic account of how adaptive phenomena can be understood.)

Hume, of course, denies that any matter of fact can be proved a priori. He accordingly has no serious interest in the ontological and cosmological arguments, although he devotes one famous paragraph to Clarke's version of the latter in the *Dialogues*.[9] The argument from design, however, wears the guise of an argument from observation and makes use, as such arguments do, of an analogy taken from experience, in this case an analogy with the known signs of the work of human craftsmen. Hume's own presentation of it, as he gives it to Cleanthes in the *Dialogues,* is this:

> Look round the world. Contemplate the whole and every part of it. You will find it to be nothing but one great machine, subdivided into an infinite number of lesser machines, which again admit of subdivisions, to a degree beyond what human senses and faculties can trace and explain. All these various machines, and even their most minute parts, are adjusted to each other with an accuracy which ravishes into admiration all men who have ever contemplated them. The curious adapting

of means to ends, throughout all nature, resembles exactly, though it much exceeds, the productions of human contrivance: of human design, thought, wisdom, and intelligence. Since therefore the effects resemble each other, we are led to infer, by all the rules of analogy, that the causes also resemble, and that the Author of nature is somewhat similar to the mind of man, though possessed of much larger faculties, proportioned to the grandeur of the work, which he has executed. By this argument *a posteriori,* and by this argument alone, we do prove at once the existence of a Deity, and his similarity to human mind and intelligence.[10]

Hume, assuming for reasons we have already discussed in Chapter Four that we can tell the difference between good and bad inductive arguments, sets out to show in section XI and later in the *Dialogues* that even though it is an argument from experience and deserves careful consideration on that count alone, it has fatal defects. It is in his view bad science.

Bad science it might be, but its cogency was part of the received wisdom of Hume's day. The deists who were Butler's target had attacked the credentials of revelation by maintaining that a rational God would have no occasion to resort to it. In attacking the belief in the miraculous, which was connected so closely in the mind of theologians in that era with the reality of revelation, Hume was following their lead in a more radical way. But the deists had not questioned the design argument. Indeed they relied on it; for it was because they thought it proved that the world was governed by a rational divine mind that they held such a mind to have no need of violating the very laws he had built into his creation. To most of us, Paley seems right in saying that if one accepts the existence of God, one should be open to evidence of the miraculous; but the deists had argued in the opposite way, and even the orthodox theologians of the time, most notably Joseph Butler, tried to refute them by showing that miracles were fully consistent with a *rational* providence. The fact that Paley responded to Hume's critique of revelation, but not to his critique of the design argument, is a reflection of the fact that in British culture, atheism, as distinct from irreligious forms of deism, was not regarded as a real option, even to most freethinkers.

For this reason, among others, Hume proceeds by indirection in section XI, as indeed he also does in the *Dialogues.* Perhaps the indirection gives Paley an excuse for not responding. In the *Dialogues,* indirection is achieved by the use of the dialogue form itself. Hume does not appear in person in that work, and although most scholars (at least since Kemp Smith)[11] consider it obvious that Hume's position is represented for the most part by the arguments of the skeptic Philo, this judgment is an interpretation. It is also an interpretation that requires us (in my view correctly) to dismiss as deliberately misleading the final remark of Pamphilus, the observer who is nominally reporting the conversations of which the work consists and who says that the one who approaches nearest to the truth is Cleanthes, the protagonist for the design argument. Hume, it must be noted, does not identify himself with Pamphilus any more than with anyone else, but his (unsupported) evaluation is the last sentence in the book.

In section XI, indirection is achieved by two devices. Neither is really misleading to the attentive reader, though both give the essay a bland and scholarly tone for readers willing to be led astray. One device is that of making the nominal subject matter something distinct from the design argument itself — namely, the question of whether someone who rejects it is committed to morally dangerous opinions. The other device is to set the whole discussion in classical times, so that the deity nominally being considered is Jupiter, not the Christian God, and the philosopher whose heresies are being defended against moral criticism is Epicurus.

The *Dialogues Concerning Natural Religion* is the greatest single work in philosophy of religion and is Hume's most carefully crafted and revised book. Section XI is earlier and briefer, but it is an exquisite piece of argument in its own right. I turn now to its contents.

❙ *The Argument of Section XI*

The essay was originally called "Of the Practical Consequences of Natural Religion," which was a better title, since Hume is arguing that there are none. That is to say, the sort of belief in God that the argument from design could establish, on the most positive reading Hume thinks is open to us, provides us with no guidance to choices in life that could not be obtained equally well without it. Epicurus can therefore say, in the face of those critics who fear his atheism as morally subversive (a charge Hume himself had had to face in Edinburgh not long before the *Enquiry* was published), that he has as much reason to uphold the moral traditions of his community as those who attack him.

We have seen that Hume's ethical theories are wholly secularized. It is vitally important to note here that Hume is arguing that those who base their theism on a posteriori arguments cannot derive from their theism any more basis for moral choice than those who do not share it. But that emphatically does not mean that Hume feels moral equality to exist between those who are as secularized as himself and those who derive their moral guidance from *revealed* religion. He makes it abundantly clear throughout his works, most obviously perhaps in his outburst against the "monkish virtues" in the second *Enquiry,*[12] that he considers the specific moral consequences of revealed Christianity to be seriously negative. This means that the design argument fails to establish the sort of Deity needed to justify the transition from natural theology to the acceptance of revelation. If it establishes a Deity at all (and we must remember that it is Epicurus speaking when this is denied here, not self-evidently Hume himself), it establishes at best a god who is far too limited for this.

There is another detail of interest here. Hume is negative about the moral consequences of revealed religion as known in his own time, that is, Calvinist Christianity most particularly. But the section does not suggest any such negativity about the popular religion of classical times. While Hume denies that the popular religion of his own day is socially beneficial in the way his critics believed, he does not seem to take the same view of the popular polytheism of the ancient world, which he seems to view as a relatively harmless form of social cement in the communities where it was practiced. His attitude here is a reflection of the view he develops at length in the *Natural History of Religion* that polytheism is morally preferable to atheism because it is localized and uncompetitive, accepting that each community has its own deities who do not claim dominance over others. Polytheism is therefore free of the tendency to foster intolerance and fanaticism, which Hume saw as endemic in the Christian tradition.

In light of this, it is intelligible that the text should tell us that Epicurus denies divine existence (and therefore providence and a future life), and yet also that Epicureans were allowed to officiate at the altar. The historical Epicurus[13] believed not that there were no gods, but that those that there were, were merely other inhabitants of the world, not creators of it; and they had no concern for, or influence on, human life. This view was compatible with conventional participation in cultic routines, which was also acceptable to the classical Skeptics. What Hume's Epicurus rejects is the single creator Deity of monotheism, supposedly established by argument.

The case given to Epicurus is this. His opponents are thinkers who have departed from the religious traditions of their forefathers, with which Epicurus does not disagree, and have tried to establish religion by rational argument. The argument they have used is based upon the order and beauty of the world, which, they say, contrary to Epicurus, could not have evolved by sheer accident but must be due to the working of intelligence. Let this be admitted.

The argument is from effect to cause. Such an argument may certainly establish that the order and beauty of the world are caused by a power (or powers) sufficient to produce it. But it cannot establish that the cause that produces it has *greater* powers than are needed to yield the results we can observe. So even if we concede that the gods are the authors of the being or order of the world, this allows us to infer only that they have the degree of power, intelligence, and goodness needed to make a world like the one we see around us. To suppose more than this is unfounded speculation, and we are never entitled to "mount up" from the world to "Jupiter" and "then descend downwards" and infer some effect of Jupiter's activity that we did not observe before; for this would involve ascribing some power to him that cannot be inferred from those effects on which we based our belief in his existence. So although priests and poets can discourse of mythical beginnings in which divine perfection was manifested in the created order, no one who claims to base his beliefs on the evidence is entitled to do this. Two things follow.

The first is that if we engage in what is called theodicy and attempt to explain the evils in the world not by reference to limitations in the power of the gods but by reference to other, special explanations such as a divine wish to create a world governed by laws, such arguments assume gratuitously that the creator has powers greater than those needed to produce the mixed world we live in. The second is that if we say there is a divine providence that orders the world so that virtue will finally triumph over vice to a degree greater than it is seen to do now, we are again ascribing to the creator powers greater than those needed to produce those effects from which we have inferred his reality. It *may* be that these special explanations of evil are true, and it *may* be that there is a special providence that guides the world toward final perfection; but if either of these things are true, they are not established by any argument that starts from the degree of order and beauty and goodness that there is.

If this is sound, then the moral consequences of natural theology are exactly the same as the moral consequences of a worldview like that of Epicurus. Epicurus believes that in this world we can see virtue to be the most prudent and satisfying form of life, and the thinker who ascribes this fact to the design of God is not able to maintain, on the basis of the evidence, that God arranges that virtue will win out to any degree greater than one can find it doing *without* ascribing its superiority to God. The case is even more clearly fallacious if someone maintains that this life is merely a prelude to another in which the problems of this world will give way to a perfect order: again, this assumes the Deity has powers far greater than those that he can be shown to have from observing the less perfect world we now inhabit.

The moral importance of a sound natural theology, then, would be zero. Having thus concluded the imaginary defense of Epicurus, Hume now considers an important counterargument. Surely we do sometimes infer causes that can produce results greater than those from which we infer them? When we find a half-finished building, we might well infer it to have been produced by a builder who is capable of completing it. If we find the imprint of a human foot in the sand, we are reasoning quite soundly if we decide that the owner of it had two feet, and the imprint of the second foot has been washed away. Is it not reasonable, therefore, to think the order and design we can see in the world is the work of a being who could do even better? The answer is that the undoubted strengths of the two imagined inferences that are compared with this one depend on the fact that we have independent knowledge that we can bring to bear on the case before us. We know from previous experience that buildings are made by builders who do not usually stop halfway. We know from previous experience that the owner of one foot usually has a second. If we had not had experience of these things, we would *not* be justified in drawing the conclusions we do. In the case of the creation of the world, we are supposed to be arguing from the evidence, and this confines us to the observed effects of the creator. We do not have the independent knowledge we would need to go beyond these effects.

This counterargument is supposedly offered by Hume in his own person and answered by his friend on behalf of Epicurus. The section concludes with another argument, more fundamental in its implications than any of the preceding, in which Hume once more speaks in his own person. He begins by saying that although the state should certainly not restrict the reasoning of philosophers in the supposed interest of morals, those philosophers who infer that the Deity will punish vice and reward virtue in the hereafter, even if their reasoning is fallacious, do good for society because they help restrain those passions that could otherwise damage it; and those who expose the weakness in their thinking may therefore not be the best corporate citizens. Even if God does not exist, those who invent him by reason may be doing society a service. But whether or not this is so, there is a deep consideration that bears upon both sides in the dispute. Epicurus has been arguing that the divine power can only be known from its effect. But the effect in this case is the universe; and the universe, necessarily, is unique. All our knowledge of causes and effects is based upon inductive reasoning: that is, it depends on *repeated* experience of instances similar to the ones being investigated. The opponents of Epicurus have argued from a unique effect (or supposed effect) to a unique cause, and Epicurus has no doubt exposed weaknesses in the results of their arguments; but the fact that the cause and effect are unique make it doubtful whether he should have conceded their argument, even for the sake of making his own. Perhaps, it is implied, a key part of the analogy between scientific inference to causes and the inference in the design argument is absent. So natural theology is not only without practical implications; it is also, perhaps, due to a misunderstanding of what causal reasoning is.

The Credentials of Natural Religion

The major themes of the *Dialogues Concerning Natural Religion,* together with the ambiguities attendant on them, can all be found, at least in embryonic form, in section XI. I concentrate first upon Hume's critique of the design argument as it is found in both works. I shall then offer some (partly speculative) comments on the more difficult and elusive matter of his views on popular and philosophical religion and their relationship.

The criticisms of the design argument in section XI are to be found, considerably elaborated, in parts ii–v and x–xi of the *Dialogues.* They are all given to Philo, who is described at the outset as a "careless" skeptic. He responds to Cleanthes, whose "accurate philosophical turn" has made Mossner suggest he represents Joseph Butler. The third character, Demea, represents "rigid inflexible orthodoxy" and for that reason is identified by Mossner with Samuel Clarke, whose version of the cosmological argument is given to Demea in part ix. These identifications are only moderately plausible, but there is no doubt that Cleanthes represents the partially secularized rational Christians of Hume's time, and Philo, prior to the concluding part xii at least, presses all the negative arguments against Cleanthes with happy abandon, and certainly does most of the talking.[14] It is noteworthy that although Philo is called a skeptic, the case he makes against Cleanthes does not, for the most part, depend upon skeptical premises, any more than the arguments of Epicurus in section XI do.

What the arguments of Epicurus and Philo do depend upon is an insistence that the likeness to scientific inference, on which the design argument is supposed to depend, is not sufficient to support the conclusion that the received wisdom of Hume's day accepted.

The central argument of Epicurus, that when treating of causes and effects, we are only entitled to ascribe those powers to the cause that are enough to produce the observed effects, and no more, reappears in part v of the *Dialogues,* where its awkward consequences are much elaborated. These are that God's creative mind must be limited in its powers if the argument is taken with any strictness; that the flaws in creation may be due to the fact that as far as we know, the universe in which we live is merely the latest in a series of attempts to produce as good a world as possible, in the way in which human craftsmen create successive prototypes; that the world may well be due to the work of a team of imperfect deities, rather than one God; and that if we are to take seriously the analogy between the creation of the world and the crafting of human artifacts, we could well infer that God's mind is lodged in a body, as our minds are. All of these awkward consequences are natural inferences from the analogy between human and divine contrivance, and one is only entitled to dismiss them if one has independent information about God, which the argument claims to do without.

The concluding argument of section XI, that causal inferences require us to have experienced repeated examples of phenomena like the cause being followed by phenomena like the effect, is one of the first to be given to Philo in the *Dialogues,* and is found in part ii. All Philo's arguments in that part have a common theme: the design argument only seems to have the same form as other inductive inferences and in fact does not. It depends on an analogy between the universe and human constructs when it is hard to see anything other than the vaguest of resemblances. The analogy it appeals to is also a very odd one — it is between some selected *parts* of the universe and the universe as a whole. Even if the analogy is accepted as a close one, we must still remember that the evidence does not show us that order and convenience are always due to intelligent minds; indeed, they are only due to such causes in the cases of human artifacts. The order and adaptability of organic bodies seems, from all the evidence, to be caused by the processes of animal and vegetable reproduction. To say that these cannot be the *real* causes is to depart from the evidence and impose the conclusion one desires before the argument starts. The fact that causal inferences depend on repeated past cases is merely one more respect in which the design argument fails to meet the standard of inductive reasoning we follow in all secular cases.

Once it is established that Cleanthes' analogy between the creation of the world and the work of human minds is so weak, Philo is able to bring out other inconveniences of "empirical theism" in ways not touched on in section XI. For example, other possible analogies seem to have as good a basis in the evidence as the one on which the design argument depends, and we can as readily speculate that the world is related to the mind of God in the way in which our bodies are related to our minds, or that the world comes into being through animal or vegetable generation. And Philo is ingeniously able to suggest something held by the ancient Epicureans themselves, that the world as we know it is the result of a purely fortuitous assemblage of atoms: once the atoms happened to combine in forms that had orderly structure, this order may have enabled the cosmos to persist in the face of forces that threatened to dissolve it. This is an interesting anticipation of Darwinism, in that it tells us that the reason our world exhibits order is merely that less orderly combinations of matter have all perished, even though the combination we have appeared by chance in the first place. All these possibilities, which are developed with great glee by Philo, are not offered as having a high degree of probability (although Hume makes it clear he is attracted to the last one), but they are theories that have as much basis in the evidence as the one the design argument presses on us. This indicates that the ready acceptance of the design argument in our culture is the result of religious traditions that have taken root for reasons quite unconnected with the quality of the evidence for them.

In parts x and xi of the *Dialogues,* there is a complex and subtle discussion of the problem of evil. The most important of Philo's arguments here is essentially the same as that put into the mouth of Epicurus in section XI. The evils in the world may, for all we can tell, be evils that a theist can explain away and *reconcile* with the moral perfection and omnipotence of God *if* these are already accepted; but the evidence does not itself *suggest* that the world is the creation of such a deity. Philo puts this central point at the beginning of part xi as follows:

> In this world considered in general, and as it appears to us in this life, different from what a man or such a limited being would, *beforehand,* expect from a very powerful, wise, and be-

nevolent Deity? It must be strange prejudice to assert the contrary. And from thence I conclude, that however consistent the world may be, allowing certain suppositions and conjectures, with the idea of such a Deity, it can never afford us an inference concerning his existence. The consistency is not absolutely denied, only the inference.[15]

Given the evils that the world contains, if we believe in a mind or minds as its cause, it is most likely, Philo thinks, that that mind is neither wholly good nor wholly bad. It will either be a mixture of both or, more likely, "have neither goodness nor malice."[16]

Most readers of the *Dialogues* would now concur with Kemp Smith that, at least to the end of part xi, the effect of the work is almost totally negative, and that Hume has exposed major defects in the argument from design. It is remarkable that Paley and others seemed to be unaffected by his arguments. What is more remarkable still is that in part xii, where Cleanthes and Philo are left to talk without Demea as an orthodox audience, Philo also seems, without formal acknowledgment, to change his mind about the cogency of the argument and to speak of its conclusion too as dubious, but as obviously true. It is clear from the manuscripts that Hume spent immense care over the wording of part xii until shortly before his death, and the ambiguities of it have caused a great deal of scholarly speculation. Part xii is also the only portion of the work in which there is discussion of the other theme of section XI, namely the moral results of rational theism. I shall now make a few comments on this latter question and try to connect it with the elaborate ambiguities of this last part. I attempt this because all agree that Hume's attitude to religion is harder to state than it seems and is also a critical element in his philosophical system.

| *True and False Religion*

There can be no doubt of Hume's strong secularizing bent. Nor can there be any doubt that he is our culture's most subtle and penetrating critic of religion, both popular and philosophical. That said, however, there are still fascinating questions about his detailed views. A great many of these questions arise in their most perplexing form when one tries to interpret part xii of the *Dialogues*. What Hume says there about the moral and social effects of religion requires comparison with the speech given to Epicurus in section XI of the *Enquiry*. But a just assessment of these passages demands that we attend to the whole range of what Hume says about religion throughout his career. We have to recognize Hume's

motives for writing with irony and circumspection on this topic,
but we must not be intimidated by this, either. If we are, we run
the risk Gaskin points out: "We should beware of so relying upon
Hume's irony that we read an often repeated declaration as an
often repeated denial."[17]

We can say with assurance that Hume, early in his life,
abandoned the popular Calvinism of his upbringing. He saw social
convention and philosophic reflection as the only possible sources
of personal moral guidance and was wholly negative in his judgment of the social effects of popular piety. He saw it not only as the
source of inner anxiety and turmoil but also as a cause of persecution, intolerance, and civil strife, the last being a major theme in
his historical writings. He is clearly an enemy of both superstition
and enthusiasm, to use his language.[18] He was aware, of course,
that religion takes politer forms, as it did in many of his friends,
and he was also aware that in British society atheism was considered both immoral and virtually unthinkable, although it might
flourish on the Continent. In its politer forms, religion received the
support of philosophical argument. Hume makes it clear in the
Natural History of Religion that he regards this alliance as a
corruption of philosophy,[19] but when the arguments purport to be
based on experience, he thinks he has an obligation to examine
them in detail.

There can be no reasonable doubt, in spite of the fact that
Philo is never formally identified with Hume himself, that Hume
judges the design argument, which was accepted unquestioningly
by deist and theist alike, to be philosophically very weak. And it
seems to me manifest from the *Dialogues* and from section XI that,
even if Hume inclined at times, as many scholars think, to accept
that the argument gives *some* degree of rational support to the
belief that the universe shows signs of the work of a designing
intelligence, he thinks it gives us no basis whatever for supposing
that this intelligence is morally perfect or even good. This is
confirmed in Philo's final speech in part xii, written as part of
Hume's last revision of the work:

> If the whole of natural theology, as some people seem to main-
> tain, resolves itself into one simple, though somewhat ambigu-
> ous, at least undefined proposition, *that the cause or causes of
> order in the universe probably bear some remote analogy to hu-
> man intelligence;* if this proposition be not capable of extension,
> variation, or more particular explication; if it afford no infer-
> ence that affects human life, or can be the source of any action
> or forbearance; and if the analogy, imperfect as it is, can be car-
> ried no farther than to the human intelligence, and cannot be
> transferred, with any appearance of probability, to the other

qualities of the mind — if this really be the case, what can the
most inquisitive, contemplative, and religious man do more
than give a plain, philosophical assent to the proposition, as
often as it occurs, and believe that the arguments, on which it
is established, exceed the objections which lie against it?[20]

While I do not know how to interpret the clause "as some people
seem to maintain" (nor, in my view, does anyone else), I find it
tempting to interpret this speech as indicating that Hume was
inclined to what Gaskin calls an attenuated deism:[21] that is, that
he thinks it weakly probable that there is an intelligent god who
accounts for the order in the world, even though the standard
arguments offered for this are poor. Certainly this is more likely
than that Hume espoused the trenchant village atheism of his
European counterparts.[22] But I merely find it tempting, and I am
not sure it is correct. It seems to me at least as likely that Hume
was, privately, an atheist (though not a dogmatic one) but that he
was affected by the sheer weight of conventional opinion that
atheism was unthinkable. He pays lip service, at least, to that
view in part xii; he has Philo say at one point, "I next turn to the
atheist, who, I assert, is only nominally so, and can never possibly
be in earnest."[23] He also has Philo talk in part xii as though his
own criticisms of the design argument were mere exercises in
skeptical dialectic that do not carry conviction,[24] and that he
shares Cleanthes' view that the world must be designed by God.

This leads us into difficult and controversial matters. If we
take seriously the things Philo is made to say in part xii, where he
talks like a deist and seems to repudiate his earlier arguments as
mere skeptical exercises, we face the suggestion that Hume
thought of belief in God as a natural belief, like those in causal
necessity or the external world.[25] This, however, seems impossible
if we give due weight to the *Natural History of Religion.* Working
there with a clearly stated distinction between the arguments that
could be offered for such a belief and the actual sources in human
nature that it has, Hume tells us that monotheism is historically a
late religious development (of which he obviously disapproves),
and that it emerges from polytheistic traditions, themselves due to
human fears in the face of unexplained calamities and misfor-
tunes. He is also at pains to tell us that religion is not universal
among mankind, but that some are free of it:

> The belief of invisible, intelligent power has been very gener-
> ally diffused over the human race, in all places and in all ages;
> but it has never perhaps been so universal as to admit of no
> exception, nor has it been, in any degree, uniform in the ideas,
> which it has suggested. Some nations have been discovered,
> who entertained no sentiments of religion, if travellers and

historians may be credited; and no two nations, and scarce any two men, have ever agreed precisely in the same sentiments. It would appear, therefore, that this preconception springs not from an original instinct or primary impression of nature, such as gives rise to self-love, affection between the sexes, love of progeny, gratitude, resentment; since every instinct of this kind has been found absolutely universal in all nations and ages, and has always a precise determinate object, which it inflexibly pursues. The first religious principles must be secondary, such as may easily be perverted by various accidents and causes, and whose operation too, in some cases, may, by an extraordinary concurrence of circumstances, be altogether prevented.[26]

The causes that actually generate religion in human beings, then, are environmental rather than inborn, and with luck we may escape them by living in a society where the influences on us are exclusively secular ones.

Hume's purpose in arguing this, I submit, is to evade a difficulty similar to the one that many readers find in the transition from the skeptical to the positive phase in his discussions of causation. If our inductive practices are never based on reason, what right does Hume have to distinguish between good and bad inductive arguments? His answer there, as we have seen, is that making inferences from customary repetition is a universal and unavoidable instinct within us that philosophers can neither justify nor dislodge, but within the inevitable acceptance of this practice it is possible to make refinements in it that help us to make only those inferences that harmonize with nature and avoid those that do not. The total abstention from inductive practice that the Skeptic affects is impossible, but this or that erroneous inference can be avoided by choice and care.[27] He offers a similar response here to those who say that if belief in God cannot be supported by rational argument, as the received wisdom thinks, this shows it to be a natural human instinct that we must accept, and that only skeptical philosophers can pretend to manage without it. (Put another way, this can be stated thus: Why criticize faith in God when inductive practice depends on faith also?[28]) As we have seen, this view could perhaps be ascribed to *Philo* in the final stages of the *Dialogues,* but the passage just quoted from the *Natural History* counts against its being *Hume's own* opinion. For what this passage tells us is that those religious beliefs from which latter-day monotheism has developed were originally due to *non*-instinctual causes, and hence that monotheism, ultimately, is also due to such causes. We must remember also that Philo, whatever his reasons, is speaking of a form of monotheism that is supposed

to be the result of philosophical argument. So unless we follow
Gaskin in taking Hume to be expressing, through Philo, an
attenuated deism of his own, we have to read Philo as expressing
indirectly Hume's recognition that the cultural forces he has
described in the *Natural History* have so entrenched belief in God
in society that the mere demolition of the rational grounds custom-
arily offered for it will not enable his readers to cast it off.

In such circumstances, what might we expect Hume to do? I
think this: in a form whose intent would be discernible by those
with objectives similar to his own but would not be alarming to the
more conventional, he will try to encourage the secularizing
tendencies in his own society in order to bring forward the day
when overt irreligiousness will be the norm rather than the rare
exception. However we may feel about the fact, this is the day in
which we are now living. Hume foresees that the development of
science and the increasing emphasis in moral and social thinking
upon purely secular risks and benefits will erode the public
influence of religion. He sees more than this, however: he is able to
perceive and encourage secularizing forces within the Christian
tradition itself.

We can now return to the moral implications of rational
theism as these are discussed in the *Dialogues* and in section XI.
We have seen that in section XI, Hume argues, through Epicurus,
that the moral impact of philosophical theism, when the reasoning
that is supposed to establish it is conducted with proper sobriety,
is in fact no different from the moral impact of socially established
practices based on common perception of what is good or bad for
oneself and society. This has two matching consequences. On the
one hand, those who attack Epicurus for undermining morals and
social order, as atheists were often attacked in Hume's time, are
mistaken, though it will take time to perceive this. On the other
hand, those who try to provide rational support for religion are
equally mistaken in supposing that their support does any real
service to the social norms and practices they think they are
serving, since these do not come from philosophical sources.

But this second consequence needs modification, for the
protagonists of philosophical religion are prone to think that their
arguments support popular religious orthodoxy, not merely
philosophical theism. And to Hume, popular orthodoxy is by no
means an unmixed blessing; he wishes to undermine it. He does,
however, see that those orthodox who are most influenced by
philosophy are moderating influences in the churches: they
progressively reduce the importance of the special obligations of

piety and are less and less inclined to demand the antisocial mortifications and to fuel the intolerance that Hume so deplored in popular religion. Their morality tends to approximate more and more closely the best secular morality, and they are increasingly embarrassed by the insistence of their more conservative religious brethren on attitudes and rules left over from previous ages. Their religion is less and less *religious* day by day. They do not, of course, see this with clarity and would reject the open statement that it is happening to them. But since Hume welcomes the implications he sees in such developments, it is more likely that he will wish to encourage them than to fan religious conservatism by an open attack on all religious forms.

We can recall here that the opening of section XI tells us that Epicurus denies providence and a future life and yet refers to the fact that his followers served as priests in the temples. This combination, which seems odd to modern readers, indicates that religion was viewed by Epicurus as a useful form of social cement that helped to inculcate and reinforce the traditions of the community. The same view, importantly, was held by the classical Skeptics, who refrained, as Hume was to do, from antireligious activity. Hume's *Dialogues* are modeled, formally speaking, on Cicero's dialogues *De Natura Deorum*.[29] In those dialogues, the Skeptic Cotta is not merely a critic of the arguments offered for the reality of the gods but also manages to combine this with a life in which he is not a mere practitioner but a functionary of the civic religion. The Skeptic attitude to religion is spelled out for us quite clearly by Sextus Empiricus: "Although, following the ordinary view, we affirm undogmatically that Gods exist and reverence Gods and ascribe to them foreknowledge, yet as against the rashness of the Dogmatists we argue as follows . . . "[30] The Skeptic may turn away from the arguments for (and against) belief in gods, but he does not have any reason to abstain from a beliefless social conformity in religious matters.[31] Hume, I suggest, takes the same view of the conventional practice of religion as we find it in the secularized liberal churches — not, of course, as we find it in their evangelical competitors. This is why he can speak through Epicurus in holding that he really is not engaged in undermining religious practice. For this is true if one is suitably selective in choosing one's examples of this practice and confining it to those religious groups most likely to be influenced by philosophy.

It is relatively easy, if all of this is close to the truth, to decode what Hume says in part xii of the *Dialogues* about "true" and "false" religion. Philo is allegedly speaking with "unfeigned intimacy" to Cleanthes, who has stood by the design argument through thick and thin; and he is apparently accepting, after all, that Cleanthes has been right. They spend the greater part of part xii discussing the relation between the "natural" or rational religious belief, in which they seem to concur, and the more popular forms of piety. Cleanthes supposes that he has been reinforcing the second by arguing for the first. Philo thinks no such thing. They spar for several pages on the issue of how far philosophical religion leads into the popular. Hume gives the following astonishing lines to Cleanthes:

> The proper office of religion is to regulate the heart of men, humanize their conduct, infuse the spirit of temperance, order, and obedience; and as its operation is silent, and only enforces the motives of morality and justice, it is in danger of being overlooked, and confounded with these other motives. When it distinguishes itself, and acts as a separate principle over men, it has departed from its proper sphere, and has become only a cover to faction and ambition.[32]

What these lines tell us is that what both call "true religion" has no independent morality or doctrine. Hume was able to see that a religious belief that seeks to gain acceptance from men of letters by the arguments he has so diligently undermined will in time turn into harmless and domesticated ethics and conventional ceremonial. While Cleanthes expresses anxiety that Philo's attacks on "false" (that is, really *religious*) religion are overzealous and might undermine the "true" faith, his own account of what the proper office of religion is leaves nothing to which Philo and other skeptics can seriously object. For they can give what Philo calls a "plain, philosophical assent" to the vague reality of the deity, and this amounts to no more than the beliefless ritual conformity that their classical Skeptic forebears showed to the religion of their own time. And the social effects of the undogmatic Sunday-morning ceremonials to which the successors of Cleanthes will adhere are even beneficial, as long as the darker, fear-ridden traditions from which they have evolved are kept firmly in the past. It is to this wholly unreligious lip service to conventional belief that I suggest Philo, Epicurus, and Hume himself are confined.

There are those, of a fideist inclination, who think that Hume and other Enlightenment critics of religion did Christian faith an unintended favor by claiming it can have no rational basis in argument. They think the acceptance of this helps faith to find its real source in divine grace and not lean on the dubious support of philosophy. They may or may not be right about this.[33] I think a careful reading of Hume's texts, however, shows that if he has done faith a favor, it is indeed a wholly unintended one. The support he gives to conformist and domesticated religious practice is no sort of evidence to the contrary.

▌*N O T E S*

1. Butler 1900, vol. 2; Stephen 1902; Penelhum 1985a, part 2.

2. *EU* X (SB 127). On the detailed understanding of Hume's verdict, see Flew 1961, chap. 8.

3. See the bibliographical material on this topic in the Appendix.

4. Paley 1838, vol. 2, 5; reprinted in Swinburne 1989, 41–48.

5. Paley 1838, vol. 1; Aquinas 1955, 59–76.

6. Hick 1971, chaps. 5 and 6; Hick and McGill 1967; Anselm 1962, 2–10; Descartes 1954, 101–8.

7. For the text of Aquinas' Five Ways (which are in the *Summa Theologiae,* part I, question ii, article 2) together with translation and detailed discussion, see Kenny 1969. See also Clarke 1738, Rowe 1975.

8. Paley 1838, vol. 1, 1.

9. *DNR* part ix (KS 189).

10. *DNR* part ii (KS 143).

11. See the introduction to his edition of the *Dialogues,* particularly 57–75.

12. *EM* IX (SB 270).

13. Rist 1972, chap. 8.

14. Mossner 1936; Jeffner 1966; Pike 1970.

15. *DNR* XI (KS 205).

16. *DNR* XI (KS 212).

17. Gaskin 1988, 220.

18. See his essay "Of Superstition and Enthusiasm" in Green and Grose 1964, vol. 1, 144–49.

19. *NHR* parts xi and xii (Root 53–65).

20. *DNR* XII (KS 227).

21. Gaskin 1988, 219–29.

22. One recalls again here the story of his encounter with Baron Holbach. See Chapter Two.

23. *DNR* XII (KS 218).

24. See also Philo's concluding speech in part x.

25. R. J. Butler 1960; Penelhum 1979 and 1983b; Gaskin 1988, chap. 2.

26. *NHR* introduction (Root 21).

27. See Chapter Four.

28. Penelhum 1983a, chaps. 5–7.

29. Cicero 1933.

30. Sextus Empiricus 1933, vol. 1, 327.

31. Penelhum 1983a, chaps. 2 and 3.

32. *DNR* XII (KS 220).

33. Penelhum 1983a, passim.

Some Notes on the Hume Literature

There is a very large literature on Hume, and it continues to grow. Much of it is of high quality, though not, of course, all of it. This Appendix is merely intended to offer the serious student suggestions for reliable and stimulating works to consult, and it makes no pretence of completeness. Full details on all the works mentioned here are to be found in the Bibliography.

Before proceeding, I should wish to refer readers to the invaluable *Fifty Years of Hume Scholarship: A Bibliographical Guide,* by Roland Hall. This is a remarkably complete listing of scholarly studies of Hume up to 1976, which has been regularly updated by supplementary lists in *Hume Studies* since it was published.

| Biography

The standard work is Mossner's *Life of David Hume* 1970. It is comprehensive, erudite, readable, and philosophically informed (though not always subtle). Most other works (like the present book) depend on it. The best supplement to it is the perusal of some of Hume's letters. These are to be found in the collected edition of J. Y. T. Greig 1932 and in *New Letters of David Hume,* edited by Klibansky and Mossner 1954.

| General Books

Norman Kemp Smith, *The Philosophy of David Hume* 1941 is the century's major work. It is best approached after reading the author's two essays on "The Naturalism of Hume" 1905. Charles W. Hendel, *Studies in the Philosophy of David Hume,* second edition 1963, is a wise and scholarly account. D. G. C. MacNabb, *David*

Hume: His Theory of Knowledge and Morality 1951 is a very read-able introduction to these two things; also recommended is the same author's article on Hume in the *Encyclopedia of Philosophy* 1967. J. A. Passmore's *Hume's Intentions* 1952 is a lively and illuminating study of the variety of motives at work in Hume's system.

Antony Flew's *Hume's Philosophy of Belief* 1961 is an excellent guide to the first *Enquiry;* it is particularly strong on the philoso-phy of mind and philosophy of religion. Jonathan Bennett, *Locke, Berkeley, Hume: Central Themes* 1973 is a philosophically acute study of the Humean teachings on perception and causation, relat-ing them to his British predecessors. James Noxon, *Hume's Philo-sophical Development* 1973 is a scholarly analysis of Hume's methods and of his indebtedness to Newton. Terence Penelhum, *Hume* 1975, is a short work that attempts to assist the serious stu-dent to come to grips with Hume's detailed arguments without los-ing sight of his general vision.

Barry Stroud, *Hume* 1977 is a fine philosophical book, treating Hume's skepticism and his naturalism as complementary, not op-posed. Nicholas Capaldi, *David Hume: The Newtonian Philosopher* 1975, which is excellently written and argued, stresses the positive and constructive side of Hume's system and firmly denies his al-leged skepticism. Peter Jones, *Hume's Sentiments: Their Ciceronian and French Context* 1982 contains penetrating analysis of some of Hume's sources and includes a ground-breaking comparison of Hume and Wittgenstein.

David Fate Norton, *David Hume: Common Sense Moralist, Sceptical Metaphysician* 1982 contains very important and learned analysis with careful comparisons between Hume and his Scottish contemporaries. It argues, as the title shows, that Hume is a skeptic about metaphysics but not about ethics, and that he accords reason a more important place than the naturalistic interpretation of him acknowledges. Donald Livingston, *Hume's Philosophy of Common Life* 1984 is a work of deep and original scholarship, showing the breadth of Hume's interests and setting his more familiar writings in the context of his conservative social and historical work. It will undoubtedly be the source of much further research. John P. Wright, *The Sceptical Realism of David Hume* 1983 makes a very strong case for the unpopular view that Hume is both a skeptic and a realist—that he believes in natural necessities and in primary and secondary qualities but holds that we do not have assured access to these realities. This study is difficult but rewarding.

A. J. Ayer, *Hume* 1980 is a short survey, not based on extensive acquaintance with Hume scholarship, but the only work on Hume written by one of our own contemporaries who was a major philoso-pher in his own right. Antony Flew, *David Hume: Philosopher of*

Moral Science 1986 is written by a distinguished thinker who admires Hume and shares his conservatism. The author stresses the important part played in Hume's thought by assumptions he inherits from Descartes and corrects the anachronisms that come from neglecting these. Nicholas Capaldi, *Hume's Place in Moral Philosophy* 1989 has wider scope than the title suggests and tries to show that Hume brought about an unnoticed "Copernican revolution" in philosophy by moving from an egocentric (or "I think") perspective to a social and pragmatic (or "we do") perspective. Like the author's 1975 work, it exaggerates; but the serious student of Hume must read it. The book contains no index.

Robert J. Fogelin, *Hume's Skepticism in the "Treatise of Human Nature"* 1985 argues for the view that Hume is indeed a skeptic of the Pyrrhonian variety and that Kemp Smith and his followers have given a "one-sided emphasis to Hume's naturalism at the expense of his skepticism." It is of high philosophical quality and fun to read. It contains two important appendixes on Hume's views about induction and causation, the first one being a vigorous criticism of Beauchamp and Rosenberg; a total contrast to Capaldi. H. H. Price, *Hume's Theory of the External World* 1940 offers a theory of perception that is inspired by Hume's treatment of the theme in *Treatise* I iv 2. It is wholly misleading if taken as a reconstruction of Hume's own views but is a superb example of how a quite different constructive use can be made of some of the elements of Hume's philosophy of mind. John V. Price, *The Ironic Hume* 1965 explores the implications of an important aspect of Hume's mode of writing. Annette Baier, *A Progress of Sentiments: Reflections on Hume's Treatise* 1991 combines textual sensitivity and philosophical sophistication to an exceptional degree and is particularly important in showing the centrality of Hume's theory of the passions.

| Collected Essays and
| General Articles

Essays on Hume appear continually in most philosophical journals. Many are listed in Hall's bibliography. The student's task has been somewhat simplified by the appearance of a number of valuable collections. Those listed below are all recommended and appear here in chronological order. The names listed are, of course, those of their editors.

Alexander Sesonske and Noel Fleming, *Human Understanding: Studies in the Philosophy of David Hume* 1965.
V. C. Chappell, *Hume: A Collection of Critical Essays* 1966.
William B. Todd, *Hume and the Enlightenment* 1974.

Donald Livingston and James King, *Hume: A Re-evaluation* 1976.
Kenneth R. Merrill and Robert W. Shahan, *David Hume: Many-Sided Genius* 1976.
George Morice, *David Hume: Bicentenary Papers* 1977.
David Norton, Nicholas Capaldi, and Wade Robison, *McGill Hume Studies* 1979.
Vincent Hope, *Philosophers of the Scottish Enlightenment* 1984.
M. A. Stewart, *Studies in the Philosophy of the Scottish Enlightenment* 1990.
David Norton, *The Cambridge Companion to Hume,* forthcoming.

While most articles on Hume deal with particular themes, there are a small number that attempt an overview of his thought. Two important ones are G. E. Moore, "Hume's Philosophy" 1922 and H. H. Price, "The Permanent Significance of Hume's Philosophy" 1940, reprinted in Sesonske and Fleming. I attempted such an overview myself in "David Hume, 1711–76: A Bicentennial Appreciation" 1977.

An important historical issue is the nature of Hume's impact on Kant. There is much of value on this in Beck 1978 and Kuehn 1983. Two commentaries on Kant's *Critique of Pure Reason* that explore this question helpfully are those by Norman Kemp Smith 1918 and Jonathan Bennett 1966.

An increasingly important source of scholarly discussion of Hume is the journal *Hume Studies.* This began as a venture of the University of Western Ontario under the editorship of John W. Davis in 1975 and is now an official publication of the Hume Society. It is essential for serious students to consult it. From 1990 it is edited by Fred Wilson.

▌ Studies of Particular Themes

Naturally the particular topics listed here are discussed in the general works mentioned above. Hence the writings listed below are for the most part specialized studies not already included.

▌ Skepticism

There have been a number of important books in recent years about the Skeptic tradition, classical and modern, all of them directly or indirectly relevant to assessing the central question of Hume's relation to that tradition. The following are recommended.

Philip P. Hallie (ed.), *Scepticism, Man and God: Selections from the Writings of Sextus Empiricus* 1964.
Charlotte Stough, *Greek Skepticism* 1969.

Richard Popkin, *The History of Scepticism from Erasmus to Spinoza* 1979; and *The High Road to Pyrrhonism* 1980.

M. Schofield, M. Burnyeat, and J. Barnes (eds.), *Doubt and Dogmatism: Studies in Hellenistic Philosophy* 1980.

Myles Burnyeat (ed.), *The Skeptical Tradition* 1983.

Barry Stroud, *The Significance of Philosophical Scepticism* 1984.

J. Annas and J. Barnes, *The Modes of Scepticism* 1985.

P. F. Strawson, *Skepticism and Naturalism: Some Varieties* 1985.

An important essay not reproduced in any of the above is Burnyeat, "Idealism and Greek Philosophy: What Descartes Saw and Berkeley Missed" 1982. A recent book that contests received interpretations, especially that of Burnyeat, is Leo Groarke, *Greek Scepticism: Antirealist Trends in Modern Thought 1990*. Since Hume seems to have been much influenced by Bayle, the reader could consult the fine short study by Elisabeth Labrousse, *Bayle* 1983, and the selections from Bayle's *Historical and Critical Dictionary* edited by Popkin 1965.

On the matter of the role of skepticism in Hume himself, in addition to the discussions in the works by Fogelin, Wright, Norton, and Capaldi listed above, there are papers by D. C. Stove, John Immerwahr, Christine Battersby, and Terence Penelhum in *McGill Hume Studies* 1979. See also John Wright, "Hume's Academic Skepticism" 1986, and Martin Bell and Marie McGinn, "Naturalism and Scepticism" 1990. I have attempted to assess both the Skeptic tradition and Hume's place in it, with special but not exclusive emphasis on the philosophy of religion, in *God and Skepticism* 1983. Further references can be found in the listing under "Causation and Induction" below.

| Philosophy of Mind

While the themes covered by this heading are pervasive, there are not so many works devoted exclusively to them. Indeed, the only book (fortunately a very good one) is John Bricke's *Hume's Philosophy of Mind* 1980. It is a rigorous and wide-ranging exploration of views Hume frequently applies but does not expound very systematically.

On the science of human nature and the doctrine of association, see James Moore's essay in *McGill Hume Studies* 1979, part 2 of Noxon 1973, the essay by Robert Anderson in Livingston and King 1976, and chapter 5 of Wright 1983. On Hume's actual or implied theory of meaning, see Flew 1961, chapter 2, and Livingston 1984, chapters 3 and 4. For the debate on how Newtonian the doctrine of association manages to be in Hume's hands, the key texts are Robert

Paul Wolff's "Hume's Theory of Mental Activity" 1960 (in Chappell) and Fred Wilson's paper of the same title in *McGill Hume Studies*.

Hume's discussions of the self have generated a great deal of debate. For my own contributions to it, refer to the Bibliography and to chapter 4 of my *Hume* 1975. There is good discussion and an excellent bibliography in Godfrey Vesey's *Personal Identity* 1974. Recommended work not included there is to be found in Lawrence Ashley and Michael Stack, "Hume's Doctrine of Personal Identity" 1974; Nelson Pike, "Hume's Bundle Theory of the Self" 1967; Jane McIntyre's essay in *McGill Hume Studies* 1979; and the debate between Beauchamp, Biro, and McIntyre in *Hume Studies* for 1979. There is important new material on this theme in Capaldi 1989, especially chapter 5. The essay "Pride, Virtue and Selfhood" by Pauline Chazan is also warmly recommended.

The contemporary debates on personal identity are very extensive. The most important contributions can be found in Derek Parfit, *Reasons and Persons* 1984; Bernard Williams, *Problems of the Self* 1973; and Sydney Shoemaker and Richard Swinburne, *Personal Identity* 1984.

∎ Causation and Induction

The literature on these themes, all of it indebted to Hume in numberless ways, is immense. I shall confine myself here to writings that deal directly with what Hume himself says. The indispensable books are these:

William Kneale, *Probability and Induction* 1949.
D. C. Stove, *Probability and Hume's Inductive Scepticism* 1973.
J. L. Mackie, *The Cement of the Universe* 1974.
Tom Beauchamp and Alexander Rosenberg, *Hume and the Problem of Causation* 1981.

Of these, Stove and Beauchamp-Rosenberg are the most detailed in their attention to the Humean text. Beauchamp-Rosenberg is criticized in an appendix to Fogelin 1985.

Articles that supplement the above in important ways, and which I have drawn upon in the commentary, are Stove, "Hume, the Causal Principle, and Kemp Smith" 1975; Fred Wilson, "Hume's Defence of Causal Inference" 1983, and "Hume's Defence of Science" 1986.

For an entry into the vast literature that Hume's discussion of induction inspired, there is the useful collection (with bibliography) edited by Richard Swinburne, *The Justification of Induction* 1974. The serious historical student needs to attend to Ian Hacking, *The Emergence of Probability* 1975.

For a debate of Hume's definitions of "cause," see the discussion between J. A. Robinson and Thomas Richards in Chappell 1966. For criticisms of Hume's views on causation, see the essays by G. E. M. Anscombe, "Causality and Determination" 1971; "Hume and Julius Caesar" 1973; and "Whatever Has a Beginning of Existence Must Have a Cause: Hume's Argument Exposed" 1974. These are all to be found in her *Collected Philosophical Papers* 1981.

| Ethics and Justice

The most important books on these themes are the following:

Rachel Kydd, *Reason and Conduct in Hume's "Treatise"* 1946.
John B. Stewart, *The Moral and Political Philosophy of David Hume* 1963.
Páll S. Árdal, *Passion and Value in Hume's Treatise* 1966.
Philip Mercer, *Sympathy and Ethics* 1972.
Jonathan Harrison, *Hume's Moral Epistemology* 1976.
J. L. Mackie, *Hume's Moral Theory* 1980.
Jonathan Harrison, *Hume's Theory of Justice* 1981.

The general listing already includes the important works by Norton 1982 and Capaldi 1989.

In addition to Árdal, one can find helpful discussion of Hume's theory of the passions in Jerome Neu, *Emotion, Thought and Therapy* 1977. See also Capaldi's essay in Livingston and King 1976, and chapter 5 of Penelhum 1975.

On the much-disputed issue of what Hume thought about the transition from "is"-judgments to "ought"-judgments, see the essays on this theme in Chappell 1966 by Alasdair MacIntyre, R. F. Atkinson, Antony Flew, Geoffrey Hunter, and W. H. Hudson, and chapter 5 of Capaldi 1989.

On the objectivity of moral judgments, or lack thereof, in Hume, the major recent studies are, once more, Norton 1982 and Capaldi 1989; but see also R. F. Atkinson's essay in Merrill and Strachan 1976. The less-discussed issue of freedom and responsibility is examined in Paul Russell, "Hume on Responsibility and Punishment" 1990.

For comparisons of Hume and his contemporaries, see Mackie 1980, Norton and Capaldi again, J. Kemp's *Reason, Action and Morality* 1964, and T. A. Roberts, *The Concept of Benevolence* 1973; also Penelhum, "Butler and Hume" 1988. A convenient range of selections from the moral thinkers of the period is available in L. A. Selby-Bigge's *British Moralists* 1897, repr. 1965. Of the classics of twentieth-century moral philosophy, the work that is closest to Hume theoretically is Stevenson's *Ethics and Language* 1944. The influential and penetrating essays in Annette Baier's *Postures of the Mind* 1985 show a deep understanding of Hume and are greatly influenced by him.

Works of recent moral philosophy that invite comparison with Hume are John Rawls, *A Theory of Justice* 1971; and David Gauthier, *Morals by Agreement* 1986. See also Gauthier's essay, "David Hume: Contractarian" 1979. For a vigorous and influential critique of Hume, see Alasdair MacIntyre, *Whose Justice? Which Rationality?* 1988.

Finally, I wish to commend the special morality issue of *Hume Studies* for April 1988 (vol. 14, number 1).

▎ Religion

The standard work here is J. C. A. Gaskin, *Hume's Philosophy of Religion,* 2nd edition, 1988. It is comprehensive, well-written, and stimulating as well as accurate. A more recent and more critical study that gives special attention to the *Natural History of Religion* is Keith E. Yandell, *Hume's "Inexplicable Mystery": His Views on Religion* 1990. A shorter and useful general treatment is the introduction to Richard Wollheim's anthology *Hume on Religion* 1963.

Section XI of the *Enquiry* is not well-blessed with commentaries, but the reader is recommended to chapter 9 of Flew's *Hume's Philosophy of Belief* 1961, and chapter 4 of his book of 1986.

For the *Dialogues,* the situation is very different. The scholarly material supplied by Kemp Smith in his 1947 edition is indispensable. The commentary and essays in Nelson Pike's edition of 1970 are very fine indeed; and it would be a mistake not to consult the introduction to Richard Popkin's edition of 1980. Discussions of the *Dialogues* abound as they should. Try the essays by Yandell and Nathan in Livingston and King 1976, those by Gaskin, Battersby, Penelhum, and Wadia in Norton, Capaldi, and Robison 1979, Noxon's contribution to Merrill and Shahan 1976, and Penelhum, "Natural Belief and Religious Belief in Hume's Philosophy" 1983, and chapter 6 of Penelhum, *God and Skepticism,* same year. For a major modern attempt to reinstate natural theology in the face of Hume's critique, see Richard Swinburne, The *Existence of God* 1979, especially chapter 8. On the vast questions of how post-Humean scientific developments affect the status of the design argument, see Richard Dawkins, *The Blind Watchmaker* 1986; and the anthology *Physical Cosmology and Philosophy,* edited by John Leslie 1990. Finally, for an important historical comparison, see Anders Jeffner, *Butler and Hume on Religion* 1966.

On miracles, the literature is very large indeed. The two best discussions remain C. D. Broad's "Hume's Theory of the Credibility of Miracles" 1916 (reprinted in Sesonske and Fleming 1965) and chapter 8 of Flew 1961. The two most substantial studies are Richard Swinburne, *The Concept of Miracle* 1970, and Michael P. Levine, *Hume and the Problem of Miracles: A Solution* 1989. An excellent place to find other discussions is Swinburne's anthology *Miracles* 1989; one thing it includes is Paley's response to Hume from his *Evidences of Christianity.* For some comment on Paley's silence on what Hume says in the *Dialogues,* see chapter 2 of D. L. LeMahieu, *The Mind of William Paley* 1976. I attempted some comment on the issue of miracles in *Religion and Rationality* 1971, chapter 19. Two final recommendations: first, the philosophy of religion issue of *Hume Studies* for November 1988 (vol. 14, number 2); and Stewart R. Sutherland, *Faith and Ambiguity* 1984.

| Other Areas of Hume's Work

It remains to make some recommendations for study in those major areas where Hume wrote, which have been left undiscussed in this book. The most important are politics and history. The best place to go for the former is the second half of Donald Livingston's book of 1984. The reader is also referred to Duncan Forbes, *Humes's Philosophical Politics* 1975; and David Miller, *Philosophy and Ideology in Hume's Political Thought* 1982. On Hume as historian, see, first, David Norton and Richard Popkin (eds.), *David Hume: Philosophical Historian* 1965; and Nicholas Phillipson, *Hume* 1989 (a work in a series entitled "Historians on Historians").

For essays, see those by Wolin, Stockton, and Walton in Livingston and King 1976, and those by Popkin and Rotwein in Merrill and Strahan 1976.

BIBLIOGRAPHY

This list includes all, and only, those works to which reference is made in the text and Appendix. Editions of books are those actually used. See the Note on Texts and Abbreviations for details of references to Hume's own writings.

Ashley, Lawrence, and Michael Stack
1974   "Hume's Doctrine of Personal Identity." *Dialogue* 13:239–54.

Atkinson, R. F.
1961   "Hume on 'Is' and 'Ought': A Reply to Mr. MacIntyre." *Philosophical Review* 70:231–38. Reprinted in Chappell 1966, 265–77.
1976   "Hume on the Standard of Morals." In Merrill and Strachan 1976, 25–44.

Augustine, Saint
1943   *Against the Academicians (Contra Academicos* 386 A.D.*).* Translated by Sister Mary Patricia Garvey. Milwaukee, Wis.: Marquette University Press.

Ayer, A. J.
1936   *Language, Truth and Logic.* London: Gollancz.
1940   *Foundations of Empirical Knowledge.* London: Macmillan.
1980   *Hume.* Oxford: Oxford University Press.

Baier, Annette
1985   *Postures of the Mind.* Minneapolis: University of Minnesota Press.
1991   *A Progress of Sentiments: Reflections on Hume's Treatise.* Cambridge, Mass.: Harvard University Press.

Battersby, Christine
1979   "The *Dialogues* as Original Imitation: Cicero and the Nature of Hume's Skepticism." In Norton, Capaldi, and Robison 1979, 239–52.

Bayle, Pierre
1965   *Historical and Critical Dictionary: Selections.* Translated and edited by Richard Popkin. Indianapolis, Ind.: Bobbs-Merrill.

Beauchamp, Tom
1979   "Self Inconsistency or Mere Self Perplexity?" *Hume Studies* 5:37–44.

Beauchamp, Tom, and Alexander Rosenberg
1981   *Hume and the Problem of Causation.* New York: Oxford University Press.

Beck, Lewis White
1978   *Essays on Kant and Hume.* New Haven, Conn.: Yale University Press.

Bell, Martin, and Marie McGinn
1990   "Naturalism and Scepticism." *Philosophy* 65:399–418.

Bennett, Jonathan
1966   *Kant's Analytic.* Cambridge: Cambridge University Press.
1971   *Locke, Berkeley, Hume: Central Themes.* Oxford: Clarendon Press.

Berkeley, George
1929   *Essay, Principles, Dialogues.* Edited by Mary Whiton Calkins. London: Charles Scribners Sons.

Biro, John
1979   "Hume's Difficulties with the Self." *Hume Studies* 5:45–54.

Boswell, James
1924   *Letters*. Edited by C. B. Tinker. 2 vols. Oxford: Oxford University Press.

Bricke, John
1980   *Hume's Philosophy of Mind*. Princeton, N.J.: Princeton University Press.
1984.   "Hume's Volitions." In Hope 1984, 70–90.

Broad, C. D.
1916   "Hume's Theory of the Credibility of Miracles." *Proceedings of the Aristotelian Society* 17:77–94. Reprinted in Sesonske and Fleming 1965, 86–98.

Burnet, John
1928   *Greek Philosophy, part 1: Thales to Plato*. London: Macmillan.

Burnyeat, Myles
1982   "Idealism and Greek Philosophy: What Descartes Saw and Berkeley Missed." *Philosophical Review* 91:3–40.
1983   *The Skeptical Tradition*. Berkeley and Los Angeles: University of California Press.

Butler, Joseph
1900   *The Works of Joseph Butler*. Edited by J. H. Bernard. 2 vols. London: Macmillan.

Butler, R. J.
1960   "Natural Belief and the Enigma of Hume." *Archiv für Geschichte der Philosophie* 42:73–100.

Capaldi, Nicholas
1975   *David Hume: The Newtonian Philosopher*. Boston: Twayne.
1976   "Hume's Theory of the Passions." In Livingston and King 1976, 172–90.
1989.   *Hume's Place in Moral Philosophy*. New York: Peter Lang.

Chappell, V. (ed.)
1966   *Hume: A Collection of Critical Essays*. Garden City, N.J.: Doubleday.

Chazan, Pauline
        "Pride, Virtue and Selfhood: A Reconstruction of Hume." *Canadian Journal of Philosophy,* forthcoming.

Cicero
1933   *De Natura Deorum and Academica*. With translation by H. Rackham. Loeb Classical Library. Cambridge, Mass.: Harvard University Press.

Clarke, Samuel
1738   *The Works of Samuel Clarke*. 4 vols. London: Paul Knapton. Facsimile reprint New York: Garland Publishing, 1978. [The Boyle Lectures of 1704, *A Demonstration of Being and Attributes of God,* are in vol. 2, 521–77. The *Discourse Concerning the Unchangeable Obligations of Natural Religion,* of 1705, is in vol. 2, 579–733.]

Descartes, René
1954   *Philosophical Writings*. Selected, edited, and translated by E. Anscombe and P. T. Geach. London: Nelson.

Dawkins, Richard
1986   *The Blind Watchmaker.* London: Longman.

Dray, William H.
1957   *Laws and Explanation in History.* Oxford: Oxford University Press.

Flew, Antony
1961   *Hume's Philosophy of Belief: A Study of his First "Inquiry."* London: Routledge and Kegan Paul.
1963   "On the Interpretation of Hume." *Philosophy* 38:178–82. Reprinted in Chappell 1966, 192–47.
1986   *David Hume: Philosopher of Moral Science.* Oxford: Basil Blackwell.

Fogelin, Robert J.
1985   *Hume's Skepticism in the "Treatise of Human Nature."* London: Routledge and Kegan Paul.

Forbes, Duncan
1975   *Hume's Philosophical Politics.* Cambridge: Cambridge University Press.

Gaskin, J. C. A.
1979   "Hume, Atheism, and the 'Interested Obligation' of Morality." In Norton, Capaldi, and Robison 1979, 147–60.
1988   *Hume's Philosophy of Religion.* 2nd edition. London: Macmillan.

Gauthier, David
1979   "David Hume: Contractarian." *Philosophical Review* 88:3–38.
1986   *Morals by Agreement.* Oxford: Clarendon Press.

Gough, J. W.
1936   *The Social Contract: A Critical History of Its Development.* Oxford: Clarendon Press.

Groarke, Leo
1990   *Greek Scepticism: Anti-realist Trends in Ancient Thought.* Montreal and Kingston: McGill-Queen's University Press.

Hacking, Ian
1975   *The Emergence of Probability.* Cambridge: Cambridge University Press.

Hall, Roland
1978   *Fifty Years of Hume Scholarship: A Bibliographical Guide.* Edinburgh: Edinburgh University Press.

Hallie, Philip P. (ed.)
1964   *Skepticism, Man and God: Selections from the Writings of Sextus Empiricus.* Middletown, Conn.: Wesleyan University Press.

Harrison, Jonathan
1976   *Hume's Moral Epistemology.* Oxford: Clarendon Press.
1981   *Hume's Theory of Justice.* Oxford: Clarendon Press.

Hendel, Charles W.
1963   *Studies in the Philosophy of David Hume.* 2nd edition. New York: Bobbs-Merrill.

Hick, John
1971   *Arguments for the Existence of God.* New York: Seabury Press.

Hick, John, and A. C. McGill (eds.)
1967   *The Many-Faced Argument: Recent Studies on the Ontological Argument of the Existence of God.* New York: Macmillan.

Hope, Vincent
1984   *Philosophers of the Scottish Enlightenment.* Edinburgh: Edinburgh University Press.

Hudson, W. D.
1964   "Hume on 'Is' and 'Ought'." *Philosophical Quarterly* 14:246–52. Reprinted in Chappell 1966, 295–307.
1967   *Ethical Intuitionism.* London: Macmillan.

Hume, David
1932   *The Letters of David Hume.* Edited by J. Y. T. Greig. Oxford: Oxford University Press.
1938   *An Abstract of a Treatise of Human Nature 1740.* Reprinted with Introduction by T. M. Keynes and P. Sraffa. Cambridge: Cambridge University Press. Reprint Hamden, Conn.: Archon Books, 1965.
1947   *Dialogues Concerning Natural Religion.* Edited by Norman Kemp Smith. Edinburgh: Thomas Nelson. Reprint Indianapolis, Ind.: Bobbs-Merrill, 1980.
1954   *New Letters of David Hume.* Edited by Raymond Klibansky and E. C. Mossner. Oxford: Clarendon Press.
1964   *Philosophical Works.* Edited by T. H. Green and T. H. Grose. 4 vols. London: Longmans Green 1878. Reprint Scientia Verlag Aalen, 1964.
1967   *A Letter from a Gentleman to His Friend in Edinburgh.* Edited by Ernest C. Mossner and John V. Price. Edinburgh: Edinburgh University Press.
1970   *Dialogues Concerning Natural Religion.* Edited with commentary by Nelson Pike. Indianapolis, Ind.: Bobbs-Merrill.
1980   *Dialogues Concerning Natural Religion.* Edited with introduction by Richard H. Popkin. Indianapolis, Ind.: Hackett.

Hunter, Geoffrey
1963   "Reply to Professor Flew." *Philosophy* 38:182–84. Reprinted in Chappell 1966, 287–94.

Immerwahr, John
1979   "A Skeptic's Progress: Hume's Preference for 'Enquiry 1.'" In Norton, Capaldi, and Robison 1979, 227–38.

Jeffner, Anders
1966   *Butler and Hume on Religion.* Stockholm: Diakonistyrelsens Bokforlag.

Jones, Peter
1982   *Hume's Sentiments: Their Ciceronian and French Context.* Edinburgh: Edinburgh University Press.

Kant, Immanuel
1929   *Immanuel Kant's Critique of Pure Reason.* Translated by Norman Kemp Smith. London: Macmillan.
1949   *The Moral Law: Or Groundwork of the Metaphysics of Morals.* Translated with Analysis and Notes by H. J. Paton. London: Hutchinson.

Kemp, John
1964   *Reason, Action and Morality.* New York: Humanities Press.

Kenny, Anthony
1969   *The Five Ways.* London: Routledge and Kegan Paul.
1973   *The Anatomy of the Soul.* Oxford: Basil Blackwell.

Kneale, William C.
1949.   *Probability and Induction.* Oxford: Clarendon Press.

Kuehn, Manfred.
1983   "Kant's Conception of 'Hume's Problem.'" *Journal of the History of Philosophy* 21:175–93.

Kydd, Rachel M.
1946   *Reason and Conduct in Hume's "Treatise."* Oxford: Clarendon Press.

Labrousse, Elisabeth
1983   *Bayle.* Oxford: Oxford University Press.

Leibniz, Gottfried Wilhelm
1898   *Leibniz: The Monadology and Other Philosophical Writings.* Translated by Robert Latta. Oxford: Oxford University Press.

LeMahieu, D. L.
1976   *The Mind of William Paley.* Lincoln: University of Nebraska Press.

Leslie, John (ed.)
1990   *Physical Cosmology and Philosophy.* New York: Macmillan.

Levine, Michael P.
1989   *Hume and the Problem of Miracles: A Solution.* Dordrecht: Kluwer.

Livingston, Donald W.
1984   *Hume's Philosophy of Common Life.* Chicago, Ill.: University of Chicago Press.

Livingston, Donald W., and James T. King (eds.)
1976   *Hume: A Re-evaluation.* New York: Fordham University Press.

Locke, John
1959   *An Essay Concerning Human Understanding.* Edited by Alexander Campbell Fraser. Oxford: Oxford University Press 1894. Reprint New York: Dover.

Mabbott, J. D.
1973   *John Locke.* London: Macmillan.

MacIntyre, Alasdair
1959   "Hume on 'Is' and 'Ought.'" *Philosophical Review* 68:451–68. Reprinted in Chappell 1966, 240–64.
1988   *Whose Justice? Which Rationality?* Notre Dame, Ind.: University of Notre Dame Press.

Mackie, John L.
1974   *The Cement of the Universe: A Study of Causation.* Oxford: Clarendon Press.
1980   *Hume's Moral Theory.* London: Routledge and Kegan Paul.

MacNabb, D. G. C.
1951   *David Hume: His Theory of Knowledge and Morality.* London: Hutchinson.
1967   "Hume." In *Encyclopedia of Philosophy,* edited by Paul Edwards. New York: Crowell Collier and Macmillan.

McIntyre, Jane
1979a   "Is Hume's Self Consistent?" In Norton, Capaldi, and Robison 1979, 79–88.
1979b   "Further Remarks on the Consistency of Hume's Account of the Self." *Hume Studies* 5:55–61.

Mercer, Philip
1972   *Sympathy and Ethics.* Oxford: Clarendon Press.

Merrill, Kenneth R., and Robert W. Shahan (eds.)
1976   *David Hume: Many-Sided Genius.* Norman: University of Oklahoma Press.

Mill, John Stuart
1897   "Utilitarianism." In *The Ethics of John Stuart Mill,* edited by Charles Douglas, 79–200. Edinburgh: Blackwood.

Miller, David
1982   *Philosophy and Ideology in Hume's Political Thought.* Oxford: Oxford University Press.

Moore, George Edward
1903   *Principia Ethica.* Cambridge: Cambridge University Press.
1922   "Hume's Philosophy." In *Philosophical Studies,* 147–67. London: Routledge and Kegan Paul.

Moore, James
1979   "The Social Background of Hume's Science of Human Nature." In Norton, Capaldi, and Robison 1979, 23–42.

Morice, George P. (ed.)
1977   *David Hume: Bicentenary Papers.* Edinburgh: Edinburgh University Press.

Mossner, Ernest Campbell
1936   "The Enigma of Hume." *Mind* 45:334–49.
1970   *The Life of David Hume.* Nelson and University of Texas Press, 1954. Reprint Oxford: Clarendon Press.

Nathan, George J.
1976   "The Existence and Nature of God in Hume's Theism." In Livingston and King 1976, 126–49.

Neu, Jerome
1977   *Emotion, Thought and Therapy.* Berkeley and Los Angeles: University of California Press.

Norton, David Fate
1975   "Hume's Commonsense Morality." *Canadian Journal of Philosophy* 5:523–44.
1982   *David Hume: Common Sense Moralist, Sceptical Metaphysician.* Princeton, N.J.: Princeton University Press.
1985   "Hume's Moral Ontology." *Hume Studies,* 10th Anniversary edition, 1985, 189–214.

Norton, David Fate (ed.)
The Cambridge Companion to Hume. New York: Cambridge University Press, forthcoming.

Norton, David, Nicholas Capaldi, and Wade L. Robison (eds.)
1979   *McGill Hume Studies.* San Diego, Tex.: Austin Hill Press.

Norton, David, and Richard Popkin (eds.)
1965   *David Hume: Philosophical Historian.* Indianapolis, Ind.: Bobbs-Merrill.

Noxon, James
1969   "Senses of Identity in Hume's 'Treatise.'" *Dialogue* 8:367–84.
1973   *Hume's Philosophical Development: A Study of His Methods.* Oxford: Clarendon Press.
1976   "Hume's Concern with Religion." In Merrill and Shahan 1976, 59–82.

Paley, William
1838   *The Works of William Paley D. D.* 4 vols. London: Longman.

Parfit, Derek
1984   *Reasons and Persons.* Oxford: Clarendon Press.

Passmore, John A.
1952   *Hume's Intentions.* Cambridge: Cambridge University Press.
1967   "The Cambridge Platonists." In *Encyclopedia of Philosophy,* edited by Paul Edwards. New York: Macmillan and the Free Press.

Paton, H. J.
1948   *The Categorical Imperative.* London: Hutchinson.

Penelhum, Terence
1955   "Hume on Personal Identity." *Philosophical Review* 44:571–89. Reprinted in Sesonske and Fleming 1965, Chappell 1966.
1971   *Religion and Rationality.* New York: Random House.
1975a   *Hume.* London: Macmillan.
1975b   "Hume's Theory of the Self Revisited." *Dialogue* 14:389–409.
1976a   "Self-Identity and Self-Regard." In *The Identities of Persons,* edited by Amelie Rorty, 253–80. Berkeley and Los Angeles: University of California Press.
1976b   "The Self in Hume's Philosophy." In Merrill and Shahan 1976, 9–24.
1977   "David Hume 1711–76: A Bicentennial Appreciation." *Transactions of the Royal Society of Canada for 1976,* 293–312.
1979   "Hume's Skepticism and the 'Dialogues.'" In Norton, Capaldi, and Robison 1979, 253–78.
1983a   *God and Skepticism.* Dordrecht: Reidel.
1983b   "Natural Belief and Religious Belief in Hume's Philosophy." *Philosophical Quarterly* 33:266–82.
1985a   *Butler.* London: Routledge and Kegan Paul.
1985b   "Scepticism, Sentiment and Common Sense in Hume." *Dialogue* 24:515–22.
1988   "Butler and Hume." *Hume Studies* 14:251–76.

Phillipson, Nicholas
1989   *Hume.* London: Weidenfeld and Nicolson.

Pike, Nelson
1967   "Hume's Bundle Theory of the Self: A Limited Defense." *American Philosophical Quarterly* 4:159–65.

Plato
1965   *Meno: Text and Criticism.* Edited by Alexander Sesonske and Noel Fleming. Belmont, Calif.: Wadsworth.
1975   *Phaedo.* Translated with notes by David Gallop. Oxford: Clarendon Press.

Popkin, Richard
1951   "Hume's Pyrrhonism and His Critique of Pyrrhonism." *Philosophical Quarterly* 1:385–407. Reprinted in Chappell 1966, Popkin 1980b.
1976   "Hume: Philosophical versus Prophetic Historian." In Merrill and Strahan 1976, 83–96.
1979   *The History of Scepticism from Erasmus to Spinoza.* Berkeley and Los Angeles: University of California Press.
1980   *The High Road to Pyrrhonism.* Edited by Richard Watson and James Force. San Diego, Tex.: Austin Hill Press.

Price, H. H.
1940a   *Hume's Theory of the External World.* Oxford: Clarendon Press.
1940b   "The Permanent Significance of Hume's Philosophy." *Philosophy* 15:10–36. Reprinted in Sesonske and Fleming 1965, 5–33.
1969   *Belief.* London: George Allen and Unwin.

Price, John Valdimir
1965   *The Ironic Hume.* Austin: University of Texas Press.

Raphael, D. D.
1947   *The Moral Sense.* Oxford: Oxford University Press.

Rawls, John
1972   *A Theory of Justice.* London: Oxford University Press.

Richards, Thomas J.
1965   "Hume's Two Definitions of 'Cause'." *Philosophical Quarterly* 15:247–53. Reprinted in Chappell 1966, 148–61.

Rist, J. M.
1969   *Stoic Philosophy.* Cambridge: Cambridge University Press.
1972   *Epicurus: An Introduction.* Cambridge: Cambridge University Press.

Roberts, T. A.
1973   *The Concept of Benevolence: Aspects of Eighteenth-Century Moral Philosophy.* London: Macmillan.

Robinson, J. A.
1962   "Hume's Two Definitions of 'Cause'." *Philosophical Quarterly* 12:162–71. Reprinted in Chappell 1966, 129–47.
1966   "Hume's Two Definitions of 'Cause' Reconsidered." In Chappell 1966, 162–68.

Rotwein, Eugene
1976   "David Hume: Philosopher-Economist." In Merrill and Strahan 1976, 117–34.

Rowe, William L.
1975 *The Cosmological Argument.* Princeton, N.J.: Princeton University Press.

Russell, Paul
1990 "Hume on Responsibility and Punishment." *Canadian Journal of Philosophy* 20:539–63.

Schneewind, J. B.
1984 "The Divine Corporation and the History of Ethics." In *Philosophy in History,* edited by R. Rorty, J. B. Schneewind, and Q. Skinner, 173–92. Cambridge: Cambridge University Press.

Schofield, M., M. Burnyeat, and J. Barnes (eds.)
1980 *Doubt and Dogmatism: Studies in Hellenistic Philosophy.* Oxford: Clarendon Press.

Selby-Bigge, L. A. (ed.)
1965 *British Moralists: Being Selections from Writers Principally of the Eighteenth Century.* 2 vols. Oxford: Clarendon Press, 1897. Reprint New York: Dover.

Sesonske, Alexander, and Noel Fleming (eds.)
1965 *Human Understanding: Studies in the Philosophy of David Hume.* Belmont, Calif.: Wadsworth.

Sextus Empiricus
1933– *Sextus Empiricus.* With English translation by R. G.
1949 Bury. 4 vols. Loeb Classical Library. Cambridge, Mass.: Harvard University Press.

Shoemaker, Sydney, and Richard Swinburne
1984 *Personal Identity.* Oxford: Basil Blackwell.

Smith, Norman Kemp
1905 "The Naturalism of Hume." *Mind,* n.s. no. 54: 149–53, 335–47.
1918 *A Commentary to Kant's 'Critique of Pure Reason.'* London: Macmillan.
1941 *The Philosophy of David Hume.* London: Macmillan.

Stephen, Leslie
1902 *A History of English Thought in the Eighteenth Century.* 3rd edition. 2 vols. London: Smith and Elder.

Stevenson, Charles L.
1944 *Ethics and Language.* New Haven, Conn.: Yale University Press.

Stewart, John B.
1963 *The Moral and Political Philosophy of David Hume.* New York: Columbia University Press.

Stewart, M. A. (ed.)
1990 *Studies in the Philosophy of the Scottish Enlightenment.* Oxford: Clarendon Press.

Stockton, C. N.
1976 "Economics and the Mechanism of Social Progress in Hume's 'History.'" In Livingston and King 1976, 296–320.

Stough, Charlotte L.
1969 *Greek Skepticism: A Study in Epistemology.* Berkeley and Los Angeles: University of California Press.

Stove, David C.
1973   *Probability and Hume's Inductive Scepticism.* Oxford: Clarendon Press.
1975   "Hume, the Causal Principle, and Kemp Smith." *Hume Studies* 1:1–24.
1979   "The Nature of Hume's Skepticism." In Norton, Capaldi, and Robison, 203–25.

Strawson P. F.
1985   *Skepticism and Naturalism: Some Varieties.* London: Methuen.

Stroud, Barry
1977   *Hume.* London: Routledge and Kegan Paul.
1984   *The Significance of Philosophical Scepticism.* Oxford: Clarendon Press.

Sutherland, Stewart R.
1977   "Hume and the Concept of Pleasure." In Morice 1977, 218–24.
1984   *Faith and Ambiguity.* London: SCM Press.

Swinburne, Richard
1970   *The Concept of Miracle.* London: Macmillan.
1979   *The Existence of God.* Oxford: Clarendon Press.
1981   *Faith and Reason.* Oxford: Clarendon Press.
1989   *Miracles.* New York: Macmillan.

Swinburne, Richard (ed.)
1974   *The Justification of Induction.* Oxford: Oxford University Press.

Taylor, A. E.
1927   *David Hume and the Miraculous.* Cambridge: Cambridge University Press.

Todd, William B. (ed.)
1974   *Hume and the Enlightenment: Essays Presented to Ernest Campbell Mossner.* Edinburgh: Edinburgh University Press.

Urmson, J. O.
1966   *Philosophical Analysis: Its Development Between the Two World Wars.* Oxford: Clarendon Press.

Vesey, Godfrey
1974   *Personal Identity.* London: Macmillan.

Wadia, Pheroze
1979   "Philo Confounded." In Norton, Capaldi, and Robison 1979, 279–90.

Walton, Craig
1976   "Hume and Jefferson on the Uses of History." In Livingston and King 1976, 389–403.

Williams, Bernard
1973   *Problems of the Self.* Cambridge: Cambridge University Press.
1978   *Descartes: The Project of Pure Enquiry.* Harmondsworth: Penguin.

Wilson, Fred
1979   "Hume's Theory of Mental Activity." In Norton, Capaldi, and Robison 1979, 101–20.

1983   "Hume's Defence of Causal Inference." *Dialogue* 22:661–94.
1985   "Hume's Cognitive Stoicism." *Hume Studies,* 10th Anniversary Issue, 1985, 52–68.
1986a   "Hume's Defence of Science." *Dialogue* 25:611–28.
1986   "Wright's Enquiry Concerning Human Understanding." *Dialogue* 25:747–52.

Winters, Barbara
1979   "Hume on Reason." *Hume Studies* 5:20–36.

Wolff, Robert Paul
1960   "Hume's Theory of Mental Activity." *Philosophical Review* 69. Reprinted in Chappell 1966, 99–128.

Wolin, Sheldon S.
1976   "Hume and Conservatism." In Livingston and King 1976, 239–56.

Wollheim, Richard (ed.)
1963   *Hume on Religion*. London: Collins.

Wright, John P.
1983   *The Sceptical Realism of David Hume*. Manchester: Manchester University Press.
1986   "Hume's Academic Skepticism: A Reappraisal of His Philosophy of Human Understanding." *Canadian Journal of Philosophy* 16:407–36.

Yandell, Keith E.
1976   "Hume on Religious Belief." In Livingston and King 1976, 109–25.
1990   *Hume's "Inexplicable Mystery": His Views on Religion*. Philadelphia, Pa.: Temple University Press.

INDEX

I Index of Names

∎ Index of Subjects